THE

POETICAL WORKS

OF

JOHN GREENLEAF WHITTIER.

COMPLETE IN TWO VOLUMES.

VOLUME I.

BOSTON:
TICKNOR AND FIELDS.
M DCCC LXVIII.

UNIVERSITY PRESS: WELCH, BIGELOW, & CO.,
CAMBRIDGE.

NOTE BY THE AUTHOR.

In these Volumes, for the first time, a complete collection of my poetical writings has been made. While it is satisfactory to know that these scattered children of my brain have found a home, I cannot but regret that I have been unable, by reason of illness, to give that attention to their revision and arrangement, which respect for the opinions of others, and my own after-thought and experience demand.

That there are pieces in this collection which I would "willingly let die," I am free to confess. But, it is now too late to disown them, and I must submit to the inevitable penalty of poetical as well as other sins. There are others, intimately connected with the author's life and times, which owe their tenacity of vitality to the circumstances under which they were written, and the events by which they were suggested.

The long poem of Mogg Megone, was, in a great measure, composed in early life; and it is scarcely necessary to say that its subject is not such as the writer would have chosen at any subsequent period.

J. G. W

Amesbury, 18th, 3d Mo., 1857.

PROEM.

I LOVE the old melodious lays
Which softly melt the ages through,
The songs of Spenser's golden days
Arcadian Sidney's silvery phrase,
Sprinkling our noon of time with freshest morning dew.

Yet, vainly in my quiet hours
To breathe their marvellous notes I try;
I feel them, as the leaves and flowers
In silence feel the dewy showers,
And drink with glad still lips the blessing of the sky.

The rigor of a frozen clime,
The harshness of an untaught ear,
The jarring words of one whose rhyme
Beat often Labor's hurried time,
Or Duty's rugged march through storm and strife, are here.

Of mystic beauty, dreamy grace,
No rounded art the lack supplies;
Unskilled the subtle lines to trace,
Or softer shades of Nature's face,
I view her common forms with unanointed eyes.

Nor mine the seer-like power to show
The secrets of the heart and mind;
To drop the plummet-line below
Our common world of joy and woe,
A more intense despair or brighter hope to find.

Yet here at least an earnest sense
Of human right and weal is shown;
A hate of tyranny intense,
And hearty in its vehemence,
As if my brother's pain and sorrow were my own.

Oh Freedom! if to me belong
Nor mighty Milton's gift divine,
Nor Marvell's wit and graceful song,
Still with a love as deep and strong
As theirs, I lay, like them, my best gifts on thy shrine!

AMESBURY, 11th mo., 1847.

CONTENTS OF VOLUME I.

POEMS.

Page
The Bridal of Pennacook.......................... 5
Mogg Megone.. 31

LEGENDARY.

The Merrimack... 71
The Norsemen... 74
Cassandra Southwick............................... 77
Funeral Tree of the Sokokis..................... 86
St. John.. 89
Pentucket... 93
The Familist's Hymn................................ 96
The Fountain... 98
The Exiles.. 102
The New Wife and the Old....................... 110

VOICES OF FREEDOM.

Toussaint L'Ouverture............................ 117
The Slave Ships...................................... 124
Stanzas. Our Countrymen in Chains.............. 128
The Yankee Girl...................................... 131
To W. L. G.. 133
Song of the Free..................................... 135
The Hunters of Men................................. 136
Clerical Oppressors................................. 138
The Christian Slave................................. 140
Stanzas for the Times............................. 142
Lines, written on reading the Message of Governor Ritner, of Pennsylvania, 1836.................. 144
The Pastoral Letter.................................. 147
Lines, written for the Meeting of the Anti-Slavery Society, at Chatham Street Chapel, N. Y., 1834. 151
Lines, written for the Celebration of the Third Anniversary of British Emancipation, 1837.......... 152

Page

Lines, written for the Anniversary of the First of August, at Milton, 1846 153
The Farewell of a Virginia Slave Mother to her Daughters sold into Southern Bondage 155
The Moral Warfare 157
The World's Convention 158
New Hampshire 164
The New Year; Addressed to the Patrons of the Pennsylvania Freeman 165
Massachusetts to Virginia 170
The Relic 176
The Branded Hand 179
Texas 182
To Faneuil Hall 185
To Massachusetts 186
The Pine-Tree 188
Lines, suggested by a Visit to the City of Washington in the 12th month of 1845 189
Lines, from a Letter to a young Clerical Friend 194
Yorktown 195
Lines, written in the Book of a Friend 198
Pæan 202
To the Memory of Thomas Shipley 204
To a Southern Statesman 207
Lines, on the Adoption of Pinckney's Resolutions 208
The Curse of the Charter-Breakers 211
The Slaves of Martinique 214
The Crisis 219
The Knight of St. John 223
The Holy Land 225

MISCELLANEOUS.

Palestine 229
Ezekiel 232
The Wife of Manoah to her Husband 235
The Cities of the Plain 238
The Crucifixion 240
The Star of Bethlehem 241
Hymns 244
The Female Martyr 248
The Frost Spirit 251
The Vaudois Teacher 252
The Call of the Christian 254
My Soul and I 256

Page

To a Friend, on her Return from Europe............ 262
The Angel of Patience............................ 264
Follen.. 265
To the Reformers of England...................... 269
The Quaker of the Olden Time..................... 271
The Reformer.................................... 272
The Prisoner for Debt............................ 275
Lines, written on reading Pamphlets published by Clergymen against the Abolition of the Gallows. 277
The Human Sacrifice.............................. 280
Randolph of Roanoke.............................. 286
Democracy.. 289
To Ronge... 292
Chalkley Hall.................................... 293
To J. P.. 295
The Cypress-Tree of Ceylon....................... 296
A Dream of Summer................................ 298
To ——.. 299
Leggett's Monument............................... 305

IN WAR TIME.

Thy Will be done................................ 311
A Word for the Hour.............................. 312
"Ein feste Burg ist unser Gott".................. 313
To John C. Fremont............................... 315
The Watchers..................................... 316
To Englishmen.................................... 319
Astræa at the Capitol............................ 320
The Battle Autumn of 1862........................ 323
Mithridates at Chios............................. 324
The Proclamation................................. 325
Anniversary Poem................................. 327
At Port Royal.................................... 330
Barbara Frietchie................................ 334

HOME BALLADS.

Cobbler Keezar's Vision.......................... 339
Amy Wentworth.................................... 345
The Countess..................................... 350

OCCASIONAL POEMS.

Naples.—1860..................................... 359
The Summons...................................... 360

Page

The Waiting.... 361

Mountain Pictures.

I. Franconia from the Pemigewasset.... 363

II. Monadnock from Wachuset.... 364

Our River.... 365

Andrew Rykman's Prayer.... 368

The Cry of a Lost Soul.... 374

Italy.... 375

The River Path.... 376

A Memorial. M. A. C.... 378

Hymn sung at Christmas by the Scholars of St. Helena's Island, S. C.... 381

NOTES.... 383

THE BRIDAL OF PENNACOOK.

1848.

POEMS.

THE BRIDAL OF PENNACOOK.[1]

We had been wandering for many days
Through the rough northern country. We had seen
The sunset, with its bars of purple cloud,
Like a new heaven, shine upward from the lake
Of Winnepiseogee; and had felt
The sunrise breezes, midst the leafy isles
Which stoop their summer beauty to the lips
Of the bright waters. We had checked our steeds,
Silent with wonder, where the mountain wall
Is piled to heaven; and, through the narrow rift
Of the vast rocks, against whose rugged feet
Beats the mad torrent with perpetual roar,
Where noonday is as twilight, and the wind
Comes burdened with the everlasting moan
Of forests and of far-off water-falls,
We had looked upward where the summer sky,
Tasselled with clouds light-woven by the sun,
Sprung its blue arch above the abutting crags
O'er-roofing the vast portal of the land
Beyond the wall of mountains We had passed
The high source of the Saco; and bewildered
In the dwarf spruce-belts of the Crystal Hills
Had heard above us, like a voice in the cloud,
The horn of Fabyan sounding; and atop
Of old Agioochook had seen the mountains
Piled to the northward, shagged with wood, and thick
As meadow mole hills—the far sea of Casco,

A white gleam on the horizon of the east;
Fair lakes, embosomed in the woods and hills;
Moosehillock's mountain range, and Kearsarge
Lifting his Titan forehead to the sun!

And we had rested underneath the oaks
Shadowing the bank, whose grassy spires are shaken
By the perpetual beating of the falls
Of the wild Ammonoosuc. We had tracked
The winding Pemigewasset, overhung
By beechen shadows, whitening down its rocks,
Or lazily gliding through its intervals,
From waving rye-fields sending up the gleam
Of sunlit waters. We had seen the moon
Rising behind Umbagog's eastern pines
Like a great Indian camp-fire; and its beams
At midnight spanning with a bridge of silver
The Merrimack by Uncanoonuc's falls.

There were five souls of us whom travel's chance
Had thrown together in these wild north hills:—
A city lawyer, for a month escaping
From his dull office, where the weary eye
Saw only hot brick walls and close thronged streets—
Briefless as yet, but with an eye to see
Life's sunniest side, and with a heart to take
Its chances all as God-sends; and his brother,
Pale from long pulpit studies, yet retaining
The warmth and freshness of a genial heart,
Whose mirror of the beautiful and true,
In Man and Nature, was as yet undimmed
By dust of theologic strife, or breath
Of sect, or cobwebs of scholastic lore;
Like a clear crystal calm of water, taking
The hue and image of o'erleaning flowers,
Sweet human faces, white clouds of the noon,
Slant starlight glimpses through the dewy leaves,

And tenderest moonrise. 'Twas, in truth, a study,
To mark his spirit, alternating between
A decent and professional gravity
And an irreverent mirthfulness, which often
Laughed in the face of his divinity,
Plucked off the sacred ephod, quite unshrined
The oracle, and for the pattern priest
Left us the man. A shrewd, sagacious merchant,
To whom the soiled sheet found in Crawford's inn
Giving the latest news of city stocks
And sales of cotton had a deeper meaning
Than the great presence of the awful mountains
Glorified by the sunset;—and his daughter,
A delicate flower on whom had blown too long
Those evil winds, which, sweeping from the ice
And winnowing the fogs of Labrador,
Shed their cold blight round Massachusetts Bay,
With the same breath which stirs Spring's opening
leaves
And lifts her half-formed flower-bell on its stem,
Poisoning our sea-side atmosphere.

It chanced
That as we turned upon our homeward way,
A drear northeastern storm came howling up,
The valley of the Saco; and that girl
Who had stood with us upon Mount Washington,
Her brown locks ruffled by the wind which whirled
In gusts around its sharp cold pinnacle,
Who had joined our gay trout-fishing in the streams
Which lave that giant's feet; whose laugh was
heard
Like a bird's carol on the sunrise breeze
Which swelled our sail amidst the lake's green
islands,
Shrank from its harsh, chill breath, and visibly
drooped
Like a flower in the frost. So, in that quiet inn
Which looks from Conway on the mountains piled

Heavily against the horizon of the north,
Like summer thunder-clouds, we made our home:
And while the mist hung over dripping hills,
And the cold wind-driven rain-drops, all day long
Beat their sad music upon roof and pane,
We strove to cheer our gentle invalid.

The lawyer in the pauses of the storm
Went angling down the Saco, and, returning,
Recounted his adventures and mishaps;
Gave us the history of his scaly clients,
Mingling with ludicrous yet apt citations
Of barbarous law Latin, passages
From Izaak Walton's Angler, sweet and fresh
As the flower-skirted streams of Staffordshire
Where, under aged trees, the southwest wind
Of soft June mornings fanned the thin, white hair
Of the sage fisher. And, if truth be told,
Our youthful candidate forsook his sermons,
His commentaries, articles and creeds
For the fair page of human loveliness—
The missal of young hearts, whose sacred text
Is music, its illumining sweet smiles.
He sang the songs she loved; and in his low,
Deep earnest voice, recited many a page
Of poetry—the holiest, tenderest lines
Of the sad bard of Olney—the sweet songs,
Simple and beautiful as Truth and Nature,
Of him whose whitened locks on Rydal Mount
Are lifted yet by morning breezes blowing
From the green hills, immortal in his lays.
And for myself, obedient to her wish,
I searched our landlord's proffered library:
A well-thumbed Bunyan, with its nice wood pictures
Of scaly fiends and angels not unlike them—
Watts' unmelodious psalms—Astrology's
Last home, a musty file of Almanacs,
And an old chronicle of border wars

And Indian history. And, as I read
A story of the marriage of the Chief
Of Saugus to the dusky Weetamoo,
Daughter of Passaconaway, who dwelt
In the old time upon Merrimack,
Our fair one, in the playful exercise
Of her prerogative—the right divine
Of youth and beauty,—bade us versify
The legend, and with ready pencil sketched
Its plan and outlines, laughingly assigning
To each his part, and barring our excuses
With absolute will. So, like the cavaliers
Whose voices still are heard in the Romance
Of silver-tongued Boccaccio, on the banks
Of Arno, with soft tales of love beguiling
The ear of languid beauty, plague-exiled
From stately Florence, we rehearsed our rhymes
To their fair auditor, and shared by turns
Her kind approval and her playful censure.

It may be that these fragments owe alone
To the fair setting of their circumstances—
The associations of time, scene and audience—
Their place amid the pictures which fill up
The chambers of my memory. Yet I trust
That some, who sigh, while wandering in thought,
Pilgrims of Romance o'er the olden world,
That our broad land—our sea-like lakes and mountains
Piled to the clouds,—our rivers overhung
By forests which have known no other change
For ages, than the budding and the fall
Of leaves—our valleys lovelier than those
Which the old poets sang of—should but figure
On the apocryphal chart of speculation
As pastures, wood-lots, mill-sites, with the privileges,
Rights and appurtenances, which make up
A Yankee Paradise—unsung, unknown,
To beautiful tradition; even their names,

Whose melody yet lingers like the last
Vibration of the red man's requiem,
Exchanged for syllables significant
Of cotton-mill and rail-car,—will look kindly
Upon this effort to call up the ghost
Of our dim Past, and listen with pleased ear
To the responses of the questioned Shade:

I. THE MERRIMACK.

Oh, child of that white-crested mountain whose springs
Gush forth in the shade of the cliff-eagle's wings,
Down whose slopes to the lowlands thy wild waters shine,
Leaping gray walls of rock, flashing through the dwarf pine.

From that cloud-curtained cradle so cold and so lone,
From the arms of that wintry-locked mother of stone,
By hills hung with forests, through vales wide and free,
Thy mountain-born brightness glanced down to the sea!

No bridge arched thy waters save that where the trees
Stretched their long arms above thee and kissed in the breeze:
No sound save the lapse of the waves on thy shores,
The plunging of otters, the light dip of oars.

Green-tufted, oak-shaded, by Amoskeag's fall
Thy twin Uncanoonucs rose stately and tall,
Thy Nashua meadows lay green and unshorn,
And the hills of Pentucket were tasselled with corn.

But thy Pennacook valley was fairer than these,
And greener its grasses and taller its trees,
Ere the sound of an axe in the forest had rung,
Or the mower his scythe in the meadows had swung

In their sheltered repose looking out from the wood
The bark-builded wigwams of Pennacook stood,
There glided the corn-dance—the Council fire shone,
And against the red war-post the hatchet was thrown.

There the old smoked in silence their pipes, and the young
To the pike and the white perch their baited lines flung;
There the boy shaped his arrows, and there the shy maid
Wove her many-hued baskets and bright wampum braid.

Oh, Stream of the Mountains! if answer of thine
Could rise from thy waters to question of mine,
Methinks through the din of thy thronged banks a moan
Of sorrow would swell for the days which have gone.

Not for thee the dull jar of the loom and the wheel,
The gliding of shuttles, the ringing of steel;
But that old voice of waters, of bird and of breeze,
The dip of the wild-fowl, the rustling of trees!

II. THE BASHABA.[2]

Lift we the twilight curtains of the Past,
And turning from familiar sight and sound
Sadly and full of reverence let us cast
A glance upon Tradition's shadowy ground,

Led by the few pale lights, which glimmering round,
That dim, strange land of Eld, seem dying fast;
And that which history gives not to the eye,
The faded coloring of Time's tapestry,
Let Fancy, with her dream-dipped brush supply

Roof of bark and walls of pine,
Through whose chinks the sunbeams shine,
Tracing many a golden line
On the ample floor within;
Where upon that earth-floor stark,
Lay the gaudy mats of bark,
With the bear's hide, rough and dark,
And the red-deer's skin.

Window-tracery, small and slight,
Woven of the willow white,
Lent a dimly-checkered light,
And the night-stars glimmered down,
Where the lodge-fire's heavy smoke,
Slowly through an opening broke,
In the low roof, ribbed with oak,
Sheathed with hemlock brown.

Gloomed behind the changeless shade,
By the solemn pine-wood made;
Through the rugged palisade,
In the open foreground planted,
Glimpses came of rowers rowing,
Stir of leaves and wild flowers blowing,
Steel-like gleams of water flowing,
In the sunlight slanted.

Here the mighty Bashaba,
Held his long-unquestioned sway,
From the White Hills, far away,
To the great sea's sounding shore;
Chief of chiefs, his regal word

All the river Sachems heard,
At his call the war-dance stirred,
Or was still once more.

There his spoils of chase and war,
Jaw of wolf and black bear's paw,
Panther's skin and eagle's claw,
Lay besides his axe and bow;
And, adown the roof-pole hung,
Loosely on a snake-skin strung,
In the smoke his scalp-locks swung
Grimly to and fro.

Nightly down the river going,
Swifter was the hunter's rowing,
When he saw that lodge-fire glowing
O'er the waters still and red;
And the squaw's dark eye burned brighter,
And she drew her blanket tighter,
As, with quicker step and lighter,
From that door she fled.

For that chief had magic skill,
And a Panisee's dark will,
Over powers of good and ill,
Powers which bless and powers which ban—
Wizard lord of Pennacook,
Chiefs upon their war-path shook,
When they met the steady look
Of that wise dark man.

Tales of him the gray squaw told,
When the winter night-wind cold
Pierced her blanket's thickest fold,
And the fire burned low and small,
Till the very child a-bed,
Drew its bear-skin over head,
Shrinking from the pale lights shed
On the trembling wall.

All the subtle spirits hiding
Under earth or wave, abiding
In the caverned rock, or riding
  Misty clouds or morning breeze;
Every dark intelligence,
Secret soul, and influence
Of all things which outward sense
  Feels, or hears or sees,—

These the wizard's skill confessed,
At his bidding banned or blessed,
Stormful woke or lulled to rest
  Wind and cloud, and fire and flood;
Burned for him the drifted snow,
Bade through ice fresh lilies blow,
And the leaves of summer grow
  Over winter's wood!

Not untrue that tale of old!
Now, as then, the wise and bold
All the powers of Nature hold
  Subject to their kingly will;
From the wondering crowds ashore,
Treading life's wild waters o'er,
As upon a marble floor,
  Moves the strong man still.

Still, to such, life's elements
With their sterner laws dispense,
And the chain of consequence
  Broken in their pathway lies;
Time and change their vassals making,
Flowers from icy pillows waking,
Tresses of the sunrise shaking
  Over midnight skies.

Still, to earnest souls, the sun
Rests on towered Gibeon,
And the moon of Ajalon

Lights the battle-grounds of life;
To his aid the strong reverses
Hidden powers and giant forces,
And the high stars in their courses
Mingle in his strife!

III. THE DAUGHTER.

THE soot-black brows of men—the yell
Of women thronging round the bed—
The tinkling charm of ring and shell—
The Powah whispering o'er the dead!—
All these the Sachem's home had known,
When, on her journey long and wild
To the dim World of Souls, alone,
In her young beauty passed the mother of his child.

Three bow-shots from the Sachem's dwelling
They laid her in the walnut shade,
Where a green hillock gently swelling
Her fitting mound of burial made.
There trailed the vine in Summer hours—
The tree-perched squirrel dropped his shell—
On velvet moss and pale-hued flowers,
Woven with leaf and spray, the softened sunshine fell!

The Indian's heart is hard and cold—
It closes darkly o'er its care,
And formed in Nature's sternest mould,
Is slow to feel, and strong to bear.
The war-paint on the Sachem's face,
Unwet with tears, shone fierce and red,
And, still in battle or in chase,
Dry leaf and snow-rime crisped beneath his foremost tread.

Yet, when her name was heard no more,
And when the robe her mother gave,

And small, light moccasin she wore,
Had slowly wasted on her grave,
Unmarked of him the dark maids sped
Their sunset dance and moonlit play;
No other shared his lonely bed,
No other fair young head upon his bosom lay.

A lone, stern man. Yet, as sometimes
The tempest-smitten tree receives
From one small root the sap which climbs
Its topmost spray and crowning leaves,
So from his child the Sachem drew
A life of Love and Hope, and felt
His cold and rugged nature through
The softness and the warmth of her young being melt.

A laugh which in the woodland rang
Bemocking April's gladdest bird—
A light and graceful form which sprang
To meet him when his step was heard—
Eyes by his lodge-fire flashing dark,
Small fingers stringing bead and shell
Or weaving mats of bright-hued bark,—
With these the household-god[3] had graced his wigwam well.

Child of the forest!—strong and free,
Slight-robed, with loosely flowing hair,
She swam the lake or climbed the tree,
Or struck the flying bird in air.
O'er the heaped drifts of Winter's moon
Her snow-shoes tracked the hunter's way;
And dazzling in the Summer noon
The blade of her light oar threw off its shower of spray!

Unknown to her the rigid rule,
The dull restraint, the chiding frown,

The weary torture of the school,
  The taming of wild nature down.
Her only lore, the legends told
  Around the hunter's fire at night;
Stars rose and set, and seasons rolled,
Flowers bloomed and snow-flakes fell, unquestioned
    in her sight.

Unknown to her the subtle skill
  With which the artist-eye can trace
In rock and tree and lake and hill
  The outlines of divinest grace;
Unknown the fine soul's keen unrest
  Which sees, admires, yet yearns alway;
Too closely on her mother's breast
To note her smiles of love the child of Nature
    lay!

It is enough for such to be
  Of common, natural things a part,
To feel with bird and stream and tree
  The pulses of the same great heart;
But we, from Nature long exiled
  In our cold homes of Art and Thought,
Grieve like the stranger-tended child,
Which seeks its mother's arms, and sees but feels
    them not.

The garden rose may richly bloom
  In cultured soil and genial air,
To cloud the light of Fashion's room
  Or droop in Beauty's midnight hair,
In lonelier grace, to sun and dew
  The sweet-briar on the hill-side shows
Its single leaf and fainter hue,
Untrained and wildly free, yet still a sister rose!

Thus o'er the heart of Weetamoo
  Their mingling shades of joy and ill

The instincts of her nature threw,—
The savage was a woman still.
Midst outlines dim of maiden schemes,
Heart-colored prophecies of life,
Rose on the ground of her young dreams
The light of a new home—the lover and the wife

IV. THE WEDDING.

Cool and dark fell the Autumn night,
But the Bashaba's wigwam glowed with light,
For down from its roof by green withes hung
Flaring and smoking the pine-knots swung.

And along the river great wood fires
Shot into the night their long red spires,
Showing behind the tall, dark wood
Flashing before on the sweeping flood.

In the changeful wind, with shimmer and shade,
Now high, now low, that fire-light played,
On tree-leaves wet with evening dews,
On gliding water and still canoes.

The trapper, that night on Turee's brook
And the weary fisher on Contoocook
Saw over the marshes and through the pine,
And down on the river the dance-lights shine

For the Saugus Sachem had come to woo
The Bashaba's daughter Weetamoo,
And laid at her father's feet that night
His softest furs and wampum white.

From the Crystal Hills to the far Southeast
The river Sagamores came to the feast;
And chiefs whose homes the sea-winds shook,
Sat down on the mats of Pennacook.

They came from Sunapee's shore of rock,
From the snowy sources of Snooganock,
And from rough Coös whose thick woods shake
Their pine-cones in Umbagog lake.

From Ammonoosuck's mountain pass
Wild as his home came Chepewass;
And the Keenomps of the hills which throw
Their shade on the Smile of Manito.

With pipes of peace and bows unstrung,
Glowing with paint came old and young,
In wampum and furs and feathers arrayed
To the dance and feast the Bashaba made.

Bird of the air and beast of the field,
All which the woods and waters yield
On dishes of birch and hemlock piled
Garnished and graced that banquet wild.

Steaks of the brown bear fat and large
From the rocky slopes of the Kearsarge;
Delicate trout from Babboosuck brook,
And salmon spear'd in the Contoocook;

Squirrels which fed where nuts fell thick
In the gravelly bed of the Otternic,
And small wild hens in reed-snares caught
From the banks of Sondagardee brought·

Pike and perch from the Suncook taken,
Nuts from the trees of the Black Hills shaken,
Cranberries picked in the Squamscot bog,
And grapes from the vines of Piscataquog:

[stands
And, drawn from that great stone vase which
In the river scooped by a spirit's hands, [4]
Garnished with spoons of shell and horn,
Stood the birchen dishes of smoking corn.

Thus bird of the air and beast of the field,
All which the woods and the waters yield,
Furnished in that olden day
The bridal feast of the Bashaba.

And merrily when that feast was done
On the fire-lit green the dance begun,
With squaws' shrill stave, and deeper hum
Of old men beating the Indian drum.

Painted and plumed, with scalp locks flowing,
And red arms tossing and black eyes glowing,
Now in the light and now in the shade
Around the fires the dancers played.

The step was quicker, the song more shrill,
And the beat of the small drums louder still
Whenever within the circle drew
The Saugus Sachem and Weetamoo.

The moons of forty winters had shed
Their snow upon that chieftain's head,
And toil and care, and battle's chance
Had seamed his hard dark countenance.

A fawn beside the bison grim—
Why turns the bride's fond eye on him,
In whose cold look is naught beside
The triumph of a sullen pride?

Ask why the graceful grape entwines
The rough oak with her arm of vines;
And why the gray rock's rugged cheek
The soft lips of the mosses seek:

Why, with wise instinct, Nature seems
To harmonize her wide extremes,
Linking the stronger with the weak,
The haughty with the soft and meek!

V. THE NEW HOME.

A wild and broken landscape, spiked with firs,
Roughening the bleak horizon's northern edge,
Steep, cavernous hill-sides, where black hemlock spurs
And sharp, gray splinters of the wind-swept ledge
Pierced the thin-glazed ice, or bristling rose,
Where the cold rim of the sky sunk down upon the snows.

And eastward cold, wide marshes stretched away,
Dull, dreary flats without a bush or tree,
O'er-crossed by icy creeks, where twice a day
Gurgled the waters of the moon-struck sea;
And faint with distance came the stifled roar,
The melancholy lapse of waves on that low shore.

No cheerful village with its mingling smokes,
No laugh of children wrestling in the snow,
No camp-fire blazing through the hill-side oaks,
No fishers kneeling on the ice below;
Yet midst all desolate things of sound and view,
Through the long winter moons smiled dark-eyed Weetamoo.

Her heart had found a home; and freshly all
Its beautiful affections overgrew
Their rugged prop. As o'er some granite wall
Soft vine leaves open to the moistening dew
And warm bright sun, the love of that young wife
Found on a hard cold breast the dew and warmth of life.

The steep bleak hills, the melancholy shore,
The long dead level of the marsh between,
A coloring of unreal beauty wore
Through the soft golden mist of young love seen.

For o'er those hills and from that dreary plain,
Nightly she welcomed home her hunter chief again

No warmth of heart, no passionate burst of feeling
Repaid her welcoming smile, and parting kiss,
No fond and playful dalliance half concealing,
Under the guise of mirth, its tenderness;
But, in their stead, the warrior's settled pride,
And vanity's pleased smile with homage satisfied.

Enough for Weetamoo, that she alone
Sat on his mat and slumbered at his side;
That he whose fame to her young ear had flown,
Now looked upon her proudly as his bride;
That he whose name the Mohawk trembling heard
Vouchsafed to her at times a kindly look or word.

For she had learned the maxims of her race,
Which teach the woman to become a slave
And feel herself the pardonless disgrace
Of love's fond weakness in the wise and brave—
The scandal and the shame which they incur,
Who give to woman all which man requires of her.

So passed the winter moons. The sun at last
Broke link by link the frost chain of the rills,
And the warm breathings of the southwest passed
Over the hoar rime of the Saugus hills,
The gray and desolate marsh grew green once more,
And the birch-tree's tremulous shade fell round the Sachem's door.

Then from far Pennacook swift runners came,
With gift and greeting for the Saugus chief;
Beseeching him in the great Sachem's name,
That, with the coming of the flower and leaf,
The song of birds, the warm breeze and the rain,
Young Weetamoo might greet her lonely sire again.

And Winnepurkit called his chiefs together,
  And a grave council in his wigwam met,
Solemn and brief in words, considering whether
  The rigid rules of forest etiquette
Permitted Weetamoo once more to look
Upon her father's face and green-banked Pennacook.

With interludes of pipe-smoke and strong water,
  The forest sages pondered, and at length,
Concluded in a body to escort her
  Up to her father's home of pride and strength,
Impressing thus on Pennacook a sense
Of Winnepurkit's power and regal consequence.

So through old woods which Aukeetamit's [5] hand,
  A soft and many-shaded greenness lent,
Over high breezy hills, and meadow land
  Yellow with flowers, the wild procession went,
Till rolling down its wooded banks between,
A broad, clear, mountain stream, the Merrimack was seen.

The hunter leaning on his bow undrawn—
  The fisher lounging on the pebbled shores,
Squaws in the clearing dropping the seed-corn,
  Young children peering through the wigwam doors,
Saw with delight, surrounded by her train
Of painted Saugus braves, their Weetamoo again.

VI. AT PENNACOOK.

The hills are dearest which our childish feet
Have climbed the earliest; and the streams most sweet,
Are ever those at which our young lips drank,
Stooped to their waters o'er the grassy bank :

Midst the cold dreary sea-watch, Home's hearth-light
Shines round the helmsman plunging through the night;
And still, with inward eye, the traveller sees
In close, dark, stranger streets his native trees.

The home-sick dreamer's brow is nightly fanned
By breezes whispering of his native land,
And, on the stranger's dim and dying eye
The soft, sweet pictures of his childhood lie

Joy then for Weetamoo, to sit once more
A child upon her father's wigwam floor!
Once more with her old fondness to beguile
From his cold eye the strange light of a smile.

The long bright days of Summer swiftly passed,
The dry leaves whirled in Autumn's rising blast,
And evening cloud and whitening sunrise rime
Told of the coming of the winter time.

But vainly looked, the while, young Weetamoo,
Down the dark river for her chief's canoe;
No dusky messenger from Saugus brought,
The grateful tidings which the young wife sought.

At length a runner from her father sent,
To Winnepurkit's sea-cooled wigwam went:
"Eagle of Saugus,—in the woods the dove,
Mourns for the shelter of thy wings of love."

But the dark chief of Saugus turned aside
In the grim anger of hard-hearted pride;
"I bore her as became a chieftain's daughter,
Up to her home beside the gliding water.

"If now no more a mat for her is found
Of all which line her father's wigwam round,

Let Pennacook call out his warrior train
And send her back with wampum gifts again."

The baffled runner turned upon his track,
Bearing the words of Winnepurkit back,
" Dog of the Marsh," cried Pennacook, " no more
Shall child of mine sit on his wigwam floor.

" Go—let him seek some meaner squaw to spread
The stolen bear-skin of his beggar's bed:
Son of a fish-hawk!—let him dig his clams
For some vile daughter of the Agawams,

" Or coward Nipmucks!—may his scalp dry black
In Mohawk smoke, before I send her back."
He shook his clenched hand towards the ocean wave,
While hoarse assent his listening council gave.

Alas poor bride!—can thy grim sire impart
His iron hardness to thy woman's heart?
Or cold self-torturing pride like his atone
For love denied and life's warm beauty flown?

On Autumn's gray and mournful grave the snow
Hung its white wreaths; with stifled voice and low
The river crept, by one vast bridge o'ercrossed,
Built by the hoar-locked artisan of Frost.

And many a Moon in beauty newly born
Pierced the red sunset with her silver horn,
Or, from the east across her azure field
Rolled the wide brightness of her full-orbed shield.

Yet Winnepurkit came not—on the mat
Of the scorned wife her dusky rival sat,
And he, the while, in Western woods afar—
Urged the long chase, or trod the path of war.

Dry up thy tears, young daughter of a chief!
Waste not on him the sacredness of grief;
Be the fierce spirit of thy sire thine own,
His lips of scorning, and his heart of stone.

What heeds the warrior of a hundred fights,
The storm-worn watcher through long hunting nights
Cold, crafty, proud of woman's weak distress,
Her home-bound grief and pining loneliness?

VII. THE DEPARTURE.

The wild March rains had fallen fast and long
The snowy mountains of the North among,
Making each vale a watercourse—each hill
Bright with the cascade of some new made rill.

Gnawed by the sunbeams, softened by the rain,
Heaved underneath by the swollen current's strain,
The ice-bridge yielded, and the Merrimack
Bore the huge ruin crashing down its track.

On that strong turbid water, a small boat
Guided by one weak hand was seen to float,
Evil the fate which loosed it from the shore,
Too early voyager with too frail an oar!

Down the vexed centre of that rushing tide,
The thick huge ice-blocks threatening either side,
The foam-white rocks of Amoskeag in view,
With arrowy swiftness sped that light canoe.

The trapper moistening his moose's meat
On the wet bank by Uncanoonuc's feet,
Saw the swift boat flash down the troubled stream—
Slept he, or waked he?—was it truth or dream?

The straining eye bent fearfully before,
The small hand clenching on the useless oar,

The bead-wrought blanket trailing o'er the water—
He knew them all—woe for the Sachem's daughter

Sick and aweary of her lonely life,
Heedless of peril the still faithful wife
Had left her mother's grave, her father's door,
To seek the wigwam of her chief once more.

Down the white rapids like a sear leaf whirled,
On the sharp rocks and piled up ices hurled,
Empty and broken, circled the canoe
In the vexed pool below—but, where was Wee-
tamoo?

VIII. SONG OF INDIAN WOMEN.

The Dark eye has left us,
The Spring-bird has flown;
On the pathway of spirits
She wanders alone.
The song of the wood-dove has died on our shore
Mat wonck kunna-monee! [6]—We hear it no more!

Oh, dark water Spirit!
We cast on thy wave
These furs which may never
Hang over her grave;
Bear down to the lost one the robes that she wore
Mat wonck kunna-monee!—We see her no more!

Of the strange land she walks in
No Powah has told:
It may burn with the sunshine,
Or freeze with the cold.
Let us give to our lost one the robes that she wore,
Mat wonck kunna-monee!—We see her no more!

The path she is treading
Shall soon be our own;

Each gliding in shadow
Unseen and alone!—
In vain shall we call on the souls gone before—
Mat wonck kunna-monee!—They hear us no more!

Oh mighty Sowanna![7]
Thy gateways unfold,
From thy wigwam of sunset
Lift curtains of gold!
Take home the poor Spirit whose journey is o'er—
Mat wonck kunna-monee!—We see her no more!

So sang the Children of the Leaves beside
The broad, dark river's coldly-flowing tide,
Now low, now harsh, with sob-like pause and swell
On the high wind their voices rose and fell.
Nature's wild music—sounds of wind-swept trees,
The scream of birds, the wailing of the breeze,
The roar of waters, steady, deep and strong,
Mingled and murmured in that farewell song.

MOGG MEGONE.

1835.

MOGG MEGONE.

PART I.

[The story of Mogg Megone has been considered by the author only as a frame-work for sketches of the scenery of New England, and of its early inhabitants. In portraying the Indian character, he has followed, as closely as his story would admit, the rough but natural delineations of Church, Mayhew, Charlevoix, and Roger Williams; and in so doing he has necessarily discarded much of the romance which poets and novelists have thrown around the ill-fated red man.]

Who stands on that cliff, like a figure of stone,
  Unmoving and tall in the light of the sky,
  Where the spray of the cataract sparkles on high,
Lonely and sternly, save Mogg Megone?[8]
Close to the verge of the rock is he,
  While beneath him the Saco its work is doing,
Hurrying down to its grave, the sea,
  And slow through the rock its pathway hewing!
Far down, through the mist of the falling river,
Which rises up like an incense ever,
The splintered points of the crags are seen,
With water howling and vexed between,
While the scooping whirl of the pool beneath
Seems an open throat, with its granite teeth!

But Mogg Megone never trembled yet
Wherever his eye or his foot was set.
He is watchful: each form in the moonlight dim,
Of rock or of tree, is seen of him:
He listens; each sound from afar is caught,
The faintest shiver of leaf and limb:

But he sees not the waters, which foam and fret,
Whose moonlit spray has his moccasin wet—
And the roar of their rushing, he hears it not.

The moonlight, through the open bough
  Of the gnarl'd beech, whose naked root
  Coils like a serpent at his foot,
Falls, checkered, on the Indian's brow.
His head is bare, save only where
Waves in the wind one lock of hair,
  Reserved for him, whoe'er he be,
More mighty than Megone in strife,
  When breast to breast and knee to knee,
Above the fallen warrior's life
Gleams, quick and keen, the scalping-knife.

Megone hath his knife and hatchet and gun,
And his gaudy and tasselled blanket on:
His knife hath a handle with gold inlaid,
And magic words on its polished blade—
'Twas the gift of Castine [9] to Mogg Megone,
For a scalp or twain from the Yengees torn:
His gun was the gift of the Tarrantine,
  And Modocawando's wives had strung
The brass and the beads, which tinkle and shine
On the polished breech, and broad bright line
  Of beaded wampum around it hung.

What seeks Megone? His foes are near—
  Grey Jocelyn's [10] eye is never sleeping,
And the garrison lights are burning clear,
  Where Phillips' [11] men their watch are keeping.
Let him hie him away through the dank river fog,
  Never rustling the boughs nor displacing the rocks,
For the eyes and the ears which are watching for Mogg,
  Are keener than those of the wolf or the fox.

He starts—there's a rustle among the leaves:
  Another—the click of his gun is heard !—
A footstep—is it the step of Cleaves,
  With Indian blood on his English sword ?
Steals Harmon [12] down from the sands of York,
With hand of iron and foot of cork ?
Has Scamman, versed in Indian wile,
For vengeance left his vine hung isle ? [13]
Hark ! at that whistle, soft and low,
  How lights the eye of Mogg Megone !
A smile gleams o'er his dusky brow—
  "Boon welcome, Johnny Bonython !"

Out steps, with cautious foot and slow,
And quick, keen glances to and fro,
  The hunted outlaw, Bonython ! [14]
A low, lean swarthy man is he,
With blanket-garb and buskin'd knee,
  And nought of English fashion on ;
For he hates the race from whence he sprung,
And he couches his words in the Indian tongue.

"Hush—let the Sachem's voice be weak ;
The water-rat shall hear him speak—
The owl shall whoop in the white man's ear,
That Mogg Megone, with his scalps, is here !"
He pauses—dark, over cheek and brow,
A flush, as of shame, is stealing now :
"Sachem !" he says, "let me have the land,
Which stretches away upon either hand,
As far about as my feet can stray
In the half of a gentle summer's day,
  From the leaping brook [15] to the Saco river—
And the fair-haired girl, thou hast sought of me,
Shall sit in the Sachem's wigwam, and be
  The wife of Mogg Megone forever."

There's a sudden light in the Indian's glance,
  A moment's trace of powerful feeling—

Of love or triumph, or both perchance,
Over his proud, calm features stealing.
"The words of my father are very good;
He shall have the land, and water, and wood;
And he who harms the Sagamore John,
Shall feel the knife of Mogg Megone;
But the fawn of the Yengees shall sleep on my breast,
And the bird of the clearing shall sing in my nest."

"But father!"—and the Indian's hand
Falls gently on the white man's arm
And with a smile as shrewdly bland
As the deep voice is slow and calm—
"Where is my father's singing-bird—
The sunny eye, and sunset hair?
I know I have my father's word,
And that his word is good and fair;
But, will my father tell me where
Megone shall go and look for his bride?—
For he sees her not by her father's side."

The dark, stern eye of Bonython
Flashes over the features of Mogg Megone,
In one of those glances which search within;
But the stolid calm of the Indian alone
Remains where the trace of emotion has been.
"Does the Sachem doubt? Let him go with me,
And the eyes of the Sachem his bride shall see."
Cautious and slow, with pauses oft,
And watchful eyes and whispers soft,
The twain are stealing through the wood,
Leaving the downward-rushing flood,
Whose deep and solemn roar behind,
Grows fainter on the evening wind

Hark!—is that the angry howl
Of the wolf, the hills among?—

Or the hooting of the owl,
  On his leafy cradle swung?—
Quickly glancing, to and fro,
Listening to each sound they go
Round the columns of the pine,
  Indistinct, in shadow, seeming
Like some old and pillared shrine;
With the soft and white moonshine,
Round the foliage-tracery shed
Of each column's branching head,
  For its lamps of worship gleaming!
And the sounds awakened there,
  In the pine leaves fine and small,
  Soft and sweetly musical,
By the fingers of the air,
For the anthem's dying fall
Lingering round some temple's wall!—
Niche and cornice round and round
Wailing like the ghost of sound!
Is not Nature's worship thus
  Ceaseless ever, going on?
Hath it not a voice for us
  In the thunder, or the tone
Of the leaf-harp faint and small,
  Speaking to the unsealed ear
  Words of blended love and fear
Of the mighty Soul of all?

Nought had the twain of thoughts like these
As they wound along through the crowded trees,
Where never had rung the axeman's stroke
On the gnarled trunk of the rough-barked oak;—
Climbing the dead tree's mossy log,
  Breaking the mesh of the bramble fine,
  Turning aside the wild grape vine,
And lightly crossing the quaking bog
Whose surface shakes at the leap of the frog,
And out of whose pools the ghostly fog
  Creeps into the chill moonshine!

Yet, even that Indian's ear had heard
The preaching of the Holy Word:
Sanchekantacket's isle of sand
Was once his father's hunting land,
Where zealous Hiacoomes [16] stood—
The wild apostle of the wood,
Shook from his soul the fear of harm,
And trampled on the Powwaw's charm;
Until the wizard's curses hung
Suspended on his palsying tongue,
And the fierce warrior, grim and tall,
Trembled before the forest Paul!

A cottage hidden in the wood—
  Red through its seams a light is glowing,
On rock and bough and tree-trunk rude,
  A narrow lustre throwing.
"Who's there?" a clear, firm voice demands:
  "Hold, Ruth—'tis I, the Sagamore!"
Quick, at the summons, hasty hands
  Unclose the bolted door;
And on the outlaw's daughter shine
The flashes of the kindled pine.

Tall and erect the maiden stands,
  Like some young priestess of the wood,
The freeborn child of Solitude,
  And bearing still the wild and rude,
Yet noble trace of Nature's hands.
Her dark brown cheek has caught its stain
More from the sunshine than the rain;
Yet, where her long fair hair is parting,
A pure white brow into light is starting;
And, where the folds of her blanket sever,
Are a neck and bosom as white as ever
The foam-wreaths rise on the leaping river.
But, in the convulsive quiver and grip
Of the muscles around her bloodless lip,
  There is something painful and sad to see;

And her eye has a glance more sternly wild
Than even that of a forest child
  In its fearless and untamed freedom should be.

Yet, seldom in hall or court are seen
So queenly a form and so noble a mien,
  As freely and smiling she welcomes them there—
Her outlawed sire and Mogg Megone:
  "Pray, father, how does thy hunting fare?
  And, Sachem, say—does Scamman wear,
In spite of thy promise, a scalp of his own?"
Hurried and light is the maiden's tone;
  But a fearful meaning lurks within
Her glance, as it questions the eye of Megone—
  An awful meaning of guilt and sin!—
The Indian hath opened his blanket, and there
Hangs a human scalp by its long damp hair!
With hand upraised, with quick-drawn breath,
She meets that ghastly sign of death.
In one long, glassy, spectral stare
The enlarging eye is fastened there,
As if that mesh of pale brown hair
  Had power to change at sight alone,
Even as the fearful locks which wound
Medusa's fatal forehead round,
  The gazer into stone.
With such a look Herodias read
The features of the bleeding head,
So looked the mad Moor on his dead,
Or the young Cenci as she stood,
O'er-dabbled with a father's blood!

Look!—feeling melts that frozen glance,
It moves that marble countenance,
As if at once within her strove
Pity with shame, and hate with love.
The Past recalls its joy and pain,
Old memories rise before her brain—
The lips which love's embraces met,

The hand her tears of parting wet,
The voice whose pleading tones beguiled
The pleased ear of the forest-child,—
And tears she may no more repress
Reveal her lingering tenderness.

Oh! woman wronged, can cherish hate
  More deep and dark than manhood may;
But, when the mockery of Fate
  Hath left Revenge its chosen way,
And the fell curse, which years have nursed,
Full on the spoiler's head hath burst—
When all her wrong, and shame, and pain,
Burns fiercely on his heart and brain—
Still lingers something of the spell
  Which bound her to the traitor's bosom—
Still, midst the vengeful fires of hell,
  Some flowers of old affection blossom.

John Bonython's eye-brows together are drawn
With a fierce expression of wrath and scorn—
He hoarsely whispers, "Ruth, beware!
  Is this the time to be playing the fool—
Crying over a paltry lock of hair,
  Like a love-sick girl at school?—
Curse on it!—an Indian can see and hear:
Away—and prepare our evening cheer!"

How keenly the Indian is watching now
Her tearful eye and her varying brow—
  With a serpent eye, which kindles and burns,
  Like a fiery star in the upper air:
On sire and daughter his fierce glance turns:—
  "Has my old white father a scalp to spare?
  For his young one loves the pale brown hair
Of the scalp of an English dog, far more
Than Mogg Megone, or his wigwam floor:
  Go—Mogg is wise: he will keep his land—
  And Sagamore John, when he feels with his hand,
Shall miss his scalp where it grew before."

The moment's gust of grief is gone—
  The lip is clenched—the tears are still—
God pity thee, Ruth Bonython!
  With what a strength of will
Are nature's feelings in thy breast,
As with an iron hand repressed!
And how, upon that nameless woe,
Quick as the pulse can come and go,
While shakes the unsteadfast knee, and yet
The bosom heaves—the eye is wet—
Has thy dark spirit power to stay
The heart's wild current on its way?
  And whence that baleful strength of guile,
Which over that still working brow
And tearful eye and cheek, can throw
  The mockery of a smile?
Warned by her father's blackening frown,
With one strong effort crushing down
Grief, hate, remorse, she meets again
  The savage murderer's sullen gaze,
  And scarcely look or tone betrays
How the heart strives beneath its chain.

"Is the Sachem angry—angry with Ruth,
Because she cries with an ache in her tooth,[17]
Which would make a Sagamore jump and cry,
And look about with a woman's eye?
No—Ruth will sit in the Sachem's door
And braid the mats for his wigwam floor,
And broil his fish and tender fawn,
And weave his wampum, and grind his corn,—
For she loves the brave and the wise, and none
Are braver and wiser than Mogg Megone!"

The Indian's brow is clear once more:
  With grave, calm face, and half-shut eye,
He sits upon the wigwam floor,
  And watches Ruth go by,
Intent upon her household care;

And ever and anon, the while,
Or on the maiden, or her fare,
Which smokes in grateful promise there,
Bestows his quiet smile.

Ah, Mogg Megone!—what dreams are thine
But those which love's own fancies dress—
The sum of Indian happiness!—
A wigwam, where the warm sunshine
Looks in among the groves of pine—
A stream, where, round thy light canoe,
The trout and salmon dart in view,
And the fair girl, before thee now,
Spreading thy mat with hand of snow,
Or plying, in the dews of morn,
Her hoe amidst thy patch of corn,
Or offering up, at eve, to thee,
Thy birchen dish of hominy!

From the rude board of Bonython,
Venison and suckatash have gone—
For long these dwellers of the wood
Have felt the gnawing want of food.
But untasted of Ruth is the frugal cheer—
With head averted, yet ready ear,
She stands by the side of her austere sire,
Feeding, at times, the unequal fire,
With the yellow knots of the pitch-pine tree,
Whose flaring light, as they kindle, falls
On the cottage-roof, and its black log walls,
And over its inmates three.

From Sagamore Bonython's hunting flask
The fire-water burns at the lip of Megone:
"Will the Sachem hear what his father shall ask?
Will he make his mark, that it may be known,
On the speaking-leaf, that he gives the land,
From the Sachem's own, to his father's hand?"

The fire-water shines in the Indian's eyes,
  As he rises, the white man's bidding to do:
"Wuttamuttata—weekan![18] Mogg is wise—
  For the water he drinks is strong and new,—
Mogg's heart is great!—will he shut his hand,
When his father asks for a little land?"—
With unsteady fingers, the Indian has drawn
  On the parchment the shape of a hunter's bow
"Boon water—boon water—Sagamore John!
  Wuttamuttata—weekan! our hearts will grow!"
He drinks yet deeper—he mutters low—
He reels on his bear-skin to and fro—
His head falls down on his naked breast—
He struggles, and sinks to a drunken rest.

"Humph—drunk as a beast!"—and Bonython's brow
  Is darker than ever with evil thought—
"The fool has signed his warrant; but how
  And when shall the deed be wrought?
Speak, Ruth! why, what the devil is there,
To fix thy gaze in that empty air?—
Speak, Ruth! by my soul, if I thought that tear,
Which shames thyself and our purpose here,
Were shed for that cursed and pale-faced dog,
Whose green scalp hangs from the belt of Mogg,
  And whose beastly soul is in Satan's keeping—
This—this!"—he dashes his hand upon
The rattling stock of his loaded gun—
  "Should send thee with him to do thy weeping."

  "Father!"—the eye of Bonython
  Sinks, at that low, sepulchral tone,
  Hollow and deep, as it were spoken
    By the unmoving tongue of death—
  Or from some statue's lips had broken—
  A sound without a breath!
  "Father!—my life I value less
  Than yonder fool his gaudy dress.

And how it ends it matters not,
By heart-break or by rifle-shot:
But spare awhile the scoff and threat—
Our business is not finished yet."

"True, true, my girl—I only meant
To draw up again the bow unbent.
Harm thee, my Ruth! I only sought
To frighten off thy gloomy thought;—
Come—let's be friends!" He seeks to clasp
His daughter's cold, damp hand in his.
Ruth startles from her father's grasp,
As if each nerve and muscle felt,
Instinctively, the touch of guilt,
Through all their subtle sympathies.

He points her to the sleeping Mogg:
"What shall be done with yonder dog?
Scamman is dead, and revenge is thine—
The deed is signed and the land is mine;
And this drunken fool is of use no more,
Save as thy hopeful bridegroom, and sooth,
'T were Christian mercy to finish him Ruth,
Now, while he lies like a beast on our floor,—
If not for thine, at least for his sake,
Rather than let the poor dog awake,
To drain my flask, and claim as his bride
Such a forest devil to run by his side—
Such a Wetuomanit[19] as thou wouldst make!"

He laughs at his jest. Hush—what is there?—
The sleeping Indian is striving to rise,
With his knife in his hand, and glaring eyes!—
"Wagh!—Mogg will have the pale-face's hair,
For his knife is sharp and his fingers can help
The hair to pull and the skin to peel—
Let him cry like a woman and twist like an eel,
The great Captain Scamman must lose his scalp!

And Ruth, when she sees it, shall dance with
Mogg."
His eyes are fixed—but his lips draw in—
With a low, hoarse chuckle, and fiendish grin,—
And he sinks again, like a senseless log.

Ruth does not speak—she does not stir;
But she gazes down on the murderer,
Whose broken and dreamful slumbers tell,
Too much for her ear, of that deed of hell.
She sees the knife, with its slaughter red,
And the dark fingers clenching the bear-skin bed!
What thoughts of horror and madness whirl
Through the burning brain of that fallen girl!

John Bonython lifts his gun to his eye,
Its muzzle is close to the Indian's ear—
But he drops it again. "Some one may be nigh,
And I would not that even the wolves should
hear."
He draws his knife from its deer-skin belt—
Its edge with his fingers is slowly felt;—
Kneeling down on one knee, by the Indian's
side,
From his throat he opens the blanket wide;
And twice or thrice he feebly essays
A trembling hand with the knife to raise.

"I cannot"—he mutters—"did he not save
My life from a cold and wintry grave,
When the storm came down from Agioochook,
And the north-wind howled, and the tree-tops
shook—
And I strove, in the drifts of the rushing snow,
Till my knees grew weak and I could not go,
And I felt the cold to my vitals creep,
And my heart's blood stiffen, and pulses sleep!
I cannot strike him—Ruth Bonython!
In the devil's name, tell me—what's to be done?"

Oh! when the soul, once pure and high,
Is stricken down from Virtue's sky,
As, with the downcast star of morn,
Some gems of light are with it drawn—
And, through its night of darkness, play
Some tokens of its primal day—
Some lofty feelings linger still—
  The strength to dare, the nerve to meet
  Whatever threatens with defeat
Its all-indomitable will!—
But lacks the mean of mind and heart,
  Though eager for the gains of crime,
  Oft, at his chosen place and time,
The strength to bear his evil part;
And, shielded by his very Vice,
Escapes from Crime by Cowardice.

Ruth starts erect—with bloodshot eye,
  And lips drawn tight across her teeth,
Showing their locked embrace beneath,
In the red fire-light:—"Mogg must die!
Give me the knife!"—The outlaw turns,
  Shuddering in heart and limb, away—
But, fitfully there, the hearth-fire burns,
  And he sees on the wall strange shadows play.
A lifted arm, a tremulous blade,
Are dimly pictured in light and shade,
  Plunging down in the darkness. Hark, that cry
Again—and again—he sees it fall—
That shadowy arm down the lighted wall!
  He hears quick footsteps—a shape flits by —
The door on its rusted hinges creaks:—
"Ruth—daughter Ruth!" the outlaw shrieks
But no sound comes back—he is standing alone
By the mangled corse of Mogg Megone!

PART II.

'Tis morning over Norridgewock—
On tree and wigwam, wave and rock.
Bathed in the autumnal sunshine, stirred
At intervals by breeze and bird,
And wearing all the hues which glow
In heaven's own pure and perfect bow,
That glorious picture of the air,
Which summer's light-robed angel forms
On the dark ground of fading storms,
With pencil dipped in sunbeams there—
And, stretching out, on either hand,
O'er all that wide and unshorn land,
Till, weary of its gorgeousness,
The aching and the dazzled eye
Rests gladdened, on the calm blue sky—
Slumbers the mighty wilderness!
The oak, upon the windy hill,
Its dark green burthen upward heaves—
The hemlock broods above its rill,
Its cone-like foliage darker still,
Against the birch's graceful stem,
And the rough walnut bough receives
The sun upon its crowded leaves,
Each colored like a topaz gem;
And the tall maple wears with them
The coronal which autumn gives,
The brief, bright sign of ruin near,
The hectic of a dying year!

The hermit priest, who lingers now
On the Bald Mountain's shrubless brow,
The gray and thunder-smitten pile
Which marks afar the Desert Isle,[20]
While gazing on the scene below,
May half forget the dreams of home,

That nightly with his slumbers come,—
The tranquil skies of sunny France,
The peasant's harvest song and dance,
The vines around the hill-sides wreathing
The soft airs midst their clusters breathing,
The wings which dipped, the stars which shone
Within thy bosom, blue Garronne!
And round the Abbey's shadowed wall,
At morning spring and even-fall,
   Sweet voices in the still air singing—
The chant of many a holy hymn—
   The solemn bell of vespers ringing—
And hallowed torch-light falling dim
   On pictured saint and seraphim!
For here beneath him lies unrolled,
Bathed deep in morning's flood of gold,
A vision gorgeous as the dream
Of the beatified may seem,
   When, as his Church's legends say,
Borne upward in ecstatic bliss,
   The rapt enthusiast soars away
Unto a brighter world than this:
A mortal's glimpse beyond the pale—
A moment's lifting of the veil!

Far eastward o'er the lovely bay,
Penobscot's clustered wigwams lay;
And gently from that Indian town
The verdant hill side slopes adown,
To where the sparkling waters play
   Upon the yellow sands below;
And shooting round the winding shores
   Of narrow capes, and isles which lie
   Slumbering to ocean's lullaby—
With birchen boat and glancing oars,
   The red men to their fishing go;
While from their planting ground is borne
The treasure of the golden corn,
By laughing girls, whose dark eyes glow

Wild through the locks which o'er them flow.
The wrinkled squaw, whose toil is done,
Sits on her bear-skin in the sun,
Watching the huskers, with a smile
For each full ear which swells the pile;
And the old chief, who never more
May bend the bow or pull the oar,
Smokes gravely in his wigwam door,
Or slowly shapes, with axe of stone,
The arrow-head from flint and bone.

Beneath the westward turning eye
A thousand wooded islands lie—
Gems of the waters!—with each hue
Of brightness set in ocean's blue.
Each bears aloft its tuft of trees
  Touched by the pencil of the frost,
And, with the motion of each breeze,
  A moment seen—a moment lost—
  Changing and blent, confused and tossed,
  The brighter with the darker crossed,
Their thousand tints of beauty glow
Down in the restless waves below,
  And tremble in the sunny skies,
As if, from waving bough to bough,
  Flitted the birds of paradise.
There sleep Placentia's group—and there
Pere Breteaux marks the hour of prayer;
And there, beneath the sea-worn cliff,
  On which the Father's hut is seen,
The Indian stays his rocking skiff,
  And peers the hemlock boughs between,
Half trembling, as he seeks to look
Upon the Jesuit's Cross and Book.[21]
There, gloomily against the sky
The Dark Isles rear their summits high;
And Desert Rock, abrupt and bare,
Lifts its gray turrets in the air—
Seen from afar, like some strong hold

Built by the ocean kings of old;
And, faint as smoke-wreath white and thin,
Swells in the north vast Katadin:
And, wandering from its marshy feet,
The broad Penobscot comes to meet
  And mingle with his own bright bay.
Slow sweep his dark and gathering floods,
Arched over by the ancient woods,
Which Time, in those dim solitudes,
  Wielding the dull axe of Decay,
  Alone hath ever shorn away.

Not thus, within the woods which hide
The beauty of thy azure tide,
  And with their falling timbers block
Thy broken currents, Kennebeck!
Gazes the white man on the wreck
  Of the down-trodden Norridgewock—
In one lone village hemmed at length,
In battle shorn of half their strength,
Turned, like the panther in his lair,
  With his fast-flowing life-blood wet,
For one last struggle of despair,
  Wounded and faint, but tameless yet!
Unreaped, upon the planting lands,
The scant, neglected harvest stands:
  No shout is there—no dance—no song:
The aspect of the very child
Scowls with a meaning sad and wild
  Of bitterness and wrong.
The almost infant Norridgewock
Essays to lift the tomahawk;
And plucks his father's knife away,
To mimic, in his frightful play,
  The scalping of an English foe:
Wreaths on his lip a horrid smile,
Burns, like a snake's, his small eye, while
  Some bough or sapling meets his blow.
The fisher, as he drops his line,

Starts, when he sees the hazles quiver
Along the margin of the river,
Looks up and down the rippling tide,
And grasps the firelock at his side.
For Bomazeen [22] from Tacconock
Has sent his runners to Norridgewock,
With tidings that Moulton and Harmon of York
Far up the river have come: [wood,
They have left their boats—they have entered the
And filled the depths of the solitude
With the sound of the ranger's drum.

On the brow of a hill, which slopes to meet
The flowing river, and bathe its feet—
The bare-washed rock, and the drooping grass,
And the creeping vine, as the waters pass—
A rude and unshapely chapel stands,
Built up in that wild by unskilled hands;
Yet the traveller knows it a place of prayer,
For the holy sign of the cross is there:
And should he chance at that place to be,
Of a sabbath morn, or some hallowed day,
When prayers are made and masses are said,
Some for the living and some for the dead,
Well might that traveller start to see
The tall dark forms, that take their way
From the birch canoe, on the river-shore,
And the forest paths, to that chapel door;
And marvel to mark the naked knees
And the dusky foreheads bending there,
While, in coarse white vesture, over these
In blessing or in prayer,
Stretching abroad his thin pale hands,
Like a shrouded ghost, the Jesuit [23] stands.

Two forms are now in that chapel dim,
The Jesuit, silent and sad and pale,
Anxiously heeding some fearful tale,
Which a stranger is telling him.

That stranger's garb is soiled and torn,
And wet with dew and loosely worn;
Her fair neglected hair falls down
O'er cheeks with wind and sunshine brown
Yet still, in that disordered face,
The Jesuit's cautious eye can trace
Those elements of former grace,
Which, half effaced, seem scarcely less,
Even now, than perfect loveliness.

With drooping head, and voice so low
That scarce it meets the Jesuit's ears—
While through her clasped fingers flow,
From the heart's fountain, hot and slow,
Her penitential tears—
She tells the story of the woe
And evil of her years.

" O Father, bear with me; my heart
Is sick and death-like, and my brain
Seems girdled with a fiery chain,
Whose scorching links will never part,
And never cool again.
Bear with me while I speak—but turn
Away that gentle eye, the while—
The fires of guilt more fiercely burn
Beneath its holy smile;
For half I fancy I can see
My mother's sainted look in thee.

"My dear lost mother! sad and pale,
Mournfully sinking day by day,
And with a hold on life as frail
As frosted leaves, that, thin and gray,
Hang feebly on their parent spray,
And tremble in the gale;
Yet watching o'er my childishness
With patient fondness—not the less
For all the agony which kept

Her blue eye wakeful, while I slept;
And checking every tear and groan
That haply might have waked my own
And bearing still, without offence,
My idle words, and petulance;
Reproving with a tear—and, while
The tooth of pain was keenly preying
Upon her very heart, repaying
My brief repentance with a smile.

'Oh, in her meek, forgiving eye
There was a brightness not of mirth—
A light, whose clear intensity
Was borrowed not of earth.
Along her cheek a deepening red
Told where the feverish hectic fed;
And yet, each fatal token gave
To the mild beauty of her face
A newer and a dearer grace,
Unwarning of the grave.
'Twas like the hue which autumn gives
To yonder changed and dying leaves,
Breathed over by his frosty breath;
Scarce can the gazer feel that this
Is but the spoiler's treacherous kiss,
The mocking-smile of Death!

"Sweet were the tales she used to tell
When summer's eve was dear to us,
And, fading from the darkening dell,
The glory of the sunset fell
On wooded Agamenticus,—
When, sitting by our cottage wall,
The murmur of the Saco's fall,
And the south wind's expiring sighs
Came, softly blending, on my ear,
With the low tones I loved to hear:
Tales of the pure—the good—the wise—
The holy men and maids of old,
In the all-sacred pages told;—

Of Rachel, stooped at Haran's fountains,
Amid her father's thirsty flock,
Beautiful to her kinsman seeming
As the bright angels of his dreaming,
On Padan-aran's holy rock;
Of gentle Ruth—and her who kept
Her awful vigil on the mountains,
By Israel's virgin daughters wept;
Of Miriam, with her maidens, singing
The song for grateful Israel meet,
While every crimson wave was bringing
The spoils of Egypt at her feet;
Of her—Samaria's humble daughter,
Who paused to hear, beside her well,
Lessons of love and truth, which fell
Softly as Shiloh's flowing water;
And saw, beneath his pilgrim guise,
The Promised One, so long foretold
By holy seer and bard of old,
Revealed before her wondering eyes!

"Slowly she faded. Day by day
Her step grew weaker in our hall,
And fainter, at each even-fall,
Her sad voice died away.
Yet on her thin, pale lip, the while,
Sat Resignation's holy smile:
And even my father checked his tread,
And hushed his voice, beside her bed:
Beneath the calm and sad rebuke
Of her meek eye's imploring look,
The scowl of hate his brow forsook,
And, in his stern and gloomy eye,
At times, a few unwonted tears
Wet the dark lashes, which for years
Hatred and pride had kept so dry.

"Calm as a child to slumber soothed,
As if an angel's hand had smoothed

The still, white features into rest,
Silent and cold, without a breath
To stir the drapery on her breast
Pain, with its keen and poisoned fang,
The horror of the mortal pang,
The suffering look her brow had worn,
The fear, the strife, the anguish gone—
She slept at last in death!

"Oh, tell me, father, *can* the dead
Walk on the earth, and look on us,
And lay upon the living's head
Their blessing or their curse?
For, oh, last night she stood by me,
As I lay beneath the woodland tree!"

The Jesuit crosses himself in awe—
"Jesu! what was it my daughter saw?"

"*She* came to me last night.
The dried leaves did not feel her tread;
She stood by me in the wan moonlight,
In the white robes of the dead!
Pale, and very mournfully
She bent her light form over me.
I heard no sound, I felt no breath
Breathe o'er me from that face of death:
Its blue eyes rested on my own,
Rayless and cold as eyes of stone;
Yet, in their fixed, unchanging gaze,
Something, which spoke of early days—
A sadness in their quiet glare,
As if love's smile were frozen there—
Came o'er me with an icy thrill;
Oh God! I feel its presence still!"

The Jesuit makes the holy sign—
"How passed the vision, daughter mine?

"All dimly in the wan moonshine,
As a wreath of mist will twist and twine,
And scatter, and melt into the light—
So scattering—melting on my sight,
The pale, cold vision passed;
But those sad eyes were fixed on mine
Mournfully to the last."

"God help thee, daughter, tell me why
That spirit passed before thine eye!"

"Father, I know not, save it be
That deeds of mine have summoned her
From the unbreathing sepulchre,
To leave her last rebuke with me.
Ah, woe for me! my mother died
Just at the moment when I stood
Close on the verge of womanhood,
A child in every thing beside;
And when my wild heart needed most
Her gentle counsels, they were lost.

"My father lived a stormy life,
Of frequent change and daily strife;
And—God forgive him! left his child
To feel, like him, a freedom wild;
To love the red man's dwelling place,
The birch boat on his shaded floods,
The wild excitement of the chase
Sweeping the ancient woods,
The camp-fire, blazing on the shore
Of the still lakes, the clear stream, where
The idle fisher sets his wear,
Or angles in the shade, far more
Than that restraining awe I felt
Beneath my gentle mother's care,
When nightly at her knee I knelt,
With childhood's simple prayer.

"There came a change. The wild, glad mood
Of unchecked freedom passed.
Amid the ancient solitude
Of unshorn grass and waving wood,
And waters glancing bright and fast,
A softened voice was in my ear,
Sweet as those lulling sounds and fine
The hunter lifts his head to hear,
Now far and faint, now full and near—
The murmur of the wind-swept pine.
A manly form was ever nigh,
A bold, free hunter, with an eye
Whose dark, keen glance had power to wake
Both fear and love—to awe and charm;
'Twas as the wizard rattlesnake,
Whose evil glances lure to harm—
Whose cold and small and glittering eye,
And brilliant coil, and changing dye,
Draw, step by step, the gazer near,
With drooping wing and cry of fear,
Yet powerless all to turn away,
A conscious, but a willing prey!

Fear, doubt, thought, life itself, ere long
Merged in one feeling deep and strong.
Faded the world which I had known,
A poor vain shadow, cold and waste,
In the warm present bliss alone
Seemed I of actual life to taste.
Fond longings dimly understood,
The glow of passion's quickening blood,
And cherished fantasies which press
The young lip with a dream's caress,—
The heart's forecast and prophecy
Took form and life before my eye,
Seen in the glance which met my own,
Heard in the soft and pleading tone,
Felt in the arms around me cast,
And warm heart-pulses beating fast.
Ah! scarcely yet to God above

With deeper trust, with stronger love
Has prayerful saint his meek heart lent,
Or cloistered nun at twilight bent,
Than I, before a human shrine,
As mortal and as frail as mine,
With heart, and soul, and mind, and form,
Knelt madly to a fellow worm.

"Full soon, upon that dream of sin,
An awful light came bursting in.
The shrine was cold, at which I knelt
The idol of that shrine was gone;
A humbled thing of shame and guilt,
Outcast, and spurned and lone,
Wrapt in the shadows of my crime,
With withering heart and burning brain,
And tears that fell like fiery rain,
I passed a fearful time.

"There came a voice—it checked the tear—
In heart and soul it wrought a change;—
My father's voice was in my ear;
It whispered of revenge!
A new and fiercer feeling swept
All lingering tenderness away;
And tiger passions, which had slept
In childhood's better day,
Unknown, unfelt, arose at length
In all their own demoniac strength.

"A youthful warrior of the wild,
By words deceived, by smiles beguiled,
Of crime the cheated instrument,
Upon our fatal errands went.
Through camp and town and wilderness
He tracked his victim; and, at last,
Just when the tide of hate had passed,
And milder thoughts came warm and fast,
Exulting, at my feet he cast
The bloody token of success.

"Oh God! with what an awful power
  I saw the buried past uprise,
And gather, in a single hour,
  Its ghost-like memories!
And then I felt—alas! too late—
That underneath the mask of hate,
That shame and guilt and wrong had thrown
O'er feelings which they might not own,
  The heart's wild love had known no change;
And still, that deep and hidden love,
With its first fondness, wept above
  The victim of its own revenge!
There lay the fearful scalp, and there
The blood was on its pale brown hair!
I thought not of the victim's scorn,
  I thought not of his baleful guile,
My deadly wrong, my outcast name,
The characters of sin and shame
On heart and forehead drawn;
  I only saw that victim's smile—
The still, green places where we met—
The moon-lit branches, dewy wet;
I only felt, I only heard
The greeting and the parting word—
The smile—the embrace—the tone, which made
An Eden of the forest shade.

"And oh, with what a loathing eye,
  With what a deadly hate, and deep,
I saw that Indian murderer lie
  Before me, in his drunken sleep!
What though for me the deed was done,
And words of mine had sped him on!
Yet when he murmured, as he slept,
  The horrors of that deed of blood,
The tide of utter madness swept
  O'er brain and bosom, like a flood.
And, father, with this hand of mine"——
  "Ha! what didst thou?" the Jesuit cries,

Shuddering, as smitten with sudden pain,
  And shading, with one thin hand, his eyes,
With the other he makes the holy sign——
"I smote him as I would a worm;—
With heart as steeled—with nerves as firm:
  He never woke again!"

"Woman of sin and blood and shame,
Speak—I would know that victim's name."

"Father," she gasped, "a chieftain, known
As Saco's Sachem—MOGG MEGONE!"

Pale priest! What proud and lofty dreams,
What keen desires, what cherished schemes,
What hopes, that time may not recall,
Are darkened by that chieftain's fall!
Was he not pledged, by cross and vow,
  To lift the hatchet of his sire,
And, round his own, the Church's foe,
  To light the avenging fire?
Who now the Tarrantine shall wake,
For thine and for the Church's sake?
  Who summon to the scene
Of conquest and unsparing strife,
And vengeance dearer than his life,
  The fiery-souled Castine? [24]
Three backward steps the Jesuit takes—
His long, thin frame as ague shakes:
  And loathing hate is in his eye,
As from his lips these words of fear
Fall hoarsely on the maiden's ear—
  "The soul that sinneth shall surely die!"

She stands, as stands the stricken deer,
  Checked midway in the fearful chase,
When bursts, upon his eye and ear,
The gaunt, gray robber, baying near,
  Between him and his hiding place;

While still behind, with yell and blow,
Sweeps, like a storm, the coming foe.
"Save me, O holy man!"—her cry
  Fills all the void, as if a tongue,
  Unseen, from rib and rafter hung,
Thrilling with mortal agony;
Her hands are clasping the Jesuit's knee,
  And her eye looks fearfully into his own;—
"Off, woman of sin!—nay, touch not me
  With those fingers of blood;—begone!"
With a gesture of horror, he spurns the form
That writhes at his feet like a trodden worm.

Ever thus the spirit must,
  Guilty in the sight of Heaven,
  With a keener woe be riven,
For its weak and sinful trust
In the strength of human dust;
  And its anguish thrill afresh,
For each vain reliance given
  To the failing arm of flesh.

PART III.

Ah, weary Priest!—with pale hands pressed
  On thy throbbing brow of pain,
Baffled in thy life-long quest,
  Overworn with toiling vain,
How ill thy troubled musings fit
  The holy quiet of a breast
  With the Dove of Peace at rest,
Sweetly brooding over it.
Thoughts are thine which have no part
With the meek and pure of heart,
Undisturbed by outward things,
Resting in the heavenly shade,

By the overspreading wings
  Of the Blessed Spirit made.
Thoughts of strife and hate and wrong
Sweep thy heated brain along—
Fading hopes, for whose success
  It were sin to breathe a prayer ;—
Schemes which heaven may never bless—
  Fears which darken to despair.
Hoary priest! thy dream is done
Of a hundred red tribes won
  To the pale of Holy Church;
And the heretic o'erthrown,
And his name no longer known,
And thy weary brethren turning,
Joyful from their years of mourning,
'Twixt the altar and the porch.
Hark! what sudden sound is heard
  In the wood and in the sky,
Shriller than the scream of bird—
  Than the trumpet's clang more high!
Every wolf-cave of the hills—
  Forest arch and mountain gorge,
  Rock and dell and river verge—
With an answering echo thrills.
Well does the Jesuit know that cry,
Which summons the Norridgewock to die,
And tells that the foe of his flock is nigh.
He listens, and hears the rangers come,
With loud hurra, and jar of drum,
And hurrying feet (for the chase is hot),
And the short, sharp sound of rifle shot,
And taunt and menace—answered well
By the Indians' mocking cry and yell—
The bark of dogs—the squaw's mad scream—
The dash of paddles along the stream—
The whistle of shot as it cuts the leaves
Of the maples around the church's eaves—
And the gride of hatchets, fiercely thrown,
On wigwam-log and tree and stone.

Black with the grime of paint and dust,
  Spotted and streaked with human gore,
A grim and naked head is thrust
  Within the chapel-door.
"Ha—Bomazeen!—In God's name say,
What mean these sounds of bloody fray?"
Silent, the Indian points his hand
  To where across the echoing glen
Sweep Harmon's dreaded ranger-band,
  And Moulton with his men.
"Where are thy warriors, Bomazeen?
Where are De Rouville [25] and Castine,
And where the braves of Sawga's queen?"
"Let my father find the winter snow
Which the sun drank up long moons ago!
Under the falls of Tacconock,
The wolves are eating the Norridgewock;
Castine with his wives lies closely hid
Like a fox in the woods of Pemaquid!
On Sawga's banks the man of war
Sits in his wigwam like a squaw—
Squando has fled, and Mogg Megone,
Struck by the knife of Sagamore John,
Lies stiff and stark and cold as a stone."

Fearfully over the Jesuit's face,
Of a thousand thoughts, trace after trace,
Like swift cloud-shadows, each other chase.
One instant, his fingers grasp his knife,
For a last vain struggle for cherished life—
The next, he hurls the blade away,
And kneels at his altar's foot to pray;
Over his beads his fingers stray,
And he kisses the cross, and calls aloud
On the Virgin and her Son;
For terrible thoughts his memory crowd
  Of evil seen and done—
Of scalps brought home by his savage flock

From Casco and Sawga and Sagadahock,
In the Church's service won.

No shrift the gloomy savage brooks,
As scowling on the priest he looks:
"Cowesass—cowesass—tawhich wessaseen?[26]
Let my father look upon Bomazeen—
My father's heart is the heart of a squaw,
But mine is so hard that it does not thaw:
Let my father ask his God to make
A dance and a feast for a great sagamore,
When he paddles across the western lake
With his dogs and his squaws to the spirit's shore
Cowesass—cowesass—tawhich wessaseen?
Let my father die like Bomazeen!"

Through the chapel's narrow doors,
And through each window in the walls,
Round the priest and warrior pours
The deadly shower of English balls.
Low on his cross the Jesuit falls;
While at his side the Norridgewock,
With failing breath, essays to mock
And menace yet the hated foe—
Shakes his scalp-trophies to and fro
Exultingly before their eyes—
Till, cleft and torn by shot and blow,
Defiant still, he dies.

"So fare all eaters of the frog!
Death to the Babylonish dog!
Down with the beast of Rome!"
With shouts like these, around the dead,
Unconscious on his bloody bed,
The rangers crowding come.
Brave men! the dead priest cannot hear
The unfeeling taunt—the brutal jeer;—
Spurn—for he sees ye not—in wrath,
The symbol of your Saviour's death;

Tear from his death-grasp, in your zeal,
And trample, as a thing accursed,
The cross he cherished in the dust:
The dead man cannot feel!

Brutal alike in deed and word,
With callous heart and hand of strife,
How like a fiend may man be made,
Plying the foul and monstrous trade
Whose harvest-field is human life,
Whose sickle is the reeking sword!
Quenching, with reckless hand in blood,
Sparks kindled by the breath of God;
Urging the deathless soul, unshriven,
Of open guilt or secret sin,
Before the bar of that pure Heaven
The holy only enter in!
Oh! by the widow's sore distress,
The orphan's wailing wretchedness,
By Virtue struggling in the accursed
Embraces of polluting Lust,
By the fell discord of the Pit,
And the pained souls that people it,
And by the blessed peace which fills
The Paradise of God forever,
Resting on all its holy hills,
And flowing with its crystal river—
Let Christian hands no longer bear
In triumph on his crimson car
The foul and idol god of war;
No more the purple wreaths prepare
To bind amid his snaky hair;
Nor Christian bards his glories tell,
Nor Christian tongues his praises swell.

Through the gun-smoke wreathing white,
Glimpses on the soldiers' sight
A thing of human shape I ween,
For a moment only seen,

With its loose hair backward streaming,
And its eyeballs madly gleaming,
Shrieking, like a soul in pain,
  From the world of light and breath,
Hurrying to its place again,
  Spectre-like it vanisheth!

Wretched girl! one eye alone
Notes the way which thou hast gone.
That great Eye, which slumbers never,
Watching o'er a lost world ever,
Tracks thee over vale and mountain,
By the gushing forest-fountain,
Plucking from the vine its fruit,
Searching for the ground-nut's root,
Peering in the she wolf's den,
Wading through the marshy fen,
Where the sluggish water-snake
Basks beside the sunny brake,
Coiling in his slimy bed,
Smooth and cold against thy tread—
Purposeless, thy mazy way
Threading through the lingering day.
And at night securely sleeping
Where the dogwood's dews are weeping!
Still, though earth and man discard thee,
Doth thy heavenly Father guard thee—
He who spared the guilty Cain,
  Even when a brother's blood,
  Crying in the ear of God,
Gave the earth its primal stain—
He whose mercy ever liveth,
Who repenting guilt forgiveth,
And the broken heart receiveth;—
Wanderer of the wilderness,
  Haunted, guilty, crazed and wild,
He regardeth thy distress,
  And careth for his sinful child!

'Tis spring time on the eastern hills!
Like torrents gush the summer rills;
Through winter's moss and dry dead leaves
The bladed grass revives and lives,
Pushes the mouldering waste away,
And glimpses to the April day.
In kindly shower and sunshine bud
The branches of the dull gray wood;
Out from its sunned and sheltered nooks
The blue eye of the violet looks;
  The southwest wind is warmly blowing,
And odors from the springing grass,
The pine-tree and the sassafras,
  Are with it on its errands going.

A band is marching through the wood
Where rolls the Kennebec his flood—
The warriors of the wilderness,
Painted, and in their battle dress;
And with them one whose bearded cheek,
And white and wrinkled brow, bespeak
  A wanderer from the shores of France.
A few long locks of scattering snow
Beneath a battered morion flow,
And from the rivets of the vest
Which girds in steel his ample breast,
  The slanted sunbeams glance.
In the harsh outlines of his face
Passion and sin have left their trace;
Yet, save worn brow and thin gray hair,
No signs of weary age are there.
  His step is firm, his eye is keen,
Nor years in broil and battle spent,
Nor toil, nor wounds, nor pain have bent
  The lordly frame of old Castine.

No purpose now of strife and blood
  Urges the hoary veteran on:
The fire of conquest, and the mood

Of chivalry have gone.
A mournful task is his—to lay
Within the earth the bones of those
Who perished in that fearful day,
When Norridgewock became the prey
Of all unsparing foes.
Sadly and still, dark thoughts between,
Of coming vengeance mused Castine,
Of the fallen chieftain Bomazeen,
Who bade for him the Norridgewocks,
Dig up their buried tomahawks
For firm defence or swift attack;
And him whose friendship formed the tie
Which held the stern self-exile back
From lapsing into savagery;
Whose garb and tone and kindly glance
Recalled a younger, happier day,
And prompted memory's fond essay,
To bridge the mighty waste which lay,
Between his wild home and that gray,
Tall chateau of his native France,
Whose chapel bell, with far-heard din
Ushered his birth hour gaily in,
And counted with its solemn toll,
The masses for his father's soul.

Hark! from the foremost of the band
Suddenly bursts the Indian yell;
For now on the very spot they stand
Where the Norridgewocks fighting fell.
No wigwam smoke is curling there;
The very earth is scorched and bare:
And they pause and listen to catch a sound
Of breathing life—but there comes not one,
Save the fox's bark and the rabbit's bound;
But here and there, on the blackened ground,
White bones are glistening in the sun.
And where the house of prayer arose,
And the holy hymn, at daylight's close,

And the aged priest stood up to bless
The children of the wilderness,
There is nought save ashes sodden and dank;
And the birchen boats of the Norridgewock,
Tethered to tree and stump and rock,
Rotting along the river bank!

Blessed Mary! who is she
Leaning against that maple tree?
The sun upon her face burns hot,
But the fixed eyelid moveth not;
The squirrel's chirp is shrill and clear
From the dry bough above her ear;
Dashing from rock and root its spray,
Close at her feet the river rushes;
The black-bird's wing against her brushes,
And sweetly through the hazel bushes
The robin's mellow music gushes;—
God save her! will she sleep alway?

Castine hath bent him over the sleeper:
"Wake daughter—wake!"—but she stirs no limb:
The eye that looks on him is fixed and dim;
And the sleep she is sleeping shall be no deeper,
Until the angel's oath is said,
And the final blast of the trump goes forth
To the graves of the sea and the graves of earth.
Ruth Bonython is dead!

LEGENDARY.

1846.

LEGENDARY.

THE MERRIMACK.

["THE Indians speak of a beautiful river, far to the South, which they call Merrimack."—SIEUR DE MONTS: 1604.]

STREAM of my fathers! sweetly still
The sunset rays thy valley fill;
Poured slantwise down the long defile,
Wave, wood, and spire beneath them smile.
I see the winding Powow fold
The green hill in its belt of gold,
And following down its wavy line,
Its sparkling waters blend with thine.
There's not a tree upon thy side,
Nor rock, which thy returning tide
As yet hath left abrupt and stark
Above thy evening water-mark;
No calm cove with its rocky hem,
No isle whose emerald swells begem
Thy broad, smooth current; not a sail
Bowed to the freshening ocean gale;
No small boat with its busy oars,
Nor gray wall sloping to thy shores;
Nor farm-house with its maple shade,
Or rigid poplar colonnade,
But lies distinct and full in sight,
Beneath this gush of sunset light.
Centuries ago, that harbor-bar,
Stretching its length of foam afar,
And Salisbury's beach of shining sand,
And yonder island's wave-smoothed strand,
Saw the adventurer's tiny sail

Flit, stooping from the eastern gale,[27]
And o'er these woods and waters broke
The cheer from Britain's hearts of oak,
As brightly on the voyager's eye,
Weary of forest, sea, and sky,
Breaking the dull continuous wood,
The Merrimack rolled down his flood;
Mingling that clear pellucid brook,
Which channels vast Agioochook
When spring-time's sun and shower unlock
The frozen fountains of the rock,
And more abundant waters given
From that pure lake, "The Smile of Heaven,"[28]
Tributes from vale and mountain side—
With ocean's dark, eternal tide!

On yonder rocky cape, which braves
The stormy challenge of the waves,
Midst tangled vine and dwarfish wood,
The hardy Anglo-Saxon stood,
Planting upon the topmost crag
The staff of England's battle-flag;
And, while from out its heavy fold
Saint George's crimson cross unrolled,
Midst roll of drum and trumpet blare,
And weapons brandishing in air,
He gave to that lone promontory
The sweetest name in all his story;[29]
Of her, the flower of Islam's daughters,
Whose harems look on Stamboul's waters—
Who, when the chance of war had bound
The Moslem chain his limbs around,
Wreathed o'er with silk that iron chain,
Soothed with her smiles his hours of pain,
And fondly to her youthful slave
A dearer gift than freedom gave.

But look!—the yellow light no more
Streams down on wave and verdant shore

And clearly on the calm air swells
The twilight voice of distant bells.
From Ocean's bosom, white and thin
The mists come slowly rolling in;
Hills, woods, the river's rocky rim,
Amidst the sea-like vapor swim,
While yonder lonely coast-light set
Within its wave-washed minaret,
Half quenched, a beamless star and pale,
Shines dimly through its cloudy veil!

Home of my fathers!—I have stood
Where Hudson rolled his lordly flood:
Seen sunrise rest and sunset fade
Along his frowning Palisade;
Looked down the Apalachian peak
On Juniata's silver streak;
Have seen along his valley gleam
The Mohawk's softly winding stream;
The level light of sunset shine
Through broad Potomac's hem of pine;
And autumn's rainbow-tinted banner
Hang lightly o'er the Susquehanna;
Yet, wheresoe'er his step might be,
Thy wandering child looked back to thee
Heard in his dreams thy river's sound
Of murmuring on its pebbly bound,
The unforgotten swell and roar
Of waves on thy familiar shore;
And saw amidst the curtained gloom
And quiet of his lonely room,
Thy sunset scenes before him pass;
As, in Agrippa's magic glass,
The loved and lost arose to view,
Remembered groves in greenness grew,
Bathed still in childhood's morning dew,
Along whose bowers of beauty swept
Whatever Memory's mourners wept,
Sweet faces, which the charnel kept,

Young, gentle eyes, which long had slept;
And while the gazer leaned to trace,
More near, some dear familiar face,
He wept to find the vision flown—
A phantom and a dream alone!

THE NORSEMEN.[80]

GIFT from the cold and silent Past!
A relic to the present cast;
Left on the ever-changing strand
Of shifting and unstable sand,
Which wastes beneath the steady chime
And beating of the waves of Time!
Who from its bed of primal rock
First wrenched thy dark, unshapely block?
Whose hand, of curious skill untaught,
Thy rude and savage outline wrought?

The waters of my native stream
Are glancing in the sun's warm beam:
From sail-urged keel and flashing oar
The circles widen to its shore;
And cultured field and peopled town
Slope to its willowed margin down.
Yet, while this morning breeze is bringing
The home-life sound of school-bells ringing,
And rolling wheel, and rapid jar
Of the fire-winged and steedless car,
And voices from the wayside near
Come quick and blended on my ear,
A spell is in this old gray stone—
My thoughts are with the Past alone!

A change!—The steepled town no more
Stretches along the sail-thronged shore;

Like palace-domes in sunset's cloud,
Fade sun-gilt spire and mansion proud.
Spectrally rising where they stood,
I see the old, primeval wood:
Dark, shadow-like, on either hand
I see its solemn waste expand:
It climbs the green and cultured hill,
It arches o'er the valley's rill;
And leans from cliff and crag, to throw
Its wild arms o'er the stream below.
Unchanged, alone, the same bright river
Flows on, as it will flow forever!
I listen, and I hear the low
Soft ripple where its waters go;
I hear behind the panther's cry,
The wild bird's scream goes thrilling by,
And shyly on the river's brink
The deer is stooping down to drink.

But hark!—from wood and rock flung back,
What sound comes up the Merrimack?
What sea-worn barks are those which throw
The light spray from each rushing prow?
Have they not in the North Sea's blast
Bowed to the waves the straining mast?
Their frozen sails the low, pale sun
Of Thulè's night has shone upon;
Flapped by the sea-wind's gusty sweep
Round icy drift, and headland steep.
Wild Jutland's wives and Lochlin's daughters
Have watched them fading o'er the waters,
Lessening through driving mist and spray,
Like white-winged sea-birds on their way!

Onward they glide—and now I view
Their iron-armed and stalwart crew;
Joy glistens in each wild blue eye,
Turned to green earth and summer sky:
Each broad, seamed breast has cast aside

Its cumbering vest of shaggy hide;
Bared to the sun and soft warm air,
Streams back the Norsemen's yellow hair.
I see the gleam of axe and spear,
The sound of smitten shields I hear,
Keeping a harsh and fitting time
To Saga's chant, and Runic rhyme;
Such lays as Zetland's Scald has sung,
His gray and naked isles among;
Or muttered low at midnight hour
Round Odin's mossy stone of power.
The wolf beneath the Arctic moon
Has answered to that startling rune;
The Gaal has heard its stormy swell,
The light Frank knows its summons well;
Iona's sable-stoled Culdee
Has heard it sounding o'er the sea,
And swept with hoary beard and hair.
His altar's foot in trembling prayer!

'T is past—the 'wildering vision dies
In darkness on my dreaming eyes!
The forest vanishes in air—
Hill-slope and vale lie starkly bare;
I hear the common tread of men,
And hum of work-day life again:
The mystic relic seems alone
A broken mass of common stone;
And if it be the chiselled limb
Of Berserkar or idol grim—
A fragment of Valhalla's Thor,
The stormy Viking's god of War,
Or Praga of the Runic lay,
Or love awakening Siona,
I know not—for no graven line,
Nor Druid mark, nor Runic sign,
Is left me here, by which to trace
Its name, or origin, or place.
Yet, for this vision of the Past,

This glance upon its darkness cast,
My spirit bows in gratitude
Before the Giver of all good,
Who fashioned so the human mind,
That, from the waste of Time behind
A simple stone, or mound of earth,
Can summon the departed forth;
Quicken the Past to life again—
The Present lose in what hath been,
And in their primal freshness show
The buried forms of long ago.
As if a portion of that Thought
By which the Eternal will is wrought,
Whose impulse fills anew with breath
The frozen solitude of Death,
To mortal mind were sometimes lent,
To mortal musings sometimes sent,
To whisper—even when it seems
But Memory's phantasy of dreams—
Through the mind's waste of woe and sin,
Of an immortal origin!

CASSANDRA SOUTHWICK.

1658.

To the God of all sure mercies let my blessing rise
to-day,
From the scoffer and the cruel He hath plucked
the spoil away,—
Yea, He who cooled the furnace around the faith-
ful three,
And tamed the Chaldean lions, hath set His hand-
maid free!

Last night I saw the sunset melt through my prison bars,
Last night across my damp earth-floor fell the pale gleam of stars;
In the coldness and the darkness all through the long night time,
My grated casement whitened with Autumn's early rime.

Alone, in that dark sorrow, hour after hour crept by;
Star after star looked palely in and sank adown the sky;
No sound amid night's stillness, save that which seemed to be
The dull and heavy beating of the pulses of the sea;

All night I sat unsleeping, for I knew that on the morrow
The ruler and the cruel priest would mock me in my sorrow,
Dragged to their place of market, and bargained for and sold,
Like a lamb before the shambles, like a heifer from the fold!

Oh, the weakness of the flesh was there—the shrinking and the shame;
And the low voice of the Tempter like whispers to me came:
"Why sit'st thou thus forlornly!" the wicked murmur said,
"Damp walls thy bower of beauty, cold earth thy maiden bed?

"Where be the smiling faces, and voices soft and sweet,
Seen in thy father's dwelling, heard in the pleasant street?

Where be the youths, whose glances the summer Sabbath through
Turned tenderly and timidly unto thy father's pew?

"Why sit'st thou here, Cassandra?—Bethink thee with what mirth
Thy happy schoolmates gather around the warm bright hearth;
How the crimson shadows tremble on foreheads white and fair,
On eyes of merry girlhood, half hid in golden hair.

"Not for thee the hearth-fire brightens, not for thee kind words are spoken,
Not for thee the nuts of Wenham woods by laughing boys are broken,
No first-fruits of the orchard within thy lap are laid,
For thee no flowers of Autumn the youthful hunters braid.

"Oh! weak, deluded maiden!—by crazy fancies led,
With wild and raving railers an evil path to tread;
To leave a wholesome worship, and teaching pure and sound;
And mate with maniac women, loose-haired and sackcloth-bound.

"Mad scoffers of the priesthood, who mock at things divine,
Who rail against the pulpit, and holy bread and wine;
Sore from their cart-tail scourgings, and from the pillory lame,
Rejoicing in their wretchedness, and glorying in their shame.

"And what a fate awaits thee?—a sadly toiling slave,
Dragging the slowly lengthening chain of bondage to the grave!

Think of thy woman's nature, subdued in hopeless thrall,
The easy prey of any, the scoff and scorn of all!"

Oh!—ever as the Tempter spoke, and feeble Nature's fears
Wrung drop by drop the scalding flow of unavailing tears,
I wrestled down the evil thoughts, and strove in silent prayer,
To feel, oh, Helper of the weak!—that Thou indeed wert there!

I thought of Paul and Silas, within Philippi's cell,
And how from Peter's sleeping limbs the prison-shackles fell,
Till I seemed to hear the trailing of an angel's robe of white,
And to feel a blessed presence invisible to sight.

Bless the Lord for all His mercies!—for the peace and love I felt,
Like dew of Hermon's holy hill, upon my spirit melt;
When, "Get behind me, Satan!" was the language of my heart,
And I felt the Evil Tempter with all his doubts depart.

Slow broke the gray cold morning; again the sunshine fell,
Flecked with the shade of bar and grate within my lonely cell;
The hoar frost melted on the wall, and upward from the street
Came careless laugh and idle word, and tread of passing feet.

At length the heavy bolts fell back, my door was open cast,

And slowly at the sheriff's side, up the long street
I passed;
I heard the murmur round me, and felt, but dared
not see,
How, from every door and window, the people
gazed on me.

And doubt and fear fell on me, shame burned upon
my cheek,
Swam earth and sky around me, my trembling
limbs grew weak:
"Oh, Lord! support thy handmaid; and from her
soul cast out
The fear of man, which brings a snare—the weak-
ness and the doubt."

Then the dreary shadows scattered like a cloud in
morning's breeze,
And a low deep voice within me seemed whispering
words like these:
"Though thy earth be as the iron, and thy heaven
a brazen wall,
Trust still His loving kindness whose power is over
all."

We paused at length, where at my feet the sunlit
waters broke
On glaring reach of shining beach, and shingly
wall of rock;
The merchant-ships lay idly there, in hard clear
lines on high,
Tracing with rope and slender spar their network
on the sky.

And there were ancient citizens, cloak-wrapped
and grave and cold,
And grim and stout sea-captains with faces bronzed
and old,

And on his horse, with Rawson, his cruel clerk at
hand,
Sat dark and haughty Endicott, the ruler of the
land.

And poisoning with his evil words the ruler's ready
ear,
The priest leaned o'er his saddle, with laugh and
scoff and jeer;
It stirred my soul, and from my lips the seal of
silence broke,
As if through woman's weakness a warning spirit
spoke.

I cried, "The Lord rebuke thee, thou smiter of the
meek,
Thou robber of the righteous, thou trampler of the
weak!
Go light the dark, cold hearth-stones—go turn the
prison lock
Of the poor hearts thou hast hunted, thou wolf
amid the flock!"

Dark lowered the brows of Endicott, and with a
deeper red
O'er Rawson's wine-empurpled cheek the flush of
anger spread;
"Good people," quoth the white-lipped priest,
"heed not her words so wild,
Her Master speaks within her—the Devil owns his
child!"

But gray heads shook, and young brows knit, the
while the sheriff read
That law the wicked rulers against the poor have
made,
Who to their house of Rimmon and idol priest-
hood bring
No bended knee of worship, nor gainful offering.

Then to the stout sea-captains the sheriff turning said:
"Which of ye, worthy seamen, will take this Quaker maid?
In the Isle of fair Barbadoes, or on Virginia's shore,
You may hold her at a higher price than Indian girl or Moor."

Grim and silent stood the captains; and when again he cried,
"Speak out, my worthy seamen!"—no voice, no sign replied;
But I felt a hard hand press my own, and kind words met my ear:
"God bless thee, and preserve thee, my gentle girl and dear!"

A weight seemed lifted from my heart,—a pitying friend was nigh,
I felt it in his hard, rough hand, and saw it in his eye;
And when again the sheriff spoke, that voice, so kind to me,
Growled back its stormy answer like the roaring of the sea:

"Pile my ship with bars of silver—pack with coins of Spanish gold,
From keel-piece up to deck-plank, the roomage of her hold,
By the living God who made me!—I would sooner in your bay
Sink ship and crew and cargo, than bear this child away!

"Well answered, worthy captain, shame on their cruel laws!"
Ran through the crowd in murmurs loud the people's just applause.

"Like the herdsman of Tekoa, in Israel of old,
Shall we see the poor and righteous again for silver sold?"

I looked on haughty Endicott; with weapon half way drawn,
Swept round the throng his lion glare of bitter hate and scorn;
Fiercely he drew his bridle rein, and turned in silence back,
And sneering priest and baffled clerk rode murmuring in his track.

Hard after them the sheriff looked, in bitterness of soul;
Thrice smote his staff upon the ground, and crushed his parchment roll.
"Good friends," he said, "since both have fled, the ruler and the priest,
Judge ye, if from their further work I be not well released."

Loud was the cheer which, full and clear, swept round the silent bay,
As, with kind words and kinder looks, he bade me go my way;
For He who turns the courses of the streamlet of the glen,
And the river of great waters, had turned the hearts of men.

Oh, at that hour the very earth seemed changed beneath my eye,
A holier wonder round me rose the blue walls of the sky,
A lovelier light on rock and hill, and stream and woodland lay,
And softer lapsed on sunnier sands the waters of the bay.

Thanksgiving to the Lord of life!—to Him all
praises be,
Who from the hands of evil men hath set His hand
maid free;
All praise to Him before whose power the mighty
are afraid,
Who takes the crafty in the snare, which for the
poor is laid!

Sing, oh, my soul, rejoicingly, on evening's twilight
calm
Uplift the loud thanksgiving—pour forth the grate-
ful psalm;
Let all dear hearts with me rejoice, as did the
saints of old,
When of the Lord's good angel the rescued Peter
told.

And weep and howl, ye evil priests and mighty
men of wrong,
The Lord shall smite the proud and lay His hand
upon the strong.
Woe to the wicked rulers in His avenging hour!
Woe to the wolves who seek the flocks to raven and
devour:

But let the humble ones arise,—the poor in heart
be glad,
And let the mourning ones again with robes of
praise be clad,
For He who cooled the furnace, and smoothed the
stormy wave,
And tamed the Chaldean lions, is mighty still to
save!

FUNERAL TREE OF THE SOKOKIS.

1756.

Around Sebago's lonely lake
There lingers not a breeze to break
The mirror which its waters make.

The solemn pines along its shore,
The firs which hang its gray rocks o'er,
Are painted on its glassy floor.

The sun looks o'er, with hazy eye,
The snowy mountain-tops which lie
Piled coldly up against the sky.

Dazzling and white! save where the bleak,
Wild winds have bared some splintering peak,
Or snow-slide left its dusky streak.

Yet green are Saco's banks below,
And belts of spruce and cedar show,
Dark fringing round those cones of snow.

The earth hath felt the breath of spring,
Though yet on her deliverer's wing
The lingering frosts of winter cling.

Fresh grasses fringe the meadow-brooks,
And mildly from its sunny nooks
The blue eye of the violet looks.

And odors from the springing grass,
The sweet birch and the sassafras,
Upon the scarce-felt breezes pass.

Her tokens of renewing care
Hath Nature scattered everywhere,
In bud and flower, and warmer air.

But in their hour of bitterness,
What reck the broken Sokokis,
Beside their slaughtered chief, of this?

The turf's red stain is yet undried—
Scarce have the death-shot echoes died
Along Sebago's wooded side:

And silent now the hunters stand,
Grouped darkly, where a swell of land
Slopes upward from the lake's white sand.

Fire and the axe have swept it bare,
Save one lone beech, unclosing there
Its light leaves in the vernal air.

With grave, cold looks, all sternly mute,
They break the damp turf at its foot,
And bare its coiled and twisted root.

They heave the stubborn trunk aside,
The firm roots from the earth divide—
The rent beneath yawns dark and wide.

And there the fallen chief is laid,
In tasselled garbs of skins arrayed,
And girded with his wampum-braid.

The silver cross he loved is pressed
Beneath the heavy arms, which rest
Upon his scarred and naked breast.

'Tis done: the roots are backward sent,
The beechen tree stands up unbent—
The Indian's fitting monument!

When of that sleeper's broken race
Their green and pleasant dwelling-place
Which knew them once, retains no trace;

O! long may sunset's light be shed
As now upon that beech's head—
A green memorial of the dead!

There shall his fitting requiem be,
In northern winds, that, cold and free,
Howl nightly in that funeral tree.

To their wild wail the waves which break
Forever round that lonely lake
A solemn under-tone shall make!

And who shall deem the spot unblest,
Where Nature's younger children rest,
Lulled on their sorrowing mother's breast?

Deem ye that mother loveth less
These bronzed forms of the wilderness
She foldeth in her long caress?

As sweet o'er them her wild flowers blow,
As if with fairer hair and brow
The blue-eyed Saxon slept below.

What though the places of their rest
No priestly knee hath ever pressed—
No funeral rite nor prayer hath blessed?

What though the bigot's ban be there,
And thoughts of wailing and despair,
And cursing in the place of prayer!

Yet Heaven hath angels watching round
The Indian's lowliest forest-mound—
And *they* have made it holy ground.

There ceases man's frail judgment; all
His powerless bolts of cursing fall
Unheeded on that grassy pall.

O, peeled, and hunted, and reviled,
Sleep on, dark tenant of the wild!
Great Nature owns her simple child!

And Nature's God, to whom alone
The secret of the heart is known—
The hidden language traced thereon;

Who from its many cumberings
Of form and creed, and outward things,
To light the naked spirit brings;

Not with our partial eye shall scan—
Not with our pride and scorn shall ban
The spirit of our brother man!

ST. JOHN.

1647.

"To the winds give our banner!
  Bear homeward again!"
Cried the Lord of Acadia,
  Cried Charles of Estienne;
From the prow of his shallop
  He gazed, as the sun,
From its bed in the ocean,
  Streamed up the St. John.

O'er the blue western waters
  That shallop had passed,
Where the mists of Penobscot
  Clung damp on her mast.
St. Saviour had look'd
  On the heretic sail,
As the songs of the Huguenot
  Rose on the gale.

The pale, ghostly fathers
  Remembered her well,
And had cursed her while passing,
  With taper and bell,
But the men of Monhegan,
  Of Papists abhorr'd,
Had welcomed and feasted
  The heretic Lord.

They had loaded his shallop
  With dun-fish and ball,
With stores for his larder,
  And steel for his wall.
Pemequid, from her bastions
  And turrets of stone,
Had welcomed his coming
  With banner and gun.

And the prayers of the elders
  Had followed his way,
As homeward he glided,
  Down Pentecost Bay.
O! well sped La Tour!
  For, in peril and pain,
His lady kept watch
  For his coming again.

O'er the Isle of the Pheasant
  The morning sun shone,
On the plane-trees which shaded
  The shores of St. John.
"Now, why from yon battlements
  Speaks not my love!
Why waves there no banner
  My fortress above?"

Dark and wild, from his deck
  St. Estienne gazed about,
On fire-wasted dwellings,
  And silent redoubt;

From the low, shattered walls
   Which the flame had o'errun,
There floated no banner,
   There thunder'd no gun!

But, beneath the low arch
   Of its doorway there stood
A pale priest of Rome,
   In his cloak and his hood.
With the bound of a lion,
   La Tour sprang to land,
On the throat of the Papist
   He fastened his hand.

"Speak, son of the Woman,
   Of scarlet and sin!
What wolf has been prowling
   My castle within?"
From the grasp of the soldier
   The Jesuit broke,
Half in scorn, half in sorrow,
   He smiled as he spoke:

"No wolf, Lord of Estienne,
   Has ravaged thy hall,
But thy red-handed rival,
   With fire, steel, and ball!
On an errand of mercy
   I hitherward came,
While the walls of thy castle
   Yet spouted with flame.

"Pentagoet's dark vessels
   Were moored in the bay,
Grim sea-lions, roaring
   Aloud for their prey."
"But what of my lady?"
   Cried Charles of Estienne:
"On the shot-crumbled turret
   Thy lady was seen:

"Half-veiled in the smoke-cloud,
   Her hand grasped thy pennon,
While her dark tresses swayed
   In the hot breath of cannon!
But woe to the heretic,
   Evermore woe!
When the son of the church
   And the cross is his foe!

"In the track of the shell,
   In the path of the ball,
Pentagoet swept over
   The breach of the wall!
Steel to steel, gun to gun,
   One moment—and then
Alone stood the victor,
   Alone with his men!

"Of its sturdy defenders,
   Thy lady alone
Saw the cross-blazon'd banner
   Float over St. John."
"Let the dastard look to it!"
   Cried fiery Estienne,
"Were D'Aulney King Louis,
   I'd free her again!

"Alas, for thy lady!
   No service from thee
Is needed by her
   Whom the Lord hath set free:
Nine days, in stern silence,
   Her thraldom she bore,
But the tenth morning came,
   And Death opened her door!

As if suddenly smitten
   La Tour stagger'd back;
His hand grasped his sword-hilt,
   His forehead grew black.

He sprang on the deck
  Of his shallop again:
"We cruise now for vengeance!
  Give way!" cried Estienne.

"Massachusetts shall hear
  Of the Huguenot's wrong,
And from island and creek-side
  Her fishers shall throng!
Pentagoet shall rue
  What his Papists have done,
When his palisades echo
  The Puritan's gun!"

O! the loveliest of heavens
  Hung tenderly o'er him,
There were waves in the sunshine,
  And green isles before him:
But a pale hand was beckoning
  The Huguenot on;
And in blackness and ashes
  Behind was St. John!

PENTUCKET.

1708.

How sweetly on the wood-girt town
The mellow light of sunset shone!
Each small, bright lake, whose waters still
Mirror the forest and the hill,
Reflected from its waveless breast
The beauty of a cloudless West,
Glorious as if a glimpse were given
Within the western gates of Heaven,
Left, by the spirit of the star
Of sunset's holy hour, ajar!

Beside the river's tranquil flood
The dark and low-wall'd dwellings stood,
Where many a rood of open land
Stretch'd up and down on either hand,
With corn-leaves waving freshly green
The thick and blacken'd stumps between.
Behind, unbroken, deep and dread,
The wild, untravell'd forest spread,
Back to those mountains, white and cold,
Of which the Indian trapper told,
Upon whose summits never yet
Was mortal foot in safety set.

Quiet and calm, without a fear
Of danger darkly lurking near,
The weary laborer left his plough—
The milk-maid caroll'd by her cow—
From cottage door and household hearth
Rose songs of praise, or tones of mirth.
At length the murmur died away,
And silence on that village lay—
So slept Pompeii, tower and hall,
Ere the quick earthquake swallow'd all,
Undreaming of the fiery fate
Which made its dwellings desolate!

Hours pass'd away. By moonlight sped
The Merrimack along his bed.
Bathed in the pallid lustre, stood
Dark cottage-wall and rock and wood,
Silent, beneath that tranquil beam,
As the hush'd grouping of a dream.
Yet on the still air crept a sound—
No bark of fox—nor rabbit's bound—
Nor stir of wings—nor waters flowing—
Nor leaves in midnight breezes blowing.

Was that the tread of many feet,
Which downward from the hill-side beat?

What forms were those which darkly stood
Just on the margin of the wood?—
Charr'd tree-stumps in the moonlight dim,
Or paling rude, or leafless limb?
No—through the trees fierce eye-balls glow'd,
Dark human forms in moonshine show'd,
Wild from their native wilderness,
With painted limbs and battle-dress!

A yell, the dead might wake to hear,
Swell'd on the night air, far and clear—
Then smote the Indian tomahawk
On crashing door and shattering lock—
Then rang the rifle-shot—and then
The shrill death-scream of stricken men—
Sank the red axe in woman's brain,
And childhood's cry arose in vain—
Bursting through roof and window came,
Red, fast and fierce, the kindled flame;
And blended fire and moonlight glared
On still dead men and weapons bared.

The morning sun looked brightly through
The river willows, wet with dew.
No sound of combat fill'd the air,—
No shout was heard,—nor gunshot there:
Yet still the thick and sullen smoke
From smouldering ruins slowly broke;
And on the greensward many a stain,
And, here and there, the mangled slain,
Told how that midnight bolt had sped,
Pentucket, on thy fated head!

Even now, the villager can tell
Where Rolfe beside his hearthstone fell,
Still show the door of wasting oak,
Through which the fatal death-shot broke,
And point the curious stranger where
De Rouville's corse lay grim and bare—

Whose hideous head, in death still fear'd,
Bore not a trace of hair or beard—
And still, within the churchyard ground,
Heaves darkly up the ancient mound,
Whose grass-grown surface overlies
The victims of that sacrifice.

THE FAMILIST'S HYMN.

FATHER! to thy suffering poor
  Strength and grace and faith impart,
And with thy own love restore
  Comfort to the broken heart!
Oh, the failing ones confirm
  With a holier strength of zeal!—
Give Thou not the feeble worm
  Helpless to the spoiler's heel!

Father! for thy holy sake
  We are spoiled and hunted thus;
Joyful, for thy truth we take
  Bonds and burthens unto us:
Poor, and weak, and robbed of all,
  Weary with our daily task,
That thy truth may never fall
  Through our weakness, Lord, we ask.

Round our fired and wasted homes
  Flits the forest-bird unscared,
And at noon the wild beast comes
  Where our frugal meal was shared;
For the song of praises there
  Shrieks the crow the livelong day,
For the sound of evening prayer
  Howls the evil beast of prey!

Sweet the songs we loved to sing
  Underneath thy holy sky—
Words and tones that used to bring
  Tears of joy in every eye,—
Dear the wrestling hours of prayer,
  When we gathered knee to knee,
Blameless youth and hoary hair,
  Bow'd, O God, alone to thee.

As thine early children, Lord,
  Shared their wealth and daily bread,
Even so, with one accord,
  We, in love, each other fed.
Not with us the miser's hoard,
  Not with us his grasping hand;
Equal round a common board,
  Drew our meek and brother band!

Safe our quiet Eden lay
  When the war-whoop stirred the land,
And the Indian turn'd away
  From our home his bloody hand.
Well that forest-ranger saw,
  That the burthen and the curse
Of the white man's cruel law
  Rested also upon us.

Torn apart, and driven forth
  To our toiling hard and long,
Father! from the dust of earth
  Lift we still our grateful song!
Grateful—that in bonds we share
  In thy love which maketh free,
Joyful—that the wrongs we bear,
  Draw us nearer, Lord, to thee!

Grateful!—that where'er we toil—
  By Wachuset's wooded side,
On Nantucket's sea-worn isle,

Or by wild Neponset's tide—
Still, in spirit, we are near,
And our evening hymns which rise
Separate and discordant here,
Meet and mingle in the skies!

Let the scoffer scorn and mock,
Let the proud and evil priest
Rob the needy of his flock,
For his wine-cup and his feast,—
Redden not thy bolts in store
Through the blackness of thy skies?
For the sighing of the poor
Wilt Thou not, at length, arise?

Worn and wasted, oh, how long
Shall thy trodden poor complain?
In thy name they bear the wrong,
In thy cause the bonds of pain!
Melt oppression's heart of steel,
Let the haughty priesthood see,
And their blinded followers feel,
That in us they mock at Thee!

In thy time, O Lord of hosts,
Stretch abroad that hand to save
Which of old, on Egypt's coasts,
Smote apart the Red Sea's wave!
Lead us from this evil land,
From the spoiler set us free,
And once more our gather'd band,
Heart to heart, shall worship Thee!

THE FOUNTAIN.

TRAVELLER! on thy journey toiling
By the swift Powow,

With the summer sunshine falling
On thy heated brow,
Listen, while all else is still
To the brooklet from the hill.

Wild and sweet the flowers are blowing
By that streamlet's side,
And a greener verdure showing
Where its waters glide—
Down the hill-slope murmuring on,
Over root and mossy stone.

Where yon oak his broad arms flingeth
O'er the sloping hill,
Beautiful and freshly springeth
That soft-flowing rill,
Through its dark roots wreath'd and bare,
Gushing up to sun and air.

Brighter waters sparkled never
In that magic well,
Of whose gift of life forever
Ancient legends tell,—
In the lonely desert wasted,
And by mortal lip untasted.

Waters which the proud Castilian [31]
Sought with longing eyes,
Underneath the bright pavilion
Of the Indian skies;
Where his forest pathway lay
Through the blooms of Florida.

Years ago a lonely stranger,
With the dusky brow
Of the outcast forest-ranger,
Crossed the swift Powow;
And betook him to the rill,
And the oak upon the hill.

O'er his face of moody sadness
  For an instant shone
Something like a gleam of gladness,
  As he stooped him down
To the fountain's grassy side
And his eager thirst supplied.

With the oak its shadow throwing
  O'er his mossy seat,
And the cool, sweet waters flowing
  Softly at his feet,
Closely by the fountain's rim
That lone Indian seated him.

Autumn's earliest frost had given
  To the woods below
Hues of beauty, such as heaven
  Lendeth to its bow;
And the soft breeze from the west
Scarcely broke their dreamy rest.

Far behind was Ocean striving
  With his chains of sand;
Southward, sunny glimpses giving,
  'Twixt the swells of land,
Of its calm and silvery track,
Rolled the tranquil Merrimack.

Over village, wood and meadow,
  Gazed that stranger man
Sadly, till the twilight shadow
  Over all things ran,
Save where spire and westward pane
Flashed the sunset back again.

Gazing thus upon the dwelling
  Of his warrior sires,
Where no lingering trace was telling
  Of their wigwam fires,

Who the gloomy thoughts might know
Of that wandering child of woe ?

Naked lay, in sunshine glowing,
   Hills that once had stood
Down their sides the shadows throwing
   Of a mighty wood,
Where the deer his covert kept,
And the eagle's pinion swept!

Where the birch canoe had glided
   Down the swift Powow,
Dark and gloomy bridges strided
   Those clear waters now;
And where once the beaver swam,
Jarred the wheel and frowned the dam.

For the wood-bird's merry singing,
   And the hunter's cheer,
Iron clang and hammer's ringing
   Smote upon his ear;
And the thick and sullen smoke
From the blackened forges broke.

Could it be, his fathers ever,
   Loved to linger here?
These bare hills—this conquer'd river—
   Could they hold them dear,
With their native loveliness
Tamed and tortured into this?

Sadly, as the shades of even
   Gathered o'er the hill,
While the western half of heaven
   Blushed with sunset still,
From the fountain's mossy seat
Turned the Indian's weary feet.

Year on year hath flown forever,
   But he came no more

To the hill-side or the river
  Where he came before.
But the villager can tell
Of that strange man's visit well.

And the merry children, laden
  With their fruits or flowers—
Roving boy and laughing maiden,
  In their school-day hours,
Love the simple tale to tell
Of the Indian and his well.

THE EXILES.

1660.

The goodman sat beside his door
  One sultry afternoon,
With his young wife singing at his side
  An old and goodly tune.

A glimmer of heat was in the air,—
  The dark green woods were still;
And the skirts of a heavy thunder-cloud
  Hung over the western hill.

Black, thick, and vast, arose that cloud
  Above the wilderness,
As some dark world from upper air
  Were stooping over this.

At times, the solemn thunder pealed,
  And all was still again,
Save a low murmur in the air
  Of coming wind and rain.

Just as the first big rain-drop fell,
  A weary stranger came,
And stood before the farmer's door,
  With travel soiled and lame.

Sad seemed he, yet sustaining hope
  Was in his quiet glance,
And peace, like autumn's moonlight, clothed
  His tranquil countenance.

A look, like that his Master wore
  In Pilate's council-hall:
It told of wrongs—but of a love
  Meekly forgiving all.

"Friend! wilt thou give me shelter here?"
  The stranger meekly said;
And, leaning on his oaken staff,
  The goodman's features read.

"My life is hunted—evil men
  Are following in my track;
The traces of the torturer's whip
  Are on my aged back.

"And much, I fear, 'twill peril thee
  Within thy doors to take
A hunted seeker of the Truth,
  Oppressed for conscience sake."

Oh, kindly spoke the goodman's wife—
  "Come in, old man!" quoth she,—
"We will not leave thee to the storm
  Whoever thou may'st be."

Then came the aged wanderer in,
  And silent sat him down;
While all within grew dark as night
  Beneath the storm-cloud's frown.

But while the sudden lightning's blaze
  Filled every cottage nook,
And with the jarring thunder-roll
  The loosened casements shook,

A heavy tramp of horses' feet
  Came sounding up the lane,
And half a score of horse, or more,
  Came plunging through the rain.

"Now, Goodman Macey, ope thy door,—
  We would not be house-breakers;
A rueful deed thou'st done this day,
  In harboring banished Quakers."

Out looked the cautious goodman then,
  With much of fear and awe,
For there, with broad wig drenched with rain,
  The parish priest he saw.

"Open thy door, thou wicked man,
  And let thy pastor in,
And give God thanks, if forty stripes
  Repay thy deadly sin."

"What seek ye?" quoth the goodman,—
  "The stranger is my guest;
He is worn with toil and grievous wrong,—
  Pray let the old man rest."

"Now, out upon thee, canting knave!"
  And strong hands shook the door,
"Believe me, Macey," quoth the priest,—
  "Thou'lt rue thy conduct sore."

Then kindled Macey's eye of fire:
  "No priest who walks the earth,
Shall pluck away the stranger-guest
  Made welcome to my hearth."

Down from his cottage wall he caught
  The matchlock, hotly tried
At Preston-pans and Marston-moor,
  By fiery Ireton's side;

Where Puritan, and Cavalier,
  With shout and psalm contended;
And Rupert's oath, and Cromwell's prayer,
  With battle-thunder blended.

Up rose the ancient stranger then:
  "My spirit is not free
To bring the wrath and violence
  Of evil men on thee:

"And for thyself, I pray forbear,—
  Bethink thee of thy Lord,
Who healed again the smitten ear,
  And sheathed his follower's sword.

"I go, as to the slaughter led:
  Friends of the poor, farewell!"
Beneath his hand the oaken door,
  Back on its hinges fell.

"Come forth, old gray-beard, yea and nay;"
  The reckless scoffers cried,
As to a horseman's saddle-bow
  The old man's arms were tied.

And of his bondage hard and long
  In Boston's crowded jail,
Where suffering woman's prayer was heard,
  With sickening childhood's wail,

It suits not with our tale to tell:
  Those scenes have passed away—
Let the dim shadows of the past
  Brood o'er that evil day.

"Ho, sheriff!" quoth the ardent priest—
"Take goodman Macey too;
The sin of this day's heresy,
His back or purse shall rue."

"Now goodwife, haste thee!" Macey cried,
She caught his manly arm:—
Behind, the parson urged pursuit,
With outcry and alarm.

Ho! speed the Maceys, neck or nought,—
The river course was near:—
The plashing on its pebbled shore
Was music to their ear.

A gray rock, tasselled o'er with birch
Above the waters hung,
And at its base, with every wave,
A small light wherry swung.

A leap—they gain the boat—and there
The goodman wields his oar:
"Ill luck betide them all"—he cried,—
"The laggards upon the shore."

Down through the crashing under-wood,
The burly sheriff came:—
"Stand, goodman Macey—yield thyself;
Yield in the King's own name."

"Now out upon thy hangman's face!"
Bold Macey answered then,—
"Whip *women*, on the village green,
But meddle not with *men*."

The priest came panting to the shore,—
His grave cocked hat was gone:
Behind him, like some owl's nest, hung
His wig upon a thorn.

"Come back—come back!" the parson cried,
"The church's curse beware."
"Curse, an' thou wilt," said Macey, "but
Thy blessing prithee spare."

"Vile scoffer!" cried the baffled priest,—
"Thou'lt yet the gallows see."
"Who's born to be hanged, will not be drowned,"
Quoth Macey, merrily;

"And so, sir sheriff and priest, good bye!"
He bent him to his oar,
And the small boat glided quietly
From the twain upon the shore.

Now in the west, the heavy clouds
Scattered and fell asunder,
While feebler came the rush of rain,
And fainter growled the thunder.

And through the broken clouds, the sun
Looked out serene and warm,
Painting its holy symbol-light
Upon the passing storm.

Oh, beautiful! that rainbow span,
O'er dim Crane-neck was bended;—
One bright foot touched the eastern hills,
And one with ocean blended.

By green Pentucket's southern slope
The small boat glided fast,—
The watchers of "the Block-house" saw
The strangers as they passed.

That night a stalwart garrison
Sat shaking in their shoes,
To hear the dip of Indian oars,—
The glide of birch canoes.

The fisher-wives of Salisbury,
  (The men were all away,)
Looked out to see the stranger oar
  Upon their waters play.

Deer-Island's rocks and fir-trees threw
  Their sunset-shadows o'er them,
And Newbury's spire and weathercock
  Peered o'er the pines before them.

Around the Black Rocks, on their left,
  The marsh lay broad and green;
And on their right, with dwarf shrubs crowned,
  Plum Island's hills were seen.

With skilful hand and wary eye
  The harbor-bar was crossed;—
A plaything of the restless wave,
  The boat on ocean tossed.

The glory of the sunset heaven
  On land and water lay,—
On the steep hills of Agawam,
  On cape, and bluff, and bay.

They passed the gray rocks of Cape Ann,
  And Gloucester's harbor-bar;
The watch-fire of the garrison
  Shone like a setting star.

How brightly broke the morning
  On Massachusetts Bay!
Blue wave, and bright green island,
  Rejoicing in the day.

On passed the bark in safety
  Round isle and headland steep—
No tempest broke above them,
  No fog-cloud veiled the deep.

Far round the bleak and stormy Cape
  The vent'rous Macey passed,
And on Nantucket's naked isle,
  Drew up his boat at last.

And how, in log-built cabin,
  They braved the rough sea-weather;
And there, in peace and quietness,
  Went down life's vale together·

How others drew around them,
  And how their fishing sped,
Until to every wind of heaven
  Nantucket's sails were spread:

How pale want alternated
  With plenty's golden smile;
Behold, is it not written
  In the annals of the isle?

And yet that isle remaineth
  A refuge of the free,
As when true-hearted Macey
  Beheld it from the sea.

Free as the winds that winnow
  Her shrubless hills of sand—
Free as the waves that batter
  Along her yielding land.

Than hers, at duty's summons,
  No loftier spirit stirs,—
Nor falls o'er human suffering
  A readier tear than hers.

God bless the sea-beat island!—
  And grant for evermore,
That charity and freedom dwell,
  As now upon her shore!

THE NEW WIFE AND THE OLD.

Dark the halls, and cold the feast—
Gone the bridemaids, gone the priest.
All is over—all is done,
Twain of yesterday are one!
Blooming girl and manhood gray,
Autumn in the arms of May!

Hushed within and hushed without,
Dancing feet and wrestlers' shout;
Dies the bonfire on the hill;
All is dark and all is still,
Save the starlight, save the breeze
Moaning through the graveyard trees;
And the great sea-waves below,
Pulse of the midnight beating slow

From the brief dream of a bride
She hath wakened, at his side.
With half uttered shriek and start—
Feels she not his beating heart?
And the pressure of his arm,
And his breathing near and warm?

Lightly from the bridal bed
Springs that fair dishevelled head,
And a feeling, new, intense,
Half of shame, half innocence,
Maiden fear and wonder speaks
Through her lips and changing cheeks.

From the oaken mantel glowing
Faintest light the lamp is throwing
On the mirror's antique mould,
High-backed chair, and wainscot old,
And, through faded curtains stealing,
His dark sleeping face revealing.

Listless lies the strong man there,
Silver-streaked his careless hair;
Lips of love have left no trace
On that hard and haughty face;
And that forehead's knitted thought
Love's soft hand hath not unwrought.

"Yet," she sighs, "he loves me well,
More than these calm lips will tell.
Stooping to my lowly state,
He hath made me rich and great,
And I bless him, though he be
Hard and stern to all save me!"

While she speaketh, falls the light
O'er her fingers small and white;
Gold and gem, and costly ring
Back the timid lustre fling—
Love's selectest gifts, and rare,
His proud hand had fastened there

Gratefully she marks the glow
From those tapering lines of snow;
Fondly o'er the sleeper bending
His black hair with golden blending,
In her soft and light caress,
Cheek and lip together press.

Ha!—that start of horror!—Why
That wild stare and wilder cry,
Full of terror, full of pain?
Is there madness in her brain?
Hark! that gasping, hoarse and low
"Spare me—spare me—let me go!"

God have mercy!—Icy cold
Spectral hands her own enfold,
Drawing silently from them
Love's fair gifts of gold and gem,

"Waken! save me!" still as death
At her side he slumbereth.

Ring and bracelet all are gone,
And that ice-cold hand withdrawn;
But she hears a murmur low,
Full of sweetness, full of woe,
Half a sigh and half a moan:
"Fear not! give the dead her own!"

Ah!—the dead wife's voice she knows!
That cold hand whose pressure froze,
Once in warmest life had borne
Gem and band her own hath worn.
"Wake thee! wake thee!" Lo, his eyes
Open with a dull surprise.

In his arms the strong man folds her,
Closer to his breast he holds her;
Trembling limbs his own are meeting,
And he feels her heart's quick beating:
"Nay, my dearest, why this fear?"
"Hush!" she saith, "the dead is here!"

"Nay, a dream—an idle dream."
But before the lamp's pale gleam
Tremblingly her hand she raises,—
There no more the diamond blazes,
Clasp of pearl, or ring of gold,—
"Ah!" she sighs, "her hand was cold!"

Broken words of cheer he saith,
But his dark lip quivereth,
And as o'er the past he thinketh,
From his young wife's arms he shrinketh;
Can those soft arms round him lie,
Underneath his dead wife's eye?

She her fair young head can rest
Soothed and childlike on his breast,

And in trustful innocence
Draw new strength and courage thence;
He, the proud man feels within
But the cowardice of sin!

She can murmur in her thought
Simple prayers her mother taught,
And his blessed angels call,
Whose great love is over all;
He, alone, in prayerless pride,
Meets the dark Past at her side!

One, who living shrank with dread,
From his look, or word, or tread,
Unto whom her early grave
Was as freedom to the slave,
Moves him at this midnight hour,
With the dead's unconscious power!

Ah, the dead, the unforgot!
From their solemn homes of thought,
Where the cypress shadows blend
Darkly over foe and friend,
Or in love or sad rebuke,
Back upon the living look.

And the tenderest ones and weakest,
Who their wrongs have borne the meekest,
Lifting from those dark, still places,
Sweet and sad-remembered faces,
O'er the guilty hearts behind
An unwitting triumph find.

VOICES OF FREEDOM.

FROM 1833 TO 1848.

VOICES OF FREEDOM.

FROM 1833 TO 1848.

TOUSSAINT L'OUVERTURE.[32]

'TWAS night. The tranquil moonlight smile
  With which Heaven dreams of Earth, shed down
Its beauty on the Indian isle—
  On broad green field and white-walled town;
And inland waste of rock and wood,
In searching sunshine, wild and rude,
Rose, mellowed through the silver gleam,
Soft as the landscape of a dream,
All motionless and dewy wet,
Tree, vine, and flower in shadow met:
The myrtle with its snowy bloom,
Crossing the nightshade's solemn gloom—
The white cecropia's silver rind
Relieved by deeper green behind,—
The orange with its fruit of gold,—
The lithe paullinia's verdant fold,—
The passion-flower, with symbol holy,
Twining its tendrils long and lowly,—
The rhexias dark, and cassia tall,
And proudly rising over all,
The kingly palm's imperial stem,
Crowned with its leafy diadem,
Star-like, beneath whose sombre shade
The fiery-winged cucullo played!

Yes—lovely was thine aspect, then,
Fair island of the Western Sea!
Lavish of beauty, even when
Thy brutes were happier than thy men,
For they, at least, were free!
Regardless of thy glorious clime,
Unmindful of thy soil of flowers,
The toiling negro sighed, that Time
No faster sped his hours.
For, by the dewy moonlight still,
He fed the weary-turning mill,
Or bent him in the chill morass,
To pluck the long and tangled grass,
And hear above his scar-worn back
The heavy slave-whip's frequent crack;
While in his heart one evil thought
In solitary madness wrought,—
One baleful fire surviving still
The quenching of the immortal mind—
One sterner passion of his kind,
Which even fetters could not kill,—
The savage hope, to deal, ere long,
A vengeance bitterer than his wrong!

Hark to that cry!—long, loud, and shrill,
From field and forest, rock and hill,
Thrilling and horrible it rang,
Around, beneath, above;—
The wild beast from his cavern sprang—
The wild bird from her grove!
Nor fear, nor joy, nor agony
Were mingled in that midnight cry;
But like the lion's growl of wrath,
When falls that hunter in his path,
Whose barbed arrow, deeply set,
Is rankling in his bosom yet,
It told of hate, full, deep, and strong,—
Of vengeance kindling out of wrong;
It was as if the crimes of years—

The unrequited toil—the tears—
The shame and hate, which liken well
Earth's garden to the nether hell,
Had found in Nature's self a tongue,
On which the gathered horror hung;
As if from cliff, and stream, and glen,
Burst, on the startled ears of men,
That voice which rises unto God,
Solemn and stern—the cry of blood!
It ceased—and all was still once more,
Save ocean chafing on his shore,
The sighing of the wind between
The broad banana's leaves of green,
Or bough by restless plumage shook,
Or murmuring voice of mountain brook.

Brief was the silence. Once again
  Pealed to the skies that frantic yell—
Glowed on the heavens a fiery stain,
  And flashes rose and fell;
And painted on the blood-red sky,
Dark, naked arms were tossed on high;
And, round the white man's lordly hall,
  Trode, fierce and free, *the brute he made*
And those who crept along the wall,
And answered to his lightest call
  With more than spaniel dread—
The creatures of his lawless beck—
Were trampling on his very neck!
And on the night-air, wild and clear,
Rose woman's shriek of more than fear;
For bloodied arms were round her thrown,
And dark cheeks pressed against her own!

Then, injured Afric!—for the shame
Of thy own daughters, vengeance came
Full on the scornful hearts of those,
Who mocked thee in thy nameless woes,
And to thy hapless children gave
One choice—pollution, or the grave!

Where then was he, whose fiery zeal
Had taught the trampled heart to feel,
Until despair itself grew strong,
And vengeance fed its torch from wrong?
Now—when the thunder-bolt is speeding;
Now—when oppression's heart is bleeding
Now—when the latent curse of Time
Is raining down in fire and blood—
That curse which, through long years of crime,
Has gathered, drop by drop, its flood—
Why strikes he not, the foremost one,
Where murder's sternest deeds are done?

He stood the aged palms beneath,
That shadowed o'er his humble door,
Listening, with half-suspended breath,
To the wild sounds of fear and death—
Toussaint l'Ouverture!
What marvel that his heart beat high!
The blow for freedom had been given;
And blood had answered to the cry
Which earth sent up to Heaven!
What marvel, that a fierce delight
Smiled grimly o'er his brow of night,
As groan, and shout, and bursting flame,
Told where the midnight tempest came,
With blood and fire along its van,
And death behind!—he was a Man!

Yes, dark-souled chieftain!—if the light
Of mild Religion's heavenly ray
Unveiled not to thy mental sight
The lowlier and the purer way,
In which the Holy Sufferer trod,
Meekly amidst the sons of crime,—
That calm reliance upon God
For justice, in his own good time,—
That gentleness, to which belongs
Forgiveness for its many wrongs,

Even as the primal martyr, kneeling
For mercy on the evil-dealing,—
Let not the favored white man name
Thy stern appeal, with words of blame.
Has *he* not, with the light of heaven
  Broadly around him, made the same?
Yea, on his thousand war-fields striven,
  And gloried in his ghastly shame?—
Kneeling amidst his brother's blood,
To offer mockery unto God,
As if the High and Holy One
Could smile on deeds of murder done!—
As if a human sacrifice
Were purer in his Holy eyes,
Though offered up by Christian hands,
Than the foul rites of Pagan lands!

* * * * *

Sternly, amidst his household band,
His carbine grasped within his hand,
  The white man stood, prepared and still,
Waiting the shock of maddened men,
Unchained, and fierce as tigers, when
  The horn winds through their caverned hill
And one was weeping in his sight—
  The sweetest flower of all the isle,—
The bride who seemed but yesternight
  Love's fair embodied smile.
And, clinging to her trembling knee,
Looked up the form of infancy,
With tearful glance in either face,
The secret of its fear to trace.

"Ha—stand or die!" The white man's eye
  His steady musket gleamed along,
As a tall Negro hastened nigh,
  With fearless step and strong.
"What, ho, Touissaint!" A moment more,
His shadow crossed the lighted floor.

"Away," he shouted; "fly with me,—
The white man's bark is on the sea;—
Her sails must catch the seaward wind,
For sudden vengeance sweeps behind.
Our brethren from their graves have spoken,
The yoke is spurned—the chain is broken;
On all the hills our fires are glowing—
Through all the vales red blood is flowing!
No more the mocking White shall rest
His foot upon the Negro's breast;
No more, at morn or eve, shall drip
The warm blood from the driver's whip;—
Yet, though Toussaint has vengeance sworn
For all the wrongs his race have borne,—
Though for each drop of Negro blood
The white man's veins shall pour a flood;
Not all alone the sense of ill
Around his heart is lingering still,
Nor deeper can the white man feel
The generous warmth of grateful zeal.
Friends of the Negro! fly with me—
The path is open to the sea:
Away, for life!"—He spoke, and pressed
The young child to his manly breast,
As, headlong, through the cracking cane,
Down swept the dark insurgent train—
Drunken and grim, with shout and yell
Howled through the dark, like sounds from hell

Far out, in peace, the white man's sail
Swayed free before the sunrise gale.
Cloud-like that island hung afar,
  Along the bright horizon's verge,
O'er which the curse of servile war
  Rolled its red torrent, surge on surge
And he—the Negro champion—where
  In the fierce tumult, struggled he?
Go trace him by the fiery glare
Of dwellings in the midnight air—

The yells of triumph and despair—
  The streams that crimson to the sea!

Sleep calmly in thy dungeon-tomb,
  Beneath Besançon's alien sky,
Dark Haytien!—for the time shall come,
Yea, even now is nigh—
When, every where, thy name shall be
Redeemed from *color's infamy;*
And men shall learn to speak of thee,
As one of earth's great spirits, born
In servitude, and nursed in scorn,
Casting aside the weary weight
And fetters of its low estate,
In that strong majesty of soul,
  Which knows no color, tongue or clime—
Which still hath spurned the base control
  Of tyrants through all time!
Far other hands than mine may wreath
The laurel round thy brow of death,
And speak thy praise, as one whose word
A thousand fiery spirits stirred,—
Who crushed his foeman as a worm—
Whose step on human hearts fell firm:—
Be mine the better task to find
A tribute for thy lofty mind,
Amidst whose gloomy vengeance shone
Some milder virtues all thine own,—
Some gleams of feeling pure and warm,
Like sunshine on a sky of storm,—
Proofs that the Negro's heart retains
Some nobleness amidst its chains,—
That kindness to the wronged is never
  Without its excellent reward,—
Holy to human-kind, and ever
  Acceptable to God.

THE SLAVE SHIPS.[34]

"———That fatal, that perfidious bark,
Built i' the eclipse, and rigged with curses dark."
Milton's Lycidas.

"All ready?" cried the captain;
"Ay, ay!" the seamen said;
"Heave up the worthless lubbers—
The dying and the dead."
Up from the slave-ship's prison
Fierce, bearded heads were thrust—
"Now let the sharks look to it—
Toss up the dead ones first!"

Corpse after corpse came up,—
Death had been busy there;
Where every blow is mercy,
Why should the spoiler spare?
Corpse after corpse they cast
Sullenly from the ship,
Yet bloody with the traces
Of fetter-link and whip.

Gloomily stood the captain,
With his arms upon his breast,
With his cold brow sternly knotted,
And his iron lip compressed.
"Are all the dead dogs over?"
Growled through that matted lip—
"The blind ones are no better,
Let's lighten the good ship."

Hark! from the ship's dark bosom,
The very sounds of hell!
The ringing clank of iron—
The maniac's short, sharp yell!—
The hoarse, low curse, throat-stifled—
The starving infant's moan—

The horror of a breaking heart
  Poured through a mother's groan

Up from that loathsome prison
  The stricken blind ones came:
Below, had all been darkness—
  Above, was still the same.
Yet the holy breath of heaven
  Was sweetly breathing there,
And the heated brow of fever
  Cooled in the soft sea air.

" Overboard with them, shipmates!
  Cutlass and dirk were plied;
Fettered and blind, one after one,
  Plunged down the vessel's side.
The sabre smote above—
  Beneath, the lean shark lay,
Waiting with wide and bloody jaw
  His quick and human prey.

God of the earth! what cries
  Rang upward unto Thee?
Voices of agony and blood,
  From ship-deck and from sea.
The last dull plunge was heard—
  The last wave caught its stain—
And the unsated shark looked up
  For human hearts in vain.

* * * *

Red glowed the western waters—
  The setting sun was there,
Scattering alike on wave and cloud
  His fiery mesh of hair.
Amidst a group in blindness,
  A solitary eye
Gazed, from the burdened slaver's deck,
  Into that burning sky.

"A storm," spoke out the gazer,
"Is gathering and at hand—
Curse on't—I'd give my other eye
For one firm rood of land."
And then he laughed—but only
His echoed laugh replied—
For the blinded and the suffering
Alone were at his side.

Night settled on the waters,
And on a stormy heaven,
While fiercely on that lone ship's track
The thunder-gust was driven.
"A sail!—thank God, a sail!"
And as the helmsman spoke,
Up through the stormy murmur,
A shout of gladness broke.

Down came the stranger vessel
Unheeding on her way,
So near, that on the slaver's deck
Fell off her driven spray.
"Ho! for the love of mercy—
We're perishing and blind!"
A wail of utter agony
Came back upon the wind:

"Help *us!* for we are stricken
With blindness every one;
Ten days we've floated fearfully,
Unnoting star or sun.
Our ship 's the slaver Leon—
We've but a score on board—
Our slaves are all gone over—
Help—for the love of God!"

On livid brows of agony
The broad red lightning shone—

But the roar of wind and thunder
  Stifled the answering groan.
Wailed from the broken waters
  A last despairing cry,
As, kindling in the stormy light,
  The stranger ship went by.

* * * *

In the sunny Guadaloupe
  A dark hulled vessel lay—
With a crew who noted never
  The night-fall or the day.
The blossom of the orange
  Was white by every stream,
And tropic leaf, and flower, ana bird
  Were in the warm sun-beam.

And the sky was bright as ever,
  And the moonlight slept as well,
On the palm-trees by the hill-side,
  And the streamlet of the dell:
And the glances of the Creole
  Were still as archly deep,
And her smiles as full as ever
  Of passion and of sleep.

But vain were bird and blossom,
  The green earth and the sky,
And the smile of human faces,
  To the slaver's darkened eye;
At the breaking of the morning,
  At the star-lit evening time,
O'er a world of light and beauty,
  Fell the blackness of his crime.

STANZAS.

["THE despotism which our fathers could not bear in their native country is expiring, and the sword of justice in her reformed hands has applied its exterminating edge to slavery. Shall the United States—the free United States, which could not bear the bonds of a king, cradle the bondage which a king is abolishing? Shall a Republic be less free than a Monarchy? Shall we, in the vigor and buoyancy of our manhood, be less energetic in righteousness than a kingdom in its age?"—*Dr. Follen's Address.*

"Genius of America!—Spirit of our free institutions—where art thou?—How art thou fallen, O Lucifer! son of the morning—how art thou fallen from Heaven! Hell from beneath is moved for thee, to meet thee at thy coming!—The kings of the earth cry out to thee, Aha! Aha!—ART THOU BECOME LIKE UNTO US?"—*Speech of Samuel J. May.*]

OUR fellow-countrymen in chains!
  Slaves—in a land of light and law!
Slaves—crouching on the very plains
  Where rolled the storm of Freedom's war!
A groan from Eutaw's haunted wood—
  A wail where Camden's martyrs fell—
By every shrine of patriot blood,
  From Moultrie's wall and Jasper's well!

By storied hill and hallowed grot,
  By mossy wood and marshy glen,
Whence rang of old the rifle-shot,
  And hurrying shout of Marion's men!
The groan of breaking hearts is there—
  The falling lash—the fetter's clank!
Slaves—SLAVES are breathing in that air,
  Which old De Kalb and Sumter drank!

What, ho!—*our* countrymen in chains!
  The whip on WOMAN'S shrinking flesh!
Our soil yet reddening with the stains,
  Caught from her scourging, warm and fresh!
What! mothers from their children riven!

What! God's own image bought and sold!
AMERICANS to market driven,
And bartered as the brute for gold!

Speak! shall their agony of prayer
Come thrilling to our hearts in vain?
To us whose fathers scorned to bear
The paltry *menace* of a chain;
To us, whose boast is loud and long
Of holy Liberty and Light—
Say, shall these writhing slaves of Wrong,
Plead vainly for their plundered Right?

What! shall we send, with lavish breath,
Our sympathies across the wave,
Where Manhood, on the field of death,
Strikes for his freedom, or a grave?
Shall prayers go up, and hymns be sung
For Greece, the Moslem fetter spurning,
And millions hail with pen and tongue
Our light on all her altars burning?

Shall Belgium feel, and gallant France,
By Vendome's pile and Schoenbrun's wall,
And Poland, gasping on her lance,
The impulse of our cheering call?
And shall the SLAVE, beneath our eye,
Clank o'er *our* fields his hateful chain?
And toss his fettered arms on high,
And groan for Freedom's gift, in vain?

Oh, say, shall Prussia's banner be
A refuge for the stricken slave?
And shall the Russian serf go free
By Baikal's lake and Neva's wave?
And shall the wintry-bosomed Dane
Relax the iron hand of pride,
And bid his bondmen cast the chain
From fettered soul and limb, aside?

Shall every flap of England's flag
  Proclaim that all around are free,
From "farthest Ind" to each blue crag
  That beetles o'er the Western Sea?
And shall we scoff at Europe's kings,
  When Freedom's fire is dim with us,
And round our country's altar clings
  The damning shade of Slavery's curse?

Go—let us ask of Constantine
  To loose his grasp on Poland's throat;
And beg the lord of Mahmoud's line
  To spare the struggling Suliote—
Will not the scorching answer come
  From turbaned Turk, and scornful Russ:
"Go, loose your fettered slaves at home,
  Then turn, and ask the like of us!"

Just God! and shall we calmly rest,
  The Christian's scorn—the heathen's mirth—
Content to live the lingering jest
  And by-word of a mocking Earth?
Shall our own glorious land retain
  That curse which Europe scorns to bear?
Shall our own brethren drag the chain
  Which not even Russia's menials wear?

Up, then, in Freedom's manly part,
  From gray-beard eld to fiery youth,
And on the nation's naked heart
  Scatter the living coals of Truth!
Up—while ye slumber, deeper yet
  The shadow of our fame is growing!
Up—while ye pause, our sun may set
  In blood, around our altars flowing!

Oh! rouse ye, ere the storm comes forth—
  The gathered wrath of God and man—
Like that which wasted Egypt's earth,
  When hail and fire above it ran.

Hear ye no warnings in the air?
  Feel ye no earthquake underneath?
Up—up—why will ye slumber where
  The sleeper only wakes in death?

Up *now* for Freedom!—not in strife
  Like that your sterner fathers saw—
The awful waste of human life—
  The glory and the guilt of war:
But break the chain—the yoke remove,
  And smite to earth Oppression's rod,
With those mild arms of Truth and Love,
  Made mighty through the living God!

Down let the shrine of Moloch sink,
  And leave no traces where it stood;
Nor longer let its idol drink
  His daily cup of human blood:
But rear another altar there,
  To Truth and Love and Mercy given,
And Freedom's gift, and Freedom's prayer,
  Shall call an answer down from Heaven!

THE YANKEE GIRL.

SHE sings by her wheel at that low cottage-door,
Which the long evening shadow is stretching before,
With a music as sweet as the music which seems
Breathed softly and faint in the ear of our dreams!

How brilliant and mirthful the light of her eye,
Like a star glancing out from the blue of the sky!
And lightly and freely her dark tresses play
O'er a brow and a bosom as lovely as they!

Who comes in his pride to that low cottage-door—
The haughty and rich to the humble and poor?
'T is the great Southern planter—the master who
waves
His whip of dominion o'er hundreds of slaves.

"Nay, Ellen—for shame! Let those Yankee fools
spin,
Who would pass for our slaves with a change of
their skin;
Let them toil as they will at the loom or the wheel,
Too stupid for shame, and too vulgar to feel!

But thou art too lovely and precious a gem
To be bound to their burdens and sullied by them—
For shame, Ellen, shame!—cast thy bondage aside,
And away to the South, as my blessing and pride.

Oh, come where no winter thy footsteps can wrong,
But where flowers are blossoming all the year long,
Where the shade of the palm-tree is over my home,
And the lemon and orange are white in their
bloom!

Oh, come to my home, where my servants shall all
Depart at thy bidding and come at thy call;
They shall heed thee as mistress with trembling
and awe,
And each wish of thy heart shall be felt as a law."

Oh, could ye have seen her—that pride of our
girls—
Arise and cast back the dark wealth of her curls,
With a scorn in her eye which the gazer could feel,
And a glance like the sunshine that flashes on
steel!

"Go back, haughty Southron! thy treasures of gold
Are dim with the blood of the hearts thou hast sold

Thy home may be lovely, but round it I hear
The crack of the whip and the footsteps of fear!

And the sky of thy South may be brighter than
ours,
And greener thy landscapes, and fairer thy flowers;
But, dearer the blast round our mountains which
raves,
Than the sweet summer zephyr which breathes
over slaves!

Full low at thy bidding thy negroes may kneel,
With the iron of bondage on spirit and heel;
Yet know that the Yankee girl sooner would be
In fetters with them, than in freedom with thee!"

TO W. L. G.

Champion of those who groan beneath
Oppression's iron hand:
In view of penury, hate, and death,
I see thee fearless stand.
Still bearing up thy lofty brow,
In the steadfast strength of truth,
In manhood sealing well the vow
And promise of thy youth.

Go on!—for thou hast chosen well;
On in the strength of God!
Long as one human heart shall swell
Beneath the tyrant's rod.
Speak in a slumbering nation's ear,
As thou hast ever spoken,
Until the dead in sin shall hear—
The fetter's link be broken!

I love thee with a brother's love,
  I feel my pulses thrill,
To mark thy spirit soar above
  The cloud of human ill.
My heart hath leaped to answer thine,
  And echo back thy words,
As leaps the warrior's at the shine
  And flash of kindred swords!

They tell me thou art rash and vain—
  A searcher after fame;
That thou art striving but to gain
  A long enduring name;
That thou hast nerved the Afric's hand
  And steeled the Afric's heart, .
To shake aloft his vengeful brand,
  And rend his chain apart.

Have I not known thee well, and read
  Thy mighty purpose long!
And watched the trials which have made
  Thy human spirit strong?
And shall the slanderer's demon breath
  Avail with one like me,
To dim the sunshine of my faith
  And earnest trust in thee?

Go on—the dagger's point may glare
  Amid thy pathway's gloom—
The fate which sternly threatens there
  Is glorious martyrdom!
Then onward with a martyr's zeal;
  And wait thy sure reward
When man to man no more shall kneel
  And God alone be Lord!

1833.

SONG OF THE FREE.

Pride of New England!
  Soul of our fathers!
Shrink we all craven-like,
  When the storm gathers?
What though the tempest be
  Over us lowering,
Where's the New Englander
  Shamefully cowering?
Graves green and holy
  Around us are lying,—
Free were the sleepers all,
  Living and dying!

Back with the Southerner's
  Padlocks and scourges!
Go—let him fetter down
  Ocean's free surges!
Go—let him silence
  Winds, clouds, and waters—
Never New England's own
  Free sons and daughters!
Free as our rivers are
  Ocean-ward going—
Free as the breezes are
  Over us blowing.

Up to our altars, then,
  Haste we, and summon
Courage and loveliness,
  Manhood and woman!
Deep let our pledges be:
  Freedom for ever!
Truce with oppression,
  Never, oh! never!
By our own birthright-gift,
  Granted of Heaven—

Freedom for heart and lip,
Be the pledge given!

If we have whispered truth,
Whisper no longer;
Speak as the tempest does,
Sterner and stronger;
Still be the tones of truth
Louder and firmer,
Startling the haughty South
With the deep murmur:
God and our charter's right,
Freedom for ever!
Truce with oppression,
Never, oh! never!

1836.

THE HUNTERS OF MEN

Have ye heard of our hunting, o'er mountain and glen,
Through cane-brake and forest—the hunting of men?
The lords of our land to this hunting have gone,
As the fox-hunter follows the sound of the horn;
Hark!—the cheer and the hallo!—the crack of the whip,
And the yell of the hound as he fastens his grip!
All blithe are our hunters, and noble their match—
Though hundreds are caught, there are millions to catch.
So speed to their hunting, o'er mountain and glen,
Through cane-brake and forest—the hunting of men!

Gay luck to our hunters!—how nobly they ride
In the glow of their zeal, and the strength of their pride!—

The priest with his cassock flung back on the wind,
Just screening the politic statesman behind—
The saint and the sinner, with cursing and prayer—
The drunk and the sober, ride merrily there.
And woman—kind woman—wife, widow, and maid,
For the good of the hunted, is lending her aid:
Her foot's in the stirrup, her hand on the rein,
How blithely she rides to the hunting of men!

Oh! goodly and grand is our hunting to see,
In this "land of the brave and this home of the free."
Priest, warrior, and statesman, from Georgia to Maine,
All mounting the saddle—all grasping the rein—
Right merrily hunting the black man, whose sin
Is the curl of his hair and the hue of his skin!
Woe, now, to the hunted who turns him at bay!
Will our hunters be turned from their purpose and prey?
Will their hearts fail within them?—their nerves tremble, when
All roughly they ride to the hunting of men?

Ho!—ALMS for our hunters! all weary and faint
Wax the curse of the sinner and prayer of the saint.
The horn is wound faintly—the echoes are still,
Over cane-brake and river, and forest and hill.
Haste—alms for our hunters! the hunted once more
Have turned from their flight with their backs to the shore:
What right have *they* here in the home of the white,
Shadowed o'er by *our* banner of Freedom and Right?
Ho!—alms for the hunters! or never again
Will they ride in their pomp to the hunting of men!

ALMS—ALMS for our hunters! why *will* ye delay,
When their pride and their glory are melting away?
The parson has turned; for, on charge of his own,
Who goeth a warfare, or hunting, alone?
The politic statesman looks back with a sigh—
There is doubt in his heart—there is fear in his eye.
Oh! haste, lest that doubting and fear shall prevail,
And the head of his steed take the place of the tail.
Oh! haste, ere he leave us! for who will ride then,
For pleasure or gain, to the hunting of men?

1835.

CLERICAL OPPRESSORS.

[IN the Report of the celebrated pro-slavery meeting in Charleston, S. C., on the 4th of the 9th month, 1835, published in the Courier of that city, it is stated, "*The* CLERGY *of all denominations attended in a body*, LENDING THEIR SANCTION TO THE PROCEEDINGS, and adding by their presence to the impressive character of the scene!"]

JUST God!—and these are they
Who minister at thine altar, God of Right!
Men who their hands with prayer and blessing lay
On Israel's Ark of light!

What! preach and kidnap men?
Give thanks—and rob thy own afflicted poor?
Talk of thy glorious liberty, and then
Bolt hard the captive's door?

What! servants of thy own
Merciful Son, who came to seek and save
The homeless and the outcast,—fettering down
The tasked and plundered slave!

Pilate and Herod, friends!
Chief priests and rulers, as of old, combine!
Just God and holy! is that church, which lends
Strength to the spoiler, thine?

Paid hypocrites, who turn
Judgment aside, and rob the Holy Book
Of those high words of truth which search and burn
In warning and rebuke;

Feed fat, ye locusts, feed!
And, in your tasselled pulpits, thank the Lord
That, from the toiling bondman's utter need,
Ye pile your own full board.

How long, O Lord! how long
Shall such a priesthood barter truth away,
And, in thy name, for robbery and wrong
At thy own altars pray?

Is not thy hand stretched forth
Visibly in the heavens, to awe and smite?
Shall not the living God of all the earth,
And heaven above, do right?

Woe, then, to all who grind
Their brethren of a common Father down!
To all who plunder from the immortal mind
Its bright and glorious crown!

Woe to the priesthood! woe
To those whose hire is with the price of blood—
Perverting, darkening, changing as they go,
The searching truths of God!

Their glory and their might
Shall perish; and their very names shall be
Vile before all the people, in the light
Of a world's liberty.

Oh! speed the moment on
When Wrong shall cease—and Liberty, and Love,
And Truth, and Right, throughout the earth be known
As in their home above.

THE CHRISTIAN SLAVE.

[In a late publication of L. F. Tasistro, "Random Shots and Southern Breezes," is a description of a slave auction at New Orleans, at which the auctioneer recommended the woman on the stand as "a good Christian!"]

A Christian! going, gone!
Who bids for God's own image?—for his grace
Which that poor victim of the market-place
Hath in her suffering won?

My God! can such things be?
Hast Thou not said that whatsoe'er is done
Unto thy weakest and thy humblest one,
Is even done to Thee?

In that sad victim, then,
Child of thy pitying love, I see Thee stand—
Once more the jest-word of a mocking band,
Bound, sold, and scourged again!

A Christian up for sale!
Wet with her blood your whips—o'ertask her frame,
Make her life loathsome with your wrong and shame,
Her patience shall not fail!

A heathen hand might deal
Back on your heads the gathered wrong of years,
But her low, broken prayer and nightly tears,
Ye neither heed nor feel.

Con well thy lesson o'er,
Thou *prudent* teacher—tell the toiling slave
No dangerous tale of Him who came to save
The outcast and the poor.

But wisely shut the ray
Of God's free Gospel from her simple heart,
And to her darkened mind alone impart
One stern command—OBEY!

So shalt thou deftly raise
The market price of human flesh; and while
On thee, their pampered guest, the planters smile,
Thy church shall praise.

Grave, reverend men shall tell
From Northern pulpits how thy work was blest,
While in that vile South Sodom, first and best,
Thy poor disciples sell.

Oh, shame! the Moslem thrall,
Who, with his master, to the Prophet kneels,
While turning to the sacred Kebla feels
His fetters break and fall.

Cheers for the turbaned Bey
Of robber-peopled Tunis! he hath torn
The dark slave-dungeons open, and hath borne
Their inmates into day:

But our poor slave in vain
Turns to the Christian shrine his aching eyes—
Its rites will only swell his market price,
And rivet on his chain.

God of all right! how long
Shall priestly robbers at thine altar stand,
Lifting in prayer to Thee, the bloody hand
And haughty brow of wrong?

Oh, from the fields of cane,
From the low rice-swamp, from the trader's cell—
From the black slave-ship's foul and loathsome hell,
And coffle's weary chain,—

Hoarse, horrible, and strong,
Rises to Heaven that agonizing cry,
Filling the arches of the hollow sky,
How long, O God, how long?

STANZAS FOR THE TIMES.

Is this the land our fathers loved,
The freedom which they toiled to win?
Is this the soil whereon they moved?
Are these the graves they slumber in?
Are *we* the sons by whom are borne
The mantles which the dead have worn?

And shall we crouch above these graves,
With craven soul and fettered lip?
Yoke in with marked and branded slaves,
And tremble at the driver's whip?
Bend to the earth our pliant knees,
And speak—but as our masters please?

Shall outraged Nature cease to feel?
Shall Mercy's tears no longer flow?
Shall ruffian threats of cord and steel—
The dungeon's gloom—the assassin's blow,
Turn back the spirit roused to save
The Truth, our Country, and the Slave?

Of human skulls that shrine was made,
Round which the priests of Mexico
Before their loathsome idol prayed—
Is Freedom's altar fashioned so?
And must we yield to Freedom's God,
As offering meet, the negro's blood?

Shall tongues be mute, when deeds are wrought
Which well might shame extremest hell?

Shall freemen lock the indignant thought?
  Shall Pity's bosom cease to swell?
Shall Honor bleed?—Shall Truth succumb?
Shall pen, and press, and soul be dumb?

No—by each spot of haunted ground,
  Where Freedom weeps her children's fall—
By Plymouth's rock, and Bunker's mound—
  By Griswold's stained and shattered wall—
By Warren's ghost—by Langdon's shade—
By all the memories of our dead!

By their enlarging souls, which burst
  The bands and fetters round them set—
By the free Pilgrim spirit nursed
  Within our inmost bosoms, yet,—
By all above—around—below—
Be ours the indignant answer—NO!

No—guided by our country's laws,
  For truth, and right, and suffering man,
Be ours to strive in Freedom's cause,
  As Christians *may*—as freemen *can!*
Still pouring on unwilling ears
That truth oppression only fears.

What! shall we guard our neighbor still,
  While woman shrieks beneath his rod,
And while he tramples down at will
  The image of a common God!
Shall watch and ward be round him set,
Of Northern nerve and bayonet?

And shall we know and share with him
  The danger and the growing shame?
And see our Freedom's light grow dim,
  Which should have filled the world with flame?
And, writhing, feel, where'er we turn,
A world's reproach around us burn?

Is't not enough that this is borne ?
  And asks our haughty neighbor more ?
Must fetters which his slaves have worn,
  Clank round the Yankee farmer's door ?
Must he be told, beside his plough,
What he must speak, and when, and how ?

Must he be told his freedom stands
  On Slavery's dark foundations strong—
On breaking hearts and fettered hands,
  On robbery, and crime, and wrong ?
That all his fathers taught is vain—
That Freedom's emblem is the chain ?

Its life—its soul, from slavery drawn ?
  False—foul—profane ! Go—teach as well
Of holy Truth from Falsehood born !
  Of Heaven refreshed by airs from Hell !
Of Virtue in the arms of Vice !
Of Demons planting Paradise !

Rail on, then, "brethren of the South"—
  Ye shall not hear the truth the less—
No seal is on the Yankee's mouth,
  No fetter on the Yankee's press !
From our Green Mountains to the Sea,
One voice shall thunder—WE ARE FREE !

LINES,

WRITTEN on reading the Message of Governor RITNER, of Pennsylvania, 1836.

THANK God for the token !—one lip is still free—
One spirit untrammelled—unbending one knee !
Like the oak of the mountain, deep-rooted and firm,
Erect, when the multitude bends to the storm ;

When traitors to Freedom, and Honor, and God,
Are bowed at an Idol polluted with blood;
When the recreant North has forgotten her trust,
And the lip of her honor is low in the dust,—
Thank God, that one arm from the shackle has
broken!
Thank God, that one man, as a *freeman* has
spoken!

O'er thy crags, Alleghany, a blast has been blown!
Down thy tide, Susquehanna, the murmur has gone!
To the land of the South—of the charter and
chain—
Of Liberty sweetened with Slavery's pain;
Where the cant of Democracy dwells on the lips
Of the forgers of fetters, and wielders of whips!
Where "chivalric" honor means really no more
Than scourging of women, and robbing the poor!
Where the Moloch of Slavery sitteth on high,
And the words which he utters are—WORSHIP, OR
DIE!

Right onward, oh, speed it! Wherever the blood
Of the wronged and the guiltless is crying to God;
Wherever a slave in his fetters is pining;
Wherever the lash of the driver is twining;
Wherever from kindred, torn rudely apart,
Comes the sorrowful wail of the broken of heart;
Wherever the shackles of tyranny bind,
In silence and darkness, the God-given mind;
There, God speed it onward!—its truth will be
felt—
The bonds shall be loosened—the iron shall melt!

And oh, will the land where the free soul of PENN
Still lingers and breathes over mountain and glen—
Will the land where a BENEZET's spirit went forth
To the peeled, and the meted, and outcast of
Earth—

Where the words of the Charter of Liberty first
From the soul of the sage and the patriot burst—
Where first for the wronged and the weak of their
kind,
The Christian and statesman their efforts combined—
Will that land of the free and the good wear a
chain?
Will the call to the rescue of Freedom be vain?

No, RITNER!—her "Friends," at thy warning shall
stand
Erect for the truth, like their ancestral band;
Forgetting the feuds and the strife of past time,
Counting coldness injustice, and silence a crime;
Turning back from the cavil of creeds, to unite
Once again for the poor in defence of the Right;
Breasting calmly, but firmly, the full tide of Wrong,
Overwhelmed, but not borne on its surges along;
Unappalled by the danger, the shame and the pain,
And counting each trial for Truth as their gain!

And that bold-hearted yeomanry, honest and true,
Who, haters of fraud, give to labor its due;
Whose fathers, of old, sang in concert with thine,
On the banks of Swetara, the songs of the Rhine—
The German-born pilgrims, who first dared to brave
The scorn of the proud in the cause of the slave:—
Will the sons of such men yield the lords of the
South
One brow for the brand—for the padlock one
mouth?
They cater to tyrants?—They rivet the chain,
Which their fathers smote off, on the negro again?

No, never!—one voice, like the sound in the cloud,
When the roar of the storm waxes loud and more
loud,
Wherever the foot of the freeman hath pressed

From the Delaware's marge to the Lake of the
West,
On the South-going breezes shall deepen and grow
Till the land it sweeps over shall tremble below!
The voice of a PEOPLE—uprisen—awake—
Pennsylvania's watchword, with Freedom at stake,
Thrilling up from each valley, flung down from
each height,
"OUR COUNTRY AND LIBERTY!—GOD FOR THE
RIGHT!"

THE PASTORAL LETTER.

So, this is all—the utmost reach
Of priestly power the mind to fetter!
When laymen think—when women preach—
A war of words—a "Pastoral Letter!"
Now, shame upon ye, parish Popes!
Was it thus with those, your predecessors,
Who sealed with racks, and fire, and ropes
Their loving kindness to transgressors?

A "Pastoral Letter," grave and dull—
Alas! in hoof and horns and features,
How different is your Brookfield bull,
From him who bellows from St. Peter's!
Your pastoral rights and powers from harm,
Think ye, can words alone preserve them?
Your wiser fathers taught the arm
And sword of temporal power to serve them.

Oh, glorious days—when church and state
Were wedded by your spiritual fathers!
And on submissive shoulders sat
Your Wilsons and your Cotton Mathers.

No vile "itinerant" then could mar
  The beauty of your tranquil Zion,
But at his peril of the scar
  Of hangman's whip and branding-iron.

Then, wholesome laws relieved the church
  Of heretic and mischief-maker,
And priest and bailiff joined in search,
  By turns, of Papist, witch, and Quaker!
The stocks were at each church's door,
  The gallows stood on Boston Common,
A Papist's ears the pillory bore,—
  The gallows-rope, a Quaker woman!

Your fathers dealt not as ye deal
  With "non-professing" frantic teachers;
They bored the tongue with red-hot steel,
  And flayed the backs of "female preachers,"
Old Newbury, had her fields a tongue,
  And Salem's streets could tell their story,
Of fainting woman dragged along,
  Gashed by the whip, accursed and gory!

And will ye ask me, why this taunt
  Of memories sacred from the scorner?
And why with reckless hand I plant
  A nettle on the graves ye honor?
Not to reproach New England's dead
  This record from the past I summon,
Of manhood to the scaffold led,
  And suffering and heroic woman.

No—for yourselves alone, I turn
  The pages of intolerance over,
That, in their spirit, dark and stern,
  Ye haply may your own discover!
For, if ye claim the "pastoral right"
  To silence Freedom's voice of warning,
And from your precincts shut the light
  Of Freedom's day around ye dawning;

If when an earthquake voice of power,
  And signs in earth and heaven are showing
That, forth, in its appointed hour,
  The Spirit of the Lord is going!
And, with that Spirit, Freedom's light
  On kindred, tongue, and people breaking,
Whose slumbering millions, at the sight,
  In glory and in strength are waking!

When for the sighing of the poor,
  And for the needy, God hath risen,
And chains are breaking, and a door
  Is opening for the souls in prison!
If then ye would, with puny hands,
  Arrest the very work of Heaven,
And bind anew the evil bands
  Which God's right arm of power hath riven—

What marvel that, in many a mind,
  Those darker deeds of bigot madness
Are closely with your own combined,
  Yet "less in anger than in sadness?"
What marvel, if the people learn
  To claim the right of free opinion?
What marvel, if at times they spurn
  The ancient yoke of your dominion?

A glorious remnant linger yet,
  Whose lips are wet at Freedom's fountains,
The coming of whose welcome feet
  Is beautiful upon our mountains!
Men, who the gospel tidings bring
  Of Liberty and Love for ever,
Whose joy is an abiding spring,
  Whose peace is as a gentle river!

But ye, who scorn the thrilling tale
  Of Carolina's high-souled daughters,
Which echoes here the mournful wail
  Of sorrow from Edisto's waters,

Close while ye may the public ear—
  With malice vex, with slander wound them—
The pure and good shall throng to hear,
  And tried and manly hearts surround them.

Oh, ever may the power which led
  Their way to such a fiery trial,
And strengthened womanhood to tread
  The wine-press of such self-denial,
Be round them in an evil land,
  With wisdom and with strength from Heaven
With Miriam's voice, and Judith's hand,
  And Deborah's song for triumph given!

And what are ye who strive with God,
  Against the ark of his salvation,
Moved by the breath of prayer abroad,
  With blessings for a dying nation?
What, but the stubble and the hay
  To perish, even as flax consuming,
With all that bars his glorious way,
  Before the brightness of his coming?

And thou sad Angel, who so long
  Hast waited for the glorious token,
That Earth from all her bonds of wrong
  To liberty and light has broken—
Angel of Freedom! soon to thee
  The sounding trumpet shall be given,
And over Earth's full jubilee
  Shall deeper joy be felt in Heaven!

LINES,

WRITTEN for the meeting of the Anti-Slavery Society, at Chatham Street Chapel, N. Y., held on the 4th of the 7th month, 1834.

O THOU, whose presence went before
  Our fathers in their weary way,
As with thy chosen moved of yore
  The fire by night—the cloud by day!

When from each temple of the free,
  A nation's song ascends to Heaven,
Most Holy Father! unto thee
  May not our humble prayer be given?

Thy children all—though hue and form
  Are varied in thine own good will—
With thy own holy breathings warm,
  And fashioned in thine image still.

We thank thee, Father!—hill and plain
  Around us wave their fruits once more,
And clustered vine, and blossomed grain,
  Are bending round each cottage door.

And peace is here; and hope and love
  Are round us as a mantle thrown,
And unto Thee, supreme above,
  The knee of prayer is bowed alone.

But oh, for those this day can bring,
  As unto us, no joyful thrill—
For those who, under Freedom's wing,
  Are bound in Slavery's fetters still:

For those to whom thy living word
  Of light and love is never given—
For those whose ears have never heard
  The promise and the hope of Heaven!

For broken heart, and clouded mind,
  Whereon no human mercies fall—
Oh, be thy gracious love inclined,
  Who, as a Father, pitiest all!

And grant, O Father! that the time
  Of Earth's deliverance may be near,
When every land, and tongue, and clime,
  The message of thy love shall hear—

When, smitten as with fire from heaven,
  The captive's chain shall sink in dust,
And to his fettered soul be given
  The glorious freedom of the just!

LINES,

WRITTEN for the celebration of the Third Anniversary of British Emancipation, at the Broadway Tabernacle, N. Y., "First of August," 1837.

O HOLY FATHER!—just and true
  Are all thy works and words and ways,
And unto Thee alone are due
  Thanksgiving and eternal praise!
As children of thy gracious care,
  We veil the eye—we bend the knee,
With broken words of praise and prayer,
  Father and God, we come to thee.

For thou hast heard, O God of Right,
  The sighing of the island slave;
And stretched for him the arm of might,
  Not shortened that it could not save.
The laborer sits beneath his vine,
  The shackled soul and hand are free—
Thanksgiving!—for the work is thine!
  Praise!—for the blessing is of Thee!

And oh, we feel thy presence here—
  Thy awful arm in judgment bare!
Thine eye hath seen the bondman's tear—
  Thine ear hath heard the bondman's prayer
Praise!—for the pride of man is low,
  The counsels of the wise are nought,
The fountains of repentance flow;
  What hath our God in mercy wrought?

Speed on thy work, Lord God of Hosts!
  And when the bondman's chain is riven,
And swells from all our guilty coasts
  The anthem of the free to Heaven,
Oh, not to those whom Thou hast led,
  As with thy cloud and fire before,
But unto Thee, in fear and dread,
  Be praise and glory ever more.

LINES,

Written for the Anniversary celebration of the First of August at Milton, 1846.

A few brief years have passed away
  Since Britain drove her million slaves
Beneath the tropic's fiery ray:
God willed their freedom; and to-day
  Life blooms above those island graves!

He spoke! across the Carib sea,
  We heard the clash of breaking chains,
And felt the heart-throb of the free,
The first, strong pulse of liberty
  Which thrilled along the bondman's veins.

Though long delayed, and far, and slow,
  The Briton's triumph shall be ours·

Wears slavery here a prouder brow
Than that which twelve short years ago
  Scowled darkly from her island bowers?

Mighty alike for good or ill
  With mother-land, we fully share
The Saxon strength—the nerve of steel—
The tireless energy of will,—
  The power to do, the pride to dare.

What she has done can we not do?
  Our hour and men are both at hand;
The blast which Freedom's angel blew
O'er her green islands, echoes through
  Each valley of our forest land.

Hear it, old Europe! we have sworn
  The death of slavery.—When it falls
Look to your vassals in their turn,
Your poor dumb millions, crushed and worn,
  Your prisons and your palace walls!

Oh kingly mockers!—scoffing show
  What deeds in Freedom's name we do;
Yet know that every taunt ye throw
Across the waters, goads our slow
  Progression towards the right and true.

Not always shall your outraged poor,
  Appalled by democratic crime,
Grind as their fathers ground before,—
The hour which sees our prison door
  Swing wide shall be *their* triumph time.

On then, my brothers! every blow
  Ye deal is felt the wide earth through;
Whatever here uplifts the low
Or humbles Freedom's hateful foe,
  Blesses the Old World through the New.

Take heart! The promised hour draws near—
  I hear the downward beat of wings,
And Freedom's trumpet sounding clear:
"Joy to the people!—woe and fear
  To new world tyrants, old world kings!"

THE FAREWELL

OF A VIRGINIA SLAVE MOTHER TO HER DAUGHTERS SOLD INTO SOUTHERN BONDAGE.

Gone, gone—sold and gone,
To the rice-swamp dank and lone.
Where the slave-whip ceaseless swings,
Where the noisome insect stings,
Where the fever demon strews
Poison with the falling dews,
Where the sickly sunbeams glare
Through the hot and misty air,—
Gone, gone—sold and gone,
To the rice-swamp dank and lone,
From Virginia's hills and waters,—
Woe is me, my stolen daughters!

Gone, gone—sold and gone,
To the rice-swamp dank and lone.
There no mother's eye is near them,
There no mother's ear can hear them;
Never, when the torturing lash
Seams their back with many a gash,
Shall a mother's kindness bless them,
Or a mother's arms caress them.
Gone, gone—sold and gone,
To the rice-swamp dank and lone,
From Virginia's hills and waters—
Woe is me, my stolen daughters!

Gone, gone—sold and gone,
To the rice-swamp dank and lone.
Oh, when weary, sad, and slow,
From the fields at night they go,
Faint with toil, and racked with pain,
To their cheerless homes again—
There no brother's voice shall greet them—
There no father's welcome meet them.
Gone, gone—sold and gone,
To the rice-swamp dank and lone,
From Virginia's hills and waters—
Woe is me, my stolen daughters!

Gone, gone—sold and gone,
To the rice-swamp dank and lone,
From the tree whose shadow lay
On their childhood's place of play—
From the cool spring where they drank—
Rock, and hill, and rivulet bank—
From the solemn house of prayer,
And the holy counsels there—
Gone, gone—sold and gone,
To the rice-swamp dank and lone,
From Virginia's hills and waters,—
Woe is me, my stolen daughters!

Gone, gone—sold and gone,
To the rice-swamp dank and lone—
Toiling through the weary day,
And at night the spoiler's prey.
Oh, that they had earlier died,
Sleeping calmly, side by side,
Where the tyrant's power is o'er,
And the fetter galls no more!
Gone, gone—sold and gone,
To the rice-swamp dank and lone,
From Virginia's hills and waters,—
Woe is me, my stolen daughters!

Gone, gone—sold and gone,
To the rice-swamp dank and lone.
By the holy love He beareth—
By the bruised reed He spareth—
Oh, may He, to whom alone
All their cruel wrongs are known,
Still their hope and refuge prove,
With a more than a mother's love.
Gone, gone—sold and gone,
To the rice-swamp dank and lone,
From Virginia's hills and waters,—
Woe is me, my stolen daughters!

THE MORAL WARFARE.

When Freedom, on her natal day,
Within her war-rocked cradle lay,
An iron race around her stood,
Baptized her infant brow in blood;
And, through the storm which round her swept,
Their constant ward and watching kept.

Then, where our quiet herds repose,
The roar of baleful battle rose,
And brethren of a common tongue
To mortal strife as tigers sprung,
And every gift on Freedom's shrine
Was man for beast, and blood for wine!

Our fathers to their graves have gone;
Their strife is past—their triumph won;
But sterner trials wait the race
Which rises in their honored place—
A moral warfare with the crime
And folly of an evil time.

So let it be. In God's own might
We gird us for the coming fight,
And, strong in Him whose cause is ours
In conflict with unholy powers,
We grasp the weapons He has given,—
The Light, and Truth, and Love of Heaven!

THE WORLD'S CONVENTION

OF THE FRIENDS OF EMANCIPATION, HELD IN LONDON IN 1840

Yes, let them gather!—Summon forth
The pledged philanthropy of Earth,
From every land, whose hills have heard
  The bugle blast of Freedom waking;
Or shrieking of her symbol-bird
  From out his cloudy eyrie breaking;
Where Justice hath one worshipper,
Or truth one altar built to her;
Where'er a human eye is weeping
  O'er wrongs which Earth's sad children know—
Where'er a single heart is keeping
  Its prayerful watch with human woe:
Thence let them come, and greet each other,
And know in each, a friend and brother!

Yes, let them come! from each green vale
  Where England's old baronial halls
  Still bear upon their storied walls
The grim crusader's rusted mail,
Battered by Paynim spear and brand
On Malta's rock or Syria's sand!
And mouldering pennon-staves once set
  Within the soil of Palestine,
By Jordan and Genessaret;
  Or, borne with England's battle line,
O'er Acre's shattered turrets stooping,
Or, 'midst the camp their banners drooping,

With dews from hallowed Hermon wet,
A holier summons now is given
Than that gray hermit's voice of old,
Which unto all the winds of heaven
The banners of the Cross unrolled!
Not for the long deserted shrine,—
Not for the dull unconscious sod,
Which tells not by one lingering sign
That there the hope of Israel trod;—
But for that TRUTH, for which alone
In pilgrim eyes are sanctified
The garden moss, the mountain stone,
Whereon his holy sandals pressed—
The fountain which his lip hath blessed—
Whate'er hath touched his garment's hem
At Bethany or Bethlehem,
Or Jordan's river side.
For FREEDOM, in the name of Him
Who came to raise Earth's drooping poor,
To break the chain from every limb—
The bolt from every prison door!
For these, o'er all the earth hath passed
An ever-deepening trumpet blast,
As if an angel's breath had lent
Its vigor to the instrument.

And Wales, from Snowden's mountain wall,
Shall startle at that thrilling call,
As if she heard her bards again;
And Erin's "harp on Tara's wall"
Give out its ancient strain,
Mirthful and sweet, yet sad withal—
The melody which Erin loves,
When o'er that harp, mid bursts of gladness
And slogan cries and lyke-wake sadness,
The hand of her O'Connell moves!
Scotland, from lake and tarn and rill,
And mountain hold, and heathery hill,
Shall catch and echo back the note,

As if she heard upon her air
Once more her Cameronian's prayer
  And song of Freedom float.
And cheering echoes shall reply
From each remote dependency,
Where Britain's mighty sway is known,
In tropic sea or frozen zone;
Where'er her sunset flag is furling,
Or morning gun-fire's smoke is curling;
From Indian Bengal's groves of palm
And rosy fields and gales of balm,
Where Eastern pomp and power are rolled
Through regal Ava's gates of gold;
And from the lakes and ancient woods
And dim Canadian solitudes,
Whence, sternly from her rocky throne,
Queen of the North, Quebec looks down;
And from those bright and ransomed Isles
Where all unwonted Freedom smiles,
And the dark laborer still retains
The scar of slavery's broken chains!

From the hoar Alps, which sentinel
The gateways of the land of Tell,
Where morning's keen and earliest glance
  On Jura's rocky wall is thrown,
And from the olive bowers of France
  And vine groves garlanding the Rhone,—
"Friends of the Blacks," as true and tried
As those who stood by Oge's side,
And heard the Haytien's tale of wrong,
Shall gather at that summons strong—
Broglie, Passy, and him whose song
Breathed over Syria's holy sod,
And in the paths which Jesus trod,
And murmured midst the hills which hem
Crownless and sad Jerusalem,
Hath echoes wheresoe'er the tone
Of Israel's prophet-lyre is known.

Still let them come—from Quito's walls,
  And from the Oronoco's tide,
From Lima's Inca-haunted halls,
From Santa Fe and Yucatan,—
  Men who by swart Guerrero's side
Proclaimed the deathless RIGHTS OF MAN,
  Broke every bond and fetter off,
  And hailed in every sable serf
A free and brother Mexican!
Chiefs who across the Andes' chain
  Have followed Freedom's flowing pennon,
And seen on Junin's fearful plain,
Glare o'er the broken ranks of Spain,
  The fire-burst of Bolivar's cannon!
And Hayti, from her mountain land,
  Shall send the sons of those who hurled
Defiance from her blazing strand—
The war-gage from her Petion's hand,
  Alone against a hostile world.

Nor all unmindful, thou, the while,
Land of the dark and mystic Nile!—
  Thy Moslem mercy yet may shame
  All tyrants of a Christian name—
When in the shade of Gezeh's pile,
Or, where from Abyssinian hills
El Gerek's upper fountain fills,
Or where from mountains of the Moon
El Abiad bears his watery boon,
Where'er thy lotus blossoms swim
  Within their ancient hallowed waters—
Where'er is heard the Coptic hymn,
  Or song of Nubia's sable daughters,—
The curse of SLAVERY and the crime,
Thy bequest from remotest time,
At thy dark Mehemet's decree
For evermore shall pass from thee;
  And chains forsake each captive's limb
Of all those tribes, whose hills around

Have echoed back the cymbal sound
  And victor horn of Ibrahim.

And thou whose glory and whose crime
To earth's remotest bound and clime,
In mingled tones of awe and scorn,
The echoes of a world have borne,
My country! glorious at thy birth,
A day-star flashing brightly forth—
  The herald-sign of Freedom's dawn!
Oh! who could dream that saw thee then,
  And watched thy rising from afar,
That vapors from oppression's fen
  Would cloud the upward tending star?
Or, that earth's tyrant powers, which heard,
  Awe-struck, the shout which hailed thy dawning,
Would rise so soon, prince, peer, and king,
To mock thee with their welcoming,
Like Hades when her thrones were stirred
  To greet the down-cast Star of Morning!
"Aha! and art thou fallen thus?
Art THOU become as one of *us?*"

Land of my fathers!—there will stand,
Amidst that world-assembled band,
Those owning thy maternal claim
Unweakened by thy crime and shame,—
The sad reprovers of thy wrong—
The children thou hast spurned so long.
Still with affection's fondest yearning
To their unnatural mother turning.
No traitors they!—but tried and leal,
Whose own is but thy general weal,
Still blending with the patriot's zeal
The Christian's love for human kind,
To caste and climate unconfined.

A holy gathering!—peaceful all—
No threat of war—on savage call

For vengeance on an erring brother;
But in their stead the God-like plan
To teach the brotherhood of man
To love and reverence one another,
As sharers of a common blood—
The children of a common God!—
Yet, even at its lightest word,
Shall Slavery's darkest depths be stirred:
Spain watching from her Moro's keep
Her slave-ships traversing the deep,
And Rio, in her strength and pride,
Lifting, along her mountain side,
Her snowy battlements and towers—
Her lemon groves and tropic bowers,
With bitter hate and sullen fear
Its freedom-giving voice shall hear;
And where my country's flag is flowing,
On breezes from Mount Vernon blowing
Above the Nation's council halls,
Where Freedom's praise is loud and long,
While, close beneath the outward walls
The driver plies his reeking thong—
The hammer of the man-thief falls,
O'er hypocritic cheek and brow
The crimson flush of shame shall glow:
And all who for their native land
Are pledging life and heart and hand—
Worn watchers o'er her changing weal,
Who for her tarnished honor feel—
Through cottage-door and council-hall
Shall thunder an awakening call.
The pen along its page shall burn
With all intolerable scorn—
An eloquent rebuke shall go
On all the winds that Southward blow
From priestly lips, now sealed and dumb,
Warning and dread appeal shall come,
Like those which Israel heard from him,
The Prophet of the Cherubim—

Or those which sad Esaias hurled
Against a sin-accursed world!
Its wizard-leaves the Press shall fling
Unceasing from its iron wing,
With characters inscribed thereon,
  As fearful in the despot's hall
As to the pomp of Babylon
  The fire-sign on the palace wall!
And, from her dark iniquities,
Methinks I see my country rise:
Not challenging the nations round
  To note her tardy justice done—
Her captives from their chains unbound,
  Her prisons opening to the sun:—
But tearfully her arms extending
Over the poor and unoffending;
  Her regal emblem now no longer
A bird of prey, with talons reeking,
Above the dying captive shrieking,
But, spreading out her ample wing—
A broad, impartial covering—
  The weaker sheltered by the stronger:—
Oh! then to Faith's anointed eyes
  The promised token shall be given;
And on a nation's sacrifice,
  Atoning for the sin of years,
And wet with penitential tears—
The fire shall fall from Heaven!

1839.

NEW HAMPSHIRE.

1845.

GOD bless New Hampshire!—from her granite peaks
Once more the voice of Stark and Langdon speaks.

The long bound vassal of the exulting South
  For very shame her self-forged chain has broken—
Torn the black seal of slavery from her mouth,
  And in the clear tones of her old time spoken!
Oh, all undreamed of, all unhoped for changes!—
  The tyrant's ally proves his sternest foe;
To all his biddings, from her mountain ranges,
  New Hampshire thunders an indignant No!
Who is it now despairs? Oh, faint of heart,
  Look upward to those Northern mountains cold,
  Flouted by Freedom's victor-flag unrolled,
And gather strength to bear a manlier part!
All is not lost. The angel of God's blessing
  Encamps with Freedom on the field of fight;
Still to her banner, day by day, are pressing,
  Unlooked for allies, striking for the right!
Courage, then, Northern hearts!—Be firm, be true:
What one brave State hath done, can ye not also
    do?

THE NEW YEAR:

ADDRESSED TO THE PATRONS OF THE PENNSYLVANIA FREEMAN.

The wave is breaking on the shore—
  The echo fading from the chime—
Again the shadow moveth o'er
  The dial-plate of time!

Oh, seer-seen Angel! waiting now
  With weary feet on sea and shore,
Impatient for the last dread vow
  That time shall be no more!

Once more across thy sleepless eye
  The semblance of a smile has passed;
The year departing leaves more nigh
  Time's fearfullest and last.

Oh! in that dying year hath been
  The sum of all since time began—
The birth and death, the joy and pain,
  Of Nature and of Man.

Spring, with her change of sun and shower,
  And streams released from winter's chain,
And bursting bud, and opening flower,
  And greenly growing grain;

And Summer's shade, and sunshine warm,
  And rainbows o'er her hill-tops bowed,
And voices in her rising storm—
  God speaking from his cloud!—

And Autumn's fruits and clustering sheaves,
  And soft, warm days of golden light,
The glory of her forest leaves,
  And harvest-moon at night;

And winter with her leafless grove,
  And prisoned stream, and drifting snow,
The brilliance of her heaven above
  And of her earth below:—

And man—in whom an angel's mind
  With earth's low instincts finds abode—
The highest of the links which bind
  Brute nature to her God;

His infant eye hath seen the light,
  His childhood's merriest laughter rung,
And active sports to manlier might
  The nerves of boyhood strung!

And quiet love, and passion's fires,
  Have soothed or burned in manhood's breast,
And lofty aims and low desires
  By turns disturbed his rest.

The wailing of the newly-born
  Has mingled with the funeral knell;
And o'er the dying's ear has gone
  The merry marriage-bell.

And Wealth has filled his halls with mirth,
  While Want, in many a humble shed,
Toiled, shivering by her cheerless hearth,
  The live-long night for bread.

And worse than all—the human slave—
  The sport of lust, and pride, and scorn!
Plucked off the crown his Maker gave—
  His regal manhood gone!

Oh! still my country! o'er thy plains,
  Blackened with slavery's blight and ban,
That human chattel drags his chains—
  An uncreated man!

And still, where'er to sun and breeze,
  My country, is thy flag unrolled,
With scorn, the gazing stranger sees
  A stain on every fold.

Oh, tear the gorgeous emblem down
  It gathers scorn from every eye,
And despots smile, and good men frown,
  Whene'er it passes by.

Shame! shame! its starry splendors glow
  Above the slaver's loathsome jail—
Its folds are ruffling even now
  His crimson flag of sale.

Still round our country's proudest hall
  The trade in human flesh is driven,
And at each careless hammer-fall
  A human heart is riven.

And this, too, sanctioned by the men,
Vested with power to shield the right,
And throw each vile and robber den
Wide open to the light.

Yet shame upon them!—there they sit,
Men of the North, subdued and still;
Meek, pliant poltroons, only fit
To work a master's will.

Sold—bargained off for Southern votes—
A passive herd of Northern mules,
Just braying through their purchased throats
Whate'er their owner rules.

And he [35]—the basest of the base—
The vilest of the vile—whose name,
Embalmed in infinite disgrace,
Is deathless in its shame!—

A tool—to bolt the people's door
Against the people clamoring there,—
An ass—to trample on their floor
A people's right of prayer!

Nailed to his self-made gibbet fast,
Self-pilloried to the public view—
A mark for every passing blast
Of scorn to whistle through;

There let him hang, and hear the boast
Of Southrons o'er their pliant tool—
A St. Stylites on his post,
"Sacred to ridicule!"

Look we at home!—our noble hall,
To Freedom's holy purpose given,
Now rears its black and ruined wall,
Beneath the wintry heaven—

Telling the story of its doom—
  The fiendish mob—the prostrate law—
The fiery jet through midnight's gloom,
  Our gazing thousands saw.

Look to our State—the poor man's right
  Torn from him:—and the sons of those
Whose blood in Freedom's sternest fight
  Sprinkled the Jersey snows,

Outlawed within the land of Penn,
  That Slavery's guilty fears might cease,
And those whom God created men,
  Toil on as brutes in peace.

Yet o'er the blackness of the storm,
  A bow of promise bends on high,
And gleams of sunshine, soft and warm,
  Break through our clouded sky.

East, West, and North, the shout is heard,
  Of freemen rising for the right:
Each valley hath its rallying word—
  Each hill its signal light.

O'er Massachusetts' rocks of grey,
  The strengthening light of freedom shines,
Rhode Island's Narragansett Bay—
  And Vermont's snow-hung pines!

From Hudson's frowning palisades
  To Alleghany's laurelled crest,
O'er lakes and prairies, streams and glades,
  It shines upon the West.

Speed on the light to those who dwell
  In Slavery's land of woe and sin,
And through the blackness of that hell,
  Let Heaven's own light break in.

So shall the Southern conscience quake,
Before that light poured full and strong,
So shall the Southern heart awake
To all the bondman's wrong.

And from that rich and sunny land
The song of grateful millions rise,
Like that of Israel's ransomed band
Beneath Arabia's skies:

And all who now are bound beneath
Our banner's shade—our eagle's wing,
From Slavery's night of moral death
To light and life shall spring.

Broken the bondman's chain—and gone
The master's guilt, and hate, and fear,
And unto both alike shall dawn,
A New and Happy Year.

1839.

MASSACHUSETTS TO VIRGINIA.

[WRITTEN on reading an account of the proceedings of the citizens of Norfolk, Va., in reference to GEORGE LATIMER, the alleged fugitive slave, the result of whose case in Massachusetts will probably be similar to that of the negro SOMERSET in England, in 1772.]

THE blast from Freedom's Northern hills, upon its Southern way,
Bears greeting to Virginia from Massachusetts Bay:—
No word of haughty challenging, nor battle bugle's peal,
Nor steady tread of marching files, nor clang of horsemen's steel.

No trains of deep-mouthed cannon along our highways go—
Around our silent arsenals untrodden lies the snow;
And to the land breeze of our ports, upon their errands far,
A thousand sails of commerce swell, but none are spread for war.

We hear thy threats, Virginia! thy stormy words and high,
Swell harshly on the Southern winds which melt along our sky;
Yet, not one brown, hard hand forgoes its honest labor here—
No hewer of our mountain oaks suspends his axe in fear.

Wild are the waves which lash the reefs along St. George's bank—
Cold on the shore of Labrador the fog lies white and dank;
Through storm, and wave, and blinding mist, stout are the hearts which man
The fishing-smacks of Marblehead, the sea-boats of Cape Ann.

The cold north light and wintry sun glare on their icy forms,
Bent grimly o'er their straining lines or wrestling with the storms;
Free as the winds they drive before, rough as the waves they roam,
They laugh to scorn the slaver's threat against their rocky home.

What means the Old Dominion? Hath she forgot the day
When o'er her conquered valleys swept the Briton's steel array?

How side by side, with sons of hers, the Massachusetts men
Encountered Tarleton's charge of fire, and stout Cornwallis, then?

Forgets she how the Bay State, in answer to the call
Of her old House of Burgesses, spoke out from Faneuil Hall?
When, echoing back her Henry's cry, came pulsing on each breath
Of Northern winds, the thrilling sounds of "LIBERTY OR DEATH!"

What asks the Old Dominion? If now her sons have proved
False to their fathers' memory—false to the faith they loved,
If she can scoff at Freedom, and its great charter spurn,
Must we of Massachusetts from truth and duty turn?

We hunt your bondmen, flying from Slavery's hateful hell—
Our voices, at your bidding, take up the bloodhound's yell—
We gather, at your summons, above our fathers' graves,
From Freedom's holy altar-horns to tear your wretched slaves!

Thank God! not yet so vilely can Massachusetts bow;
The spirit of her early time is with her even now;
Dream not because her Pilgrim blood moves slow, and calm, and cool,
She thus can stoop her chainless neck, a sister's slave and tool!

All that a *sister* State should do, all that a *free* State may,
Heart, hand, and purse we proffer, as in our early day;
But that one dark loathsome burden ye must stagger with alone,
And reap the bitter harvest which ye yourselves have sown!

Hold, while ye may, your struggling slaves, and burden God's free air
With woman's shriek beneath the lash, and manhood's wild despair;
Cling closer to the "cleaving curse" that writes upon your plains
The blasting of Almighty wrath against a land of chains.

Still shame your gallant ancestry, the cavaliers of old,
By watching round the shambles where human flesh is sold—
Gloat o'er the new-born child, and count his market value, when
The maddened mother's cry of woe shall pierce the slaver's den!

Lower than plummet soundeth, sink the Virginian name;
Plant, if ye will, your fathers' graves with rankest weeds of shame;
Be, if ye will, the scandal of God's fair universe—
We wash our hands forever, of your sin, and shame, and curse.

A voice from lips whereon the coal from Freedom's shrine hath been,
Thrilled, as but yesterday, the hearts of Berkshire's mountain men:

The echoes of that solemn voice are sadly lingering
still
In all our sunny valleys, on every wind-swept hill.

And when the prowling man-thief came hunting
for his prey
Beneath the very shadow of Bunker's shaft of
gray,
How, through the free lips of the son, the father's
warning spoke;
How, from its bonds of trade and sect, the Pilgrim
city broke!

A hundred thousand right arms were lifted up on
high,—
A hundred thousand voices sent back their loud
reply;
Through the thronged towns of Essex the startling
summons rang,
And up from bench and loom and wheel her young
mechanics sprang!

The voice of free, broad Middlesex—of thousands
as of one—
The shaft of Bunker calling to that of Lexington—
From Norfolk's ancient villages; from Plymouth's
rocky bound
To where Nantucket feels the arms of ocean close
her round;—

From rich and rural Worcester, where through the
calm repose
Of cultured vales and fringing woods the gentle
Nashua flows,
To where Wachuset's wintry blasts the mountain
larches stir,
Swelled up to Heaven the thrilling cry of "God
save Latimer!"

And sandy Barnstable rose up, wet with the salt sea spray—
And Bristol sent her answering shout down Narragansett Bay!
Along the broad Connecticut old Hampden felt the thrill,
And the cheer of Hampshire's woodmen swept down from Holyoke Hill.

The voice of Massachusetts! Of her free sons and daughters—
Deep calling unto deep aloud—the sound of many waters!
Against the burden of that voice what tyrant power shall stand?
No fetters in the Bay State! No slave upon her land!

Look to it well, Virginians! In calmness we have borne,
In answer to our faith and trust, your insult and your scorn;
You've spurned our kindest counsels—you've hunted for our lives—
And shaken round our hearths and homes your manacles and gyves!

We wage no war—we lift no arm—we fling no torch within
The fire-damps of the quaking mine beneath your soil of sin;
We leave ye with your bondmen, to wrestle, while ye can,
With the strong upward tendencies and God-like soul of man!

But for us and for our children, the vow which we have given
For freedom and humanity, is registered in Heaven;

No slave-hunt in our borders—no pirate on our strand!
No fetters in the Bay State—no slave upon our land!

THE RELIC.

[PENNSYLVANIA HALL, dedicated to Free Discussion and the cause of human liberty, was destroyed by a mob in 1838. The following was written on receiving a cane wrought from a fragment of the wood-work which the fire had spared.]

TOKEN of friendship true and tried,
From one whose fiery heart of youth
With mine has beaten, side by side,
For Liberty and Truth;
With honest pride the gift I take,
And prize it for the giver's sake.

But not alone because it tells
Of generous hand and heart sincere;
Around that gift of friendship dwells
A memory doubly dear—
Earth's noblest aim—man's holiest thought,
With that memorial frail inwrought!

Pure thoughts and sweet, like flowers unfold,
And precious memories round it cling,
Even as the Prophet's rod of old
In beauty blossoming:
And buds of feeling pure and good
Spring from its cold unconscious wood.

Relic of Freedom's shrine!—a brand
Plucked from its burning!—let it be
Dear as a jewel from the hand
Of a lost friend to me!—
Flower of a perished garland left,
Of life and beauty unbereft!

Oh! if the young enthusiast bears,
  O'er weary waste and sea, the stone
Which crumbled from the Forum's stairs,
  Or round the Parthenon;
Or olive bough from some wild tree
Hung over old Thermopylæ:

If leaflets from some hero's tomb,
  Or moss-wreath torn from ruins hoary,—
Or faded flowers whose sisters bloom
  On fields renowned in story,—
Or fragment from the Alhambra's crest,
Or the gray rock by Druids blessed;

Sad Erin's shamrock greenly growing
  Where Freedom led her stalwart kern,
Or Scotia's "rough bur thistle" blowing
  On Bruce's Bannockburn—
Or Runnymede's wild English rose,
Or lichen plucked from Sempach's snows!—

If it be true that things like these
  To heart and eye bright visions bring,
Shall not far holier memories
  To this memorial cling?
Which needs no mellowing mist of time
To hide the crimson stains of crime!

Wreck of a temple, unprofaned—
  Of courts where Peace with Freedom trod,
Lifting on high, with hands unstained,
  Thanksgiving unto God;
Where Mercy's voice of love was pleading
For human hearts in bondage bleeding!—

Where midst the sound of rushing feet
  And curses on the night air flung,
That pleading voice rose calm and sweet
  From woman's earnest tongue;

And Riot turned his scowling glance,
Awed, from her tranquil countenance!

That temple now in ruin lies!—
  The fire-stain on its shattered wall,
And open to the changing skies
  Its black and roofless hall,
It stands before a nation's sight,
A gravestone over buried Right!

But from that ruin, as of old,
  The fire-scorched stones themselves are
    crying,
And from their ashes white and cold
  Its timbers are replying!
A voice which slavery cannot kill
Speaks from the crumbling arches still!

And even this relic from thy shrine,
  Oh, holy Freedom!—hath to me
A potent power, a voice and sign
  To testify of thee;
And, grasping it, methinks I feel
A deeper faith, a stronger zeal.

And not unlike that mystic rod,
  Of old stretched o'er the Egyptian wave,
Which opened, in the strength of God,
  A pathway for the slave,
It yet may point the bondman's way,
And turn the spoiler from his prey.

THE BRANDED HAND.

1846.

WELCOME home again, brave seaman! with thy thoughtful brow and gray,
And the old heroic spirit of our earlier, better day—
With that front of calm endurance, on whose steady nerve, in vain
Pressed the iron of the prison, smote the fiery shafts of pain!

Is the tyrant's brand upon thee? Did the brutal cravens aim
To make God's truth thy falsehood, his holiest work thy shame?
When, all blood-quenched, from the torture the iron was withdrawn,
How laughed their evil angel the baffled fools to scorn!

They change to wrong, the duty which God hath written out
On the great heart of humanity too legible for doubt!
They, the loathsome moral lepers, blotched from footsole up to crown,
Give to shame what God hath given unto honor and renown!

Why, that brand is highest honor!—than its traces never yet
Upon old armorial hatchments was a prouder blazon set;
And thy unborn generations, as they tread our rocky strand,
Shall tell with pride the story of their father's BRANDED HAND!

As the Templar home was welcome, bearing back
from Syrian wars
The scars of Arab lances, and of Paynim scimetars,
The pallor of the prison and the shackle's crimson
span,
So we meet thee, so we greet thee, truest friend of
God and man!

He suffered for the ransom of the dear Redeemer's
grave,
Thou for his living presence in the bound and
bleeding slave;
He for a soil no longer by the feet of angels trod,
Thou for the true Shechinah, the present home of
God!

For, while the jurist sitting with the slave-whip o'er
him swung,
From the tortured truths of freedom the lie of
slavery wrung,
And the solemn priest to Moloch, on each God-deserted shrine,
Broke the bondman's heart for bread, poured the
bondman's blood for wine—

While the multitude in blindness to a far-off Saviour
knelt,
And spurned, the while, the temple where a present Saviour dwelt;
Thou beheld'st Him in the task-field, in the prison
shadows dim,
And thy mercy to the bondman, it was mercy unto
Him!

In thy lone and long night watches, sky above and
wave below,
Thou did'st learn a higher wisdom than the babbling school-men know;

God's stars and silence taught thee, as his angels only can,
That the one, sole sacred thing beneath the cope of heaven, is Man!

That he who treads profanely on the scrolls of law and creed,
In the depth of God's great goodness may find mercy in his need;
But woe to him who crushes the SOUL with chain and rod,
And herds with lower natures the awful form of God!

Then lift that manly right hand, bold ploughman of the wave!
Its branded palm shall prophesy, "SALVATION TO THE SLAVE!"
Hold up its fire-wrought language, that whoso reads may feel
His heart swell strong within him, his sinews change to steel.

Hold it up before our sunshine, up against our Northern air—
Ho! men of Massachusetts, for the love of God look there!
Take it henceforth for your standard—like the Bruce's heart of yore,
In the dark strife closing round ye, let that hand be seen before!

And the tyrants of the slave-land shall tremble at that sign,
When it points its finger Southward along the Puritan line:
Woe to the State-gorged leeches, and the Church's locust band,
When they look from slavery's ramparts on the coming of that hand!

TEXAS.

VOICE OF NEW ENGLAND.

Up the hill-side, down the glen,
Rouse the sleeping citizen;
Summon out the might of men!

Like a lion growling low—
Like a night-storm rising slow—
Like the tread of unseen foe—

It is coming—it is nigh!
Stand your homes and altars by;
On your own free thresholds die.

Clang the bells in all your spires;
On the grey hills of your sires
Fling to heaven your signal fires.

From Wachuset, lone and bleak,
Unto Berkshire's tallest peak,
Let the flame-tongued heralds speak.

O! for God and duty stand,
Heart to heart and hand to hand,
Round the old graves of the land.

Whoso shrinks or falters now,
Whoso to the yoke would bow,
Brand the craven on his brow!

Freedom's soil hath only place
For a free and fearless race—
None for traitors false and base.

Perish party—perish clan;
Strike together while ye can,
Like the arm of one strong man.

Like that angel's voice sublime,
Heard above a world of crime.
Crying of the end of time—

With one heart and with one mouth,
Let the North unto the South
Speak the word befitting both:

"What though Issachar be strong!
Ye may load his back with wrong
Overmuch and over long:

Patience with her cup o'errun,
With her weary thread outspun,
Murmurs that her work is done.

Make our Union-bond a chain,
Weak as tow in Freedom's strain
Link by link shall snap in twain.

Vainly shall your sand-wrought rope
Bind the starry cluster up,
Shattered over heaven's blue cope!

Give us bright though broken rays,
Rather than eternal haze,
Clouding o'er the full-orbed blaze.

Take your land of sun and bloom;
Only leave to Freedom room
For her plough, and forge, and loom;

Take your slavery-blackened vales;
Leave us but our own free gales,
Blowing on our thousand sails.

Boldly, or with treacherous art,
Strike the blood-wrought chain apart·
Break the Union's mighty heart·

Work the ruin, if ye will;
Pluck upon your heads an ill
Which shall grow and deepen still.

With your bondman's right arm bare,
With his heart of black despair,
Stand alone, if stand ye dare!

Onward with your fell design;
Dig the gulf and draw the line:
Fire beneath your feet the mine:

Deeply, when the wide abyss
Yawns between your land and this,
Shall ye feel your helplessness.

By the hearth, and in the bed,
Shaken by a look or tread,
Ye shall own a guilty dread.

And the curse of unpaid toil,
Downward through your generous soil
Like a fire shall burn and spoil.

Our bleak hills shall bud and blow,
Vines our rocks shall overgrow,
Plenty in our valleys flow;—

And when vengeance clouds your skies,
Hither shall ye turn your eyes,
As the lost on Paradise!

We but ask our rocky strand,
Freedom's true and brother hand,
Freedom's strong and honest hand,—

Valleys by the slave untrod,
And the Pilgrim's mountain sod,
Blessed of our fathers' God!"

TO FANEUIL HALL

1844.

MEN !—if manhood still ye claim,
  If the Northern pulse can thrill,
Roused by wrong or stung by shame,
  Freely, strongly still :—
Let the sounds of traffic die :
  Shut the mill-gate—leave the stall—
Fling the axe and hammer by—
  Throng to Faneuil Hall !

Wrongs which freemen never brooked—
  Dangers grim and fierce as they,
Which, like couching lions, looked
  On your fathers' way ;—
These your instant zeal demand,
  Shaking with their earthquake-call
Every rood of Pilgrim land—
  Ho, to Faneuil Hall !

From your capes and sandy bars—
  From your mountain-ridges cold,
Through whose pines the westering stars
  Stoop their crowns of gold—
Come, and with your footsteps wake
  Echoes from that holy wall :
Once again, for Freedom's sake,
  Rock your fathers' hall !

Up, and tread beneath your feet
  Every cord by party spun ;
Let your hearts together beat
  As the heart of one.
Banks and tariffs, stocks and trade,
  Let them rise or let them fall :

Freedom asks your common aid—
 Up, to Faneuil Hall!

Up, and let each voice that speaks
 Ring from thence to Southern plains,
Sharply as the blow which breaks
 Prison-bolts and chains!
Speak as well becomes the free—
 Dreaded more than steel or ball,
Shall your calmest utterance be,
 Heard from Faneuil Hall!

Have they wronged us? Let us then
 Render back nor threats nor prayers;
Have they chained our free-born men?
 LET US UNCHAIN THEIRS!
Up! your banner leads the van,
 Blazoned "Liberty for all!"
Finish what your sires began—
 Up, to Faneuil Hall!

TO MASSACHUSETTS.

1844.

WHAT though around thee blazes
 No fiery rallying sign?
From all thy own high places,
 Give heaven the light of thine!
What though unthrilled, unmoving,
 The statesman stands apart,
And comes no warm approving
 From Mammon's crowded mart?

Still, let the land be shaken
 By a summons of thine own!

By all save truth forsaken,
  Why, stand with that alone!
Shrink not from strife unequal!
  With the best is always hope;
And ever in the sequel
  God holds the right side up!

But when, with thine uniting,
  Come voices long and loud,
And far-off hills are writing
  Thy fire-words on the cloud:
When from Penobscot's fountains
  A deep response is heard,
And across the Western mountains
  Rolls back thy rallying word;

Shall thy line of battle falter,
  With its allies just in view?
Oh, by hearth and holy altar,
  My Father-land be true!
Fling abroad thy scrolls of Freedom!
  Speed them onward far and fast!
Over hill and valley speed them,
  Like the Sibyl's on the blast!

Lo! the Empire State is shaking
  The shackles from her hand;
With the rugged North is waking
  The level sunset land!
On they come—the free battalions!
  East and West and North they come,
And the heart-beat of the millions
  Is the beat of Freedom's drum.

"To the tyrant's plot no favor!
  No heed to place-fed knaves!
Bar and bolt the door forever
  Against the land of Slaves!"

Hear it, mother Earth, and hear it,
The Heavens above us spread!
The land is roused—its spirit
Was sleeping, but not dead!

THE PINE-TREE.

1846.

Lift again the stately emblem on the Bay State's rusted shield,
Give to Northern winds the Pine-Tree on our banner's tattered field,
Sons of men who sat in council with their Bibles round the board,
Answering England's royal missive with a firm, "Thus saith the Lord!"
Rise again for home and freedom!—set the battle in array!—
What the fathers did of old time we their sons must do to-day.

Tell us not of banks and tariffs—cease your paltry peddler cries—
Shall the good State sink her honor that your gambling stocks may rise?
Would ye barter man for cotton?—That your gains may sum up higher,
Must we kiss the feet of Moloch, pass our children through the fire?
Is the dollar only real?—God and truth and right a dream?
Weighed against your lying ledgers must our manhood kick the beam?

Oh, my God!—for that free spirit, which of old in Boston town

Smote the Province House with terror, struck the
crest of Andros down!—
For another strong-voiced Adams in the city's
streets to cry:
"Up for God and Massachusetts!—Set your feet
on Mammon's lie!
Perish banks and perish traffic—spin your cotton's
latest pound—
But in Heaven's name keep your honor—keep the
heart o' the Bay State sound!"

Where's the MAN for Massachusetts?—Where's the
voice to speak her free?—
Where's the hand to light up bonfires from her
mountains to the sea?
Beats her Pilgrim pulse no longer?—Sits she dumb
in her despair?—
Has she none to break the silence?—Has she none
to do and dare?
Oh my God! for one right worthy to lift up her
rusted shield,
And to plant again the Pine-Tree in her banner's
tattered field!

LINES,

SUGGESTED BY A VISIT TO THE CITY OF WASHINGTON IN THE 12TH MONTH OF 1845.

WITH a cold and wintry noon-light,
On its roofs and steeples shed,
Shadows weaving with the sunlight
From the gray sky overhead,
Broadly, vaguely, all around me, lies the half-built
town outspread.

Through this broad street, restless ever,
Ebbs and flows a human tide,
Wave on wave a living river;
Wealth and fashion side by side;
Toiler, idler, slave and master, in the same quick current glide.

Underneath yon dome, whose coping
Springs above them, vast and tall,
Grave men in the dust are groping
For the largess, base and small,
Which the hand of Power is scattering, crumbs which from its table fall.

Base of heart! They vilely barter
Honor's wealth for party's place:
Step by step on Freedom's charter
Leaving footprints of disgrace;
For to-day's poor pittance turning from the great hope of their race.

Yet, where festal lamps are throwing
Glory round the dancer's hair,
Gold-tressed, like an angel's flowing
Backward on the sunset air;
And the low quick pulse of music beats its measures sweet and rare:

There to-night shall woman's glances,
Star-like, welcome give to them,
Fawning fools with shy advances
Seek to touch their garments' hem,
With the tongue of flattery glozing deeds which God and Truth condemn.

From this glittering lie my vision
Takes a broader, sadder range,
Full before me have arisen
Other pictures dark and strange;

From the parlor to the prison must the scene and witness change.

Hark! the heavy gate is swinging
On its hinges, harsh and slow;
One pale prison lamp is flinging
On a fearful group below
Such a light as leaves to terror whatsoe'er it does not show.

Pitying God!—Is that a WOMAN
On whose wrist the shackles clash?
Is that shriek she utters human,
Underneath the stinging lash?
Are they MEN whose eyes of madness from that sad procession flash?

Still the dance goes gayly onward!
What is it to Wealth and Pride?
That without the stars are looking
On a scene which earth should hide?
That the SLAVE-SHIP lies in waiting, rocking on Potomac's tide!

Vainly to that mean Ambition
Which, upon a rival's fall,
Winds above its old condition,
With a reptile's slimy crawl,
Shall the pleading voice of sorrow, shall the slave in anguish call.

Vainly to the child of Fashion,
Giving to ideal woe
Graceful luxury of compassion,
Shall the stricken mourner go;
Hateful seems the earnest sorrow, beautiful the hollow show!

Nay, my words are all too sweeping:
In this crowded human mart,

Feeling is not dead, but sleeping;
Man's strong will and woman's heart,
In the coming strife for Freedom, yet shall bear their generous part.

And from yonder sunny valleys,
Southward in the distance lost,
Freedom yet shall summon allies
Worthier than the North can boast,
With the Evil by their hearth-stones grappling at severer cost.

Now, the soul alone is willing:
Faint the heart and weak the knee;
And as yet no lip is thrilling
With the mighty words "BE FREE!"
Tarrieth long the land's Good Angel, but his advent is to be!

Meanwhile, turning from the revel
To the prison-cell my sight,
For intenser hate of evil,
For a keener sense of right,
Shaking off thy dust, I thank thee, City of the Slaves, to-night!

"To thy duty now and ever!
Dream no more of rest or stay;
Give to Freedom's great endeavor
All thou art and hast to-day:"—
Thus, above the city's murmur, saith a Voice, or seems to say.

Ye with heart and vision gifted
To discern and love the right,
Whose worn faces have been lifted
To the slowly-growing light,
Where from Freedom's sunrise drifted slowly back the murk of night!—

Ye who through long years of trial
Still have held your purpose fast,
While a lengthening shade the dial
From the westering sunshine cast,
And of hope each hour's denial seemed an echo of the last!—

Oh, my brothers! oh, my sisters!
Would to God that ye were near,
Gazing with me down the vistas
Of a sorrow strange and drear;
Would to God that ye were listeners to the Voice I seem to hear!

With the storm above us driving,
With the false earth mined below—
Who shall marvel if thus striving
We have counted friend as foe;
Unto one another giving in the darkness blow for blow.

Well it may be that our natures
Have grown sterner and more hard,
And the freshness of their features
Somewhat harsh and battle-scarred,
And their harmonies of feeling overtasked and rudely jarred.

Be it so. It should not swerve us
From a purpose true and brave;
Dearer Freedom's rugged service
Than the pastime of the slave;
Better is the storm above it than the quiet of the grave.

Let us then, uniting, bury
All our idle feuds in dust,
And to future conflicts carry

Mutual faith and common trust;
Always he who most forgiveth in his brother is most just.

From the eternal shadow rounding
All our sun and starlight here,
Voices of our lost ones sounding
Bid us be of heart and cheer,
Through the silence, down the spaces, falling on the inward ear.

Know we not our dead are looking
Downward with a sad surprise,
All our strife of words rebuking
With their mild and loving eyes?
Shall we grieve the holy angels? Shall we cloud their blessed skies?

Let us draw their mantles o'er us
Which have fallen in our way;
Let us do the work before us,
Cheerly, bravely, while we may,
Ere the long night-silence cometh, and with us it is not day!

LINES,

FROM A LETTER TO A YOUNG CLERICAL FRIEND.

A STRENGTH thy service cannot tire—
A faith which doubt can never dim—
A heart of love, a lip of fire—
Oh! Freedom's God! be thou to him!

Speak through him words of power and fear,
As through thy prophet bards of old,

And let a scornful people hear
  Once more thy Sinai-thunders rolled.

For lying lips thy blessing seek,
  And hands of blood are raised to Thee,
And on thy children, crushed and weak,
  The oppressor plants his kneeling knee.

Let then, O God! thy servant dare
  Thy truth in all its power to tell,
Unmask the priestly thieves, and tear
  The Bible from the grasp of hell!

From hollow rite and narrow span
  Of law and sect by Thee released,
Oh! teach him that the Christian man
  Is holier than the Jewish priest.

Chase back the shadows, gray and old,
  Of the dead ages, from his way,
And let his hopeful eyes behold
  The dawn of thy millennial day;—

That day when fettered limb and mind
  Shall know the truth which maketh free,
And he alone who loves his kind
  Shall, child-like, claim the love of Thee!

YORKTOWN.[36]

From Yorktown's ruins, ranked and still,
Two lines stretch far o'er vale and hill:
Who curbs his steed at head of one?
Hark! the low murmur: Washington!
Who bends his keen, approving glance

Where down the gorgeous line of France
Shine knightly star and plume of snow?
Thou too art victor, Rochambeau!

The earth which bears this calm array
Shook with the war-charge yesterday,
Ploughed deep with hurrying hoof and wheel,
Shot-sown and bladed thick with steel;
October's clear and noonday sun
Paled in the breath-smoke of the gun,
And down night's double blackness fell,
Like a dropped star, the blazing shell.

Now all is hushed: the gleaming lines
Stand moveless as the neighboring pines;
While through them, sullen, grim, and slow,
The conquered hosts of England go:
O'Hara's brow belies his dress,
Gay Tarleton's troop rides bannerless:
Shout, from thy fired and wasted homes,
Thy scourge, Virginia, captive comes!

Nor thou alone: with one glad voice
Let all thy sister States rejoice;
Let Freedom, in whatever clime
She waits with sleepless eye her time,
Shouting from cave and mountain wood,
Make glad her desert solitude,
While they who hunt her quail with fear:
The New World's chain lies broken here!

But who are they, who, cowering, wait
Within the shattered fortress gate?
Dark tillers of Virginia's soil,
Classed with the battle's common spoil,
With household stuffs, and fowl, and swine,
With Indian weed and planters' wine,
With stolen beeves, and foraged corn—
Are they not men, Virginian born?

Oh! veil your faces, young and brave!
Sleep, Scammel, in thy soldier grave!
Sons of the Northland, ye who set
Stout hearts against the bayonet,
And pressed with steady footfall near
The moated battery's blazing tier,
Turn your scarred faces from the sight,
Let shame do homage to the right!

Lo! threescore years have passed; and where
The Gallic timbrel stirred the air,
With Northern drum-roll, and the clear,
Wild horn-blow of the mountaineer,
While Britain grounded on that plain
The arms she might not lift again,
As abject as in that old day
The slave still toils his life away.

Oh! fields still green and fresh in story,
Old days of pride, old names of glory,
Old marvels of the tongue and pen,
Old thoughts which stirred the hearts of men,
Ye spared the wrong; and over all
Behold the avenging shadow fall!
Your world-wide honor stained with shame—
Your freedom's self a hollow name!

Where's now the flag of that old war?
Where flows its stripe? Where burns its star?
Bear witness, Palo Alto's day,
Dark Vale of Palms, red Monterey,
Where Mexic Freedom, young and weak,
Fleshes the Northern eagle's beak:
Symbol of terror and despair,
Of chains and slaves, go seek it there!

Laugh, Prussia, midst thy iron ranks!
Laugh, Russia, from thy Neva's banks!
Brave sport to see the fledgling born

Of Freedom by its parent torn!
Safe now is Speilberg's dungeon cell,
Safe drear Siberia's frozen hell:
With Slavery's flag o'er both unrolled,
What of the New World fears the Old?

LINES,

WRITTEN IN THE BOOK OF A FRIEND.

On page of thine I cannot trace
The cold and heartless common-place—
A statue's fixed and marble grace.

For ever as these lines I penned,
Still with the thought of thee will blend
That of some loved and common friend.

Who in life's desert track has made
His pilgrim tent with mine, or strayed
Beneath the same remembered shade.

And hence my pen unfettered moves
In freedom which the heart approves—
The negligence which friendship loves.

And wilt thou prize my poor gift less
For simple air and rustic dress,
And sign of haste and carelessness?—

Oh! more than specious counterfeit
Of sentiment or studied wit,
A heart like thine should value it.

Yet half I fear my gift will be
Unto thy book, if not to thee,
Of more than doubtful courtesy.

A banished name from fashion's sphere,
A lay unheard of Beauty's ear,
Forbid, disowned,—what do they here?—

Upon my ear not all in vain
Came the sad captive's clanking chain—
The groaning from his bed of pain.

And sadder still, I saw the woe
Which only wounded spirits know
When Pride's strong footsteps o'er them go

Spurned not alone in walks abroad,
But from the "temples of the Lord"
Thrust out apart, like things abhorred.

Deep as I felt, and stern and strong,
In words which Prudence smothered long,
My soul spoke out against the wrong;

Not mine alone the task to speak
Of comfort to the poor and weak,
And dry the tear on Sorrow's cheek;

But, mingled in the conflict warm,
To pour the fiery breath of storm
Through the harsh trumpet of Reform;

To brave Opinion's settled frown,
From ermined robe and saintly gown,
While wrestling reverenced Error down

Founts gushed beside my pilgrim way,
Cool shadows on the greensward lay,
Flowers swung upon the bending spray.

And, broad and bright, on either hand,
Stretched the green slopes of Fairy land,
With Hope's eternal sunbow spanned;

Whence voices called me like the flow,
Which on the listener's ear will grow,
Of forest streamlets soft and low.

And gentle eyes, which still retain
Their picture on the heart and brain,
Smiled, beckoning from that path of pain.

In vain!—nor dream, nor rest, nor pause
Remain for him who round him draws
The battered mail of Freedom's cause.

From youthful hopes—from each green spot
Of young Romance, and gentle Thought,
Where storm and tumult enter not—

From each fair altar, where belong
The offerings Love requires of Song
In homage to her bright-eyed throng—

With soul and strength, with heart and hand,
I turned to Freedom's struggling band—
To the sad Helots of our land.

What marvel then that Fame should turn
Her notes of praise to those of scorn—
Her gifts reclaimed—her smiles withdrawn?

What matters it!—a few years more,
Life's surge so restless heretofore
Shall break upon the unknown shore!

In that far land shall disappear
The shadows which we follow here—
The mist-wreaths of our atmosphere!

Before no work of mortal hand,
Of human will or strength expand
The pearl gates of the Better Land;

Alone in that great love which gave
Life to the sleeper of the grave,
Resteth the power to "seek and save."

Yet, if the spirit gazing through
The vista of the past can view
One deed to Heaven and virtue true—

If through the wreck of wasted powers,
Of garlands wreathed from Folly's bowers,
Of idle aims and misspent hours—

The eye can note one sacred spot
By Pride and Self profaned not—
A green place in the waste of thought—

Where deed or word hath rendered less
"The sum of human wretchedness,"
And Gratitude looks forth to bless—

The simple burst of tenderest feeling
From sad hearts worn by evil-dealing,
For blessing on the hand of healing,—

Better than Glory's pomp will be
That green and blessed spot to me—
A palm-shade in Eternity!—

Something of Time which may invite
The purified and spiritual sight
To rest on with a calm delight.

And when the summer winds shall sweep
With their light wings my place of sleep,
And mosses round my head-stone creep—

If still, as Freedom's rallying sign,
Upon the young heart's altars shine
The very fires they caught from mine—

If words my lips once uttered still,
In the calm faith and steadfast will
Of other hearts, their work fulfill—

Perchance with joy the soul may learn
These tokens, and its eye discern
The fires which on those altars burn—

A marvellous joy that even then,
The spirit hath its life again,
In the strong hearts of mortal men.

Take, lady, then, the gift I bring,
No gay and graceful offering—
No flower-smile of the laughing spring.

Midst the green buds of Youth's fresh May,
With Fancy's leaf-enwoven bay,
My sad and sombre gift I lay.

And if it deepens in thy mind
A sense of suffering human kind—
The outcast and the spirit-blind:

Oppressed and spoiled on every side,
By Prejudice, and Scorn, and Pride,
Life's common courtesies denied;

Sad mothers mourning o'er their trust,
Children by want and misery nursed,
Tasting life's bitter cup at first;

If to their strong appeals which come
From fireless hearth, and crowded room,
And the close alley's noisome gloom—

Though dark the hands upraised to thee
In mute beseeching agony,
Thou lend'st thy woman's sympathy—

Not vainly on thy gentle shrine,
Where Love, and Mirth, and Friendship twine
Their varied gifts, I offer mine.

PÆAN.

1848.

Now, joy and thanks forevermore!
  The dreary night has wellnigh passed,
The slumbers of the North are o'er—
  The Giant stands erect at last!

More than we hoped in that dark time,
  When, faint with watching, few and worn,
We saw no welcome day-star climb
  The cold gray pathway of the morn!

O weary hours! O night of years!
  What storms our darkling pathway swept,
Where, beating back our thronging fears,
  By Faith alone our march we kept.

How jeered the scoffing crowd behind,
  How mocked before the tyrant train,
As, one by one, the true and kind
  Fell fainting in our path of pain.

They died—their brave hearts breaking slow—
  But, self-forgetful to the last,
In words of cheer and bugle blow
  Their breath upon the darkness passed.

A mighty host, on either hand,
  Stood waiting for the dawn of day
To crush like reeds our feeble band;
  The morn has come—and where are they?

Troop after troop their line forsakes;
With peace-white banners waving free,
And from our own the glad shout breaks,
Of Freedom and Fraternity!

Like mist before the growing light,
The hostile cohorts melt away;
Our frowning foemen of the night
Are brothers at the dawn of day!

As unto these repentant ones
We open wide our toil-worn ranks,
Along our line a murmur runs
Of song, and praise, and grateful thanks.

Sound for the onset!—Blast on blast!
Till Slavery's minions cower and quail;
One charge of fire shall drive them fast
Like chaff before our Northern gale!

O, prisoners in your house of pain,
Dumb, toiling millions, bound and sold,
Look! stretched o'er Southern vale and plain,
The Lord's delivering hand behold!

Above the tyrant's pride of power,
His iron gates and guarded wall,
The bolts which shattered Shinar's tower,
Hang, smoking, for a fiercer fall.

Awake! awake! my Father-land!
It is thy Northern light that shines;
This stirring march of Freedom's band
The storm-song of thy mountain pines.

Wake, dwellers where the day expires!
And hear, in winds that sweep your lakes
And fan your prairies' roaring fires,
The signal-call that Freedom makes!

TO THE MEMORY OF THOMAS SHIPLEY,

GONE to thy Heavenly Father's rest!
  The flowers of Eden round thee blowing,
And on thine ear the murmurs blest
  Of Siloa's waters softly flowing!
Beneath that Tree of Life which gives
To all the earth its healing leaves
In the white robe of angels clad,
  And wandering by that sacred river,
Whose streams of holiness make glad
  The city of our God forever!

Gentlest of spirits!—not for thee
  Our tears are shed, our sighs are given:
Why mourn to know thou art a free
  Partaker of the joys of Heaven?
Finished thy work, and kept thy faith
In Christian firmness unto death:
And beautiful as sky and earth,
  When Autumn's sun is downward going
The blessed memory of thy worth
  Around thy place of slumber glowing!

But woe for us! who linger still
  With feebler strength and hearts less lowly,
And minds less steadfast to the will
  Of Him whose every work is holy.
For not like thine, is crucified
The spirit of our human pride:
And at the bondman's tale of woe,
  And for the outcast and forsaken,
Not warm like thine, but cold and slow,
  Our weaker sympathies awaken.

Darkly upon our struggling way
  The storm of human hate is sweeping;
Hunted and branded, and a prey,
  Our watch amidst the darkness keeping,
Oh! for that hidden strength which can
Nerve unto death the inner man!
Oh! for thy spirit, tried and true,
  And constant in the hour of trial,
Prepared to suffer, or to do,
  In meekness and in self-denial.

Oh! for that spirit, meek and mild,
  Derided, spurned, yet uncomplaining—
By man deserted and reviled,
  Yet faithful to its trust remaining.
Still prompt and resolute to save
From scourge and chain the hunted slave!
Unwavering in the Truth's defence,
  Even where the fires of Hate were burning,
Th' unquailing eye of innocence
  Alone upon th' oppressor turning!

O loved of thousands! to thy grave,
  Sorrowing of heart, thy brethren bore thee
The poor man and the rescued slave
  Wept as the broken earth closed o'er thee;
And grateful tears, like summer rain,
Quickened its dying grass again!
And there, as to some pilgrim-shrine,
  Shall come the outcast and the lowly,
Of gentle deeds and words of thine
  Recalling memories sweet and holy!

Oh! for the death the righteous die!
  An end, like Autumn's day declining,
On human hearts, as on the sky,
  With holier, tenderer beauty shining;
As to the parting soul were given
The radiance of an opening Heaven!

As if that pure and blessed light,
  From off th' Eternal altar flowing,
Were bathing, in its upward flight,
  The spirit to its worship going!

TO A SOUTHERN STATESMAN.

1846.

Is this thy voice, whose treble notes of fear
Wail in the wind? And dost thou shake to hear,
Actæon-like, the bay of thine own hounds,
Spurning the leash, and leaping o'er their bounds?
Sore-baffled statesman! when thy eager hand,
With game afoot, unslipped the hungry pack,
To hunt down Freedom in her chosen land,
Hadst thou no fear, that, ere long, doubling back,
These dogs of thine might snuff on Slavery's track?
Where's now the boast, which even thy guarded tongue,
Cold, calm and proud, in the teeth o' the Senate flung,
O'er the fulfilment of thy baleful plan,
Like Satan's triumph at the fall of man?
How stood'st thou then, thy feet on Freedom planting,
And pointing to the lurid heaven afar,
Whence all could see, through the south windows slanting,
Crimson as blood, the beams of that Lone Star!
The Fates are just; they give us but our own;
Nemesis ripens what our hands have sown.
There is an Eastern story, not unknown,
Doubtless, to thee, of one whose magic skill
Called demons up his water-jars to fill;
Deftly and silently, they did his will,

But, when the task was done, kept pouring still,
In vain with spell and charm the wizard wrought,
Faster and faster were the buckets brought,
Higher and higher rose the flood around,
Till the fiends clapped their hands above their
    master drowned!
So, Carolinian, it may prove with thee,
For God still overrules man's schemes, and takes
Craftiness in its self-set snare, and makes
The wrath of man to praise Him. It may be,
That the roused spirits of Democracy
May leave to freer States the same wide door
Through which thy slave-cursed Texas entered in,
From out the blood and fire, the wrong and sin,
Of the stormed city and the ghastly plain,
Beat by hot hail, and wet with bloody rain,
A myriad-handed Aztec host may pour,
And swarthy South with pallid North combine
Back on thyself to turn thy dark design.

LINES,

Written on the adoption of Pinckney's Resolutions, in the House of Representatives, and the passage of Calhoun's "Bill for excluding papers written or printed, touching the subject of Slavery from the U. S. Post-office," in the Senate of the United States.

Men of the North-land! where's the manly spirit
  Of the true-hearted and the unshackled gone?
Sons of old freemen, do we but inherit
    Their names alone?

Is the old Pilgrim spirit quenched within us,
  Stoops the strong manhood of our souls so low,
That Mammon's lure or Party's wile can win us
    To silence now?

Now, when our land to ruin's brink is verging,
  In God's name, let us speak while there is time!
Now, when the padlocks for our lips are forging,
      Silence is crime!

What! shall we henceforth humbly ask as favors
  Rights all our own? In madness shall we barter,
For treacherous peace, the freedom Nature gave us,
      God and our charter?

Here shall the statesman forge his human fetters,
  Here the false jurist human rights deny,
And, in the church, their proud and skilled abettors
      Make truth a lie?

Torture the pages of the hallowed Bible,
  To sanction crime, and robbery, and blood?
And, in Oppression's hateful service, libel
      Both man and God?

Shall our New England stand erect no longer,
  But stoop in chains upon her downward way,
Thicker to gather on her limbs and stronger
      Day after day?

Oh, no; methinks from all her wild, green mountains—
  From valleys where her slumbering fathers lie—
From her blue rivers and her welling fountains,
      And clear, cold sky—

From her rough coast, and isles, which hungry Ocean
  Gnaws with his surges—from the fisher's skiff,
With white sail swaying to the billows' motion
      Round rock and cliff—

From the free fire-side of her unbought farmer—
  From her free laborer at his loom and wheel—

From the brown smith-shop, where, beneath the hammer,
Rings the red steel—

From each and all, if God hath not forsaken
Our land, and left us to an evil choice,
Loud as the summer thunderbolt shall waken
A People's voice

Startling and stern! the Northern winds shall bear it
Over Potomac's to St. Mary's wave;
And buried Freedom shall awake to hear it
Within her grave.

Oh, let that voice go forth! The bondman sighing
By Santee's wave, in Mississippi's cane,
Shall feel the hope, within his bosom dying,
Revive again.

Let it go forth! The millions who are gazing
Sadly upon us from afar, shall smile,
And unto God devout thanksgiving raising,
Bless us the while.

Oh, for your ancient freedom, pure and holy,
For the deliverance of a groaning earth,
For the wronged captive, bleeding, crushed, and lowly,
Let it go forth!

Sons of the best of fathers! will ye falter
With all they left ye perilled and at stake?
Ho! once again on Freedom's holy altar
The fire awake!

Prayer-strengthened for the trial, come together,
Put on the harness for the moral fight,
And, with the blessing of your Heavenly Father,
MAINTAIN THE RIGHT!

THE CURSE OF THE CHARTER-BREAKERS.[37]

In Westminster's royal halls,
Robed in their pontificals,
England's ancient prelates stood
For the people's right and good.

Closed around the waiting crowd,
Dark and still, like winter's cloud,
King and council, lord and knight,
Squire and yeoman, stood in sight—

Stood to hear the priest rehearse,
In God's name, the Church's curse,
By the tapers round them lit,
Slowly, sternly uttering it.

"Right of voice in framing laws,
Right of peers to try each cause;
Peasant homestead, mean and small,
Sacred as the monarch's hall—

"Whoso lays his hand on these,
England's ancient liberties—
Whoso breaks, by word or deed,
England's vow at Runnymede—

"Be he Prince or belted knight,
Whatsoe'er his rank or might,
If the highest, then the worst,
Let him live and die accursed.

"Thou, who to thy Church hast given
Keys alike, of hell and heaven,
Make our word and witness sure,
Let the curse we speak endure!"

Silent, while that curse was said,
Every bare and listening head
Bowed in reverent awe, and then
All the people said, Amen!

Seven times the bells have tolled,
For the centuries gray and old,
Since that stoled and mitred band
Cursed the tyrants of their land.

Since the priesthood, like a tower,
Stood between the poor and power;
And the wronged and trodden down
Blessed the abbot's shaven crown.

Gone, thank God, their wizard spell,
Lost, their keys of heaven and hell;
Yet I sigh for men as bold
As those bearded priests of old.

Now, too oft the priesthood wait
At the threshold of the state—
Waiting for the beck and nod
Of its power as law and God.

Fraud exults, while solemn words
Sanctify his stolen hoards;
Slavery laughs, while ghostly lips
Bless his manacles and whips.

Not on them the poor rely,
Not to them looks liberty,
Who with fawning falsehood cower
To the wrong, when clothed with power.

Oh! to see them meanly cling,
Round the master, round the king,
Sported with, and sold and bought—
Pitifuller sight is not!

Tell me not that this must be:
God's true priest is always free;
Free, the needed truth to speak,
Right the wronged, and raise the weak.

Not to fawn on wealth and state,
Leaving Lazarus at the gate—
Not to peddle creeds like wares—
Not to mutter hireling prayers—

Nor to paint the new life's bliss
On the sable ground of this—
Golden streets for idle knave,
Sabbath rest for weary slave!

Not for words and works like these,
Priest of God, thy mission is;
But to make earth's desert glad,
In its Eden greenness clad;

And to level manhood bring
Lord and peasant, serf and king;
And the Christ of God to find
In the humblest of thy kind!

Thine to work as well as pray
Clearing thorny wrongs away;
Plucking up the weeds of sin,
Letting heaven's warm sunshine in—

Watching on the hills of Faith;
Listening what the spirit saith,
Of the dimseen light afar,
Growing like a nearing star.

God's interpreter art thou,
To the waiting ones below;
'Twixt them and its light midway
Heralding the better day—

Catching gleams of temple spires,
Hearing notes of angel choirs,
Where, as yet unseen of them,
Comes the New Jerusalem!

Like the seer of Patmos gazing,
On the glory downward blazing;
Till upon Earth's grateful sod
Rests the City of our God!

THE SLAVES OF MARTINIQUE.

SUGGESTED BY A DAGUERREOTYPE FROM A FRENCH ENGRAVING.

Beams of noon, like burning lances, through the tree-tops flash and glisten,
As she stands before her lover, with raised face to look and listen.

Dark, but comely, like the maiden in the ancient Jewish song:
Scarcely has the toil of task-fields done her graceful beauty wrong.

He, the strong one and the manly, with the vassal's garb and hue,
Holding still his spirit's birthright, to his higher nature true;

Hiding deep the strengthening purpose of a freeman in his heart,
As the greegree holds his Fetich from the white man's gaze apart.

Ever foremost of his comrades, when the drivers morning horn
Calls away to stifling mill-house, to the fields of cane and corn:

Fall the keen and burning lashes, never on his back or limb;
Scarce with look or word of censure, turns the driver unto him.

Yet, his brow is always thoughtful, and his eye is hard and stern;
Slavery's last and humblest lesson, he has never deigned to learn.

And, at evening, when his comrades dance before their master's door,
Folding arms and knitting forehead, stands he silent evermore.

God be praised for every instinct which rebels against a lot,
Where the brute survives the human, and man's upright form is not!

As the serpent-like bejuco winds his spiral fold on fold,
Round the tall and stately ceiba, till it withers in his hold;—

Slow decays the forest monarch, closer girds the fell embrace,
Till the tree is seen no longer, and the vine is in its place—

So a base and bestial nature, round the vassal's manhood twines,
And the spirit wastes beneath it, like the ceiba choked with vines.

God is Love, saith the Evangel; and our world of woe and sin
Is made light and happy only, when a Love is shining in.

Ye whose lives are free as sunshine, finding where-
soe'er ye roam,
Smiles of welcome, looks of kindness, making all
the world like home;

In the veins of whose affections, kindred blood is
but a part,
Of one kindly current throbbing from the universal
heart;

Can ye know the deeper meaning of a love in
Slavery nursed,
Last flower of a lost Eden, blooming in that Soil
accursed?

Love of Home, and Love of Woman!—dear to all,
but doubly dear
To the heart whose pulses elsewhere measure only
hate and fear.

All around the desert circles, underneath a brazen
sky,
Only one green spot remaining where the dew is
never dry!

From the horror of that desert, from its atmosphere
of hell,
Turns the fainting spirit thither, as the diver seeks
his bell.

'Tis the fervid tropic noontime; faint and low the
sea-waves beat;
Hazy rise the inland mountains through the glim-
mer of the heat,—

Where, through mingled leaves and blossoms ar-
rowy sunbeams flash and glisten,
Speaks her lover to the slave girl, and she lifts her
head to listen:—

"We shall live as slaves no longer! Freedom's
hour is close at hand!
Rocks her bark upon the waters, rests the boat
upon the strand!

"I have seen the Haytien Captain; I have seen
his swarthy crew,
Haters of the pallid faces, to their race and color
true.

"They have sworn to wait our coming till the night
has passed its noon,
And the gray and darkening waters roll above the
sunken moon!"

Oh! the blessed hope of freedom! how with joy
and glad surprise,
For an instant throbs her bosom, for an instant
beam her eyes!

But she looks across the valley, where her mother's
hut is seen,
Through the snowy bloom of coffee, and the lemon
leaves so green.

And she answers, sad and earnest: "It were wrong
for thee to stay;
God hath heard thy prayer for freedom, and his
finger points the way.

"Well I know with what endurance, for the sake
of me and mine,
Thou hast borne too long a burden, never meant
for souls like thine.

"Go; and at the hour of midnight, when our last
farewell is o'er,
Kneeling on our place of parting, I will bless thee
from the shore.

"But for me, my mother, lying on her sick bed all the day,
Lifts her weary head to watch me, coming through the twilight gray.

"Should I leave her sick and helpless, even freedom, shared with thee,
Would be sadder far than bondage, lonely toil, and stripes to me.

"For my heart would die within me, and my brain would soon be wild:
I should hear my mother calling through the twilight for her child!"

Blazing upward from the ocean, shines the sun of morning time,
Through the coffee-trees in blossom, and green hedges of the lime.

Side by side, amidst the slave gang, toil the lover and the maid;
Wherefore looks he o'er the waters, leaning forward on his spade?

Sadly looks he, deeply sighs he: 'tis the Haytien's sail he sees,
Like a white cloud of the mountains, driven seaward by the breeze!

But his arm a light hand presses, and he hears a low voice call:
Hate of Slavery, hope of Freedom, Love is mightier than all.

THE CRISIS.

WRITTEN ON LEARNING THE TERMS OF THE TREATY WITH MEXICO.

Across the Stony Mountains, o'er the desert's drouth and sand,
The circles of our empire touch the Western Ocean's strand;
From slumberous Timpanogos, to Gila, wild and free,
Flowing down from Neuva Leon to California's sea;
And from the mountains of the East, to Santa Rosa's shore,
The eagles of Mexitli shall beat the air no more.

O Vale of Rio Bravo! Let thy simple children weep;
Close watch about their holy fire let maids of Pecos keep;
Let Taos send her cry across Sierra Madre's pines,
And Algodones toll her bells amidst her corn and vines;
For lo! the pale land-seekers come, with eager eyes of gain,
Wide scattering, like the bison herds on broad Salada's plain.

Let Sacramento's herdsmen heed what sound, the winds bring down,
Of footsteps on the crisping snow, from cold Neveda's crown!
Full hot and fast the Saxon rides, with rein of travel slack,
And, bending o'er his saddle, leaves the sunrise at his back;

By many a lonely river, and gorge of fir and pine,
On many a wintry hill-top, his nightly camp-fires
shine.

O countrymen and brothers! that land of lake and
plain,
Of salt wastes alternating with valleys fat with
grain;
Of mountains white with winter, looking down-
ward, cold, serene,
On their feet with spring-vines tangled and lapped
in softest green;
Swift through whose black volcanic gates, o'er
many a sunny vale,
Wind-like the Arapahoe sweeps the bison's dusty
trail!

Great spaces yet untravelled, great lakes whose
mystic shores
The Saxon rifle never heard, nor dip of Saxon
oars;
Great herds that wander all unwatched, wild steeds
that none have tamed,
Strange fish in unknown streams, and birds the
Saxon never named;
Deep mines, dark mountain crucibles, where Na-
ture's chemic powers
Work out the Great Designer's will:—all these ye
say are ours!

Forever ours! for good or ill, on us the burden
lies;
God's balance, watched by angels, is hung across
the skies.
Shall Justice, Truth, and Freedom, turn the poised
and trembling scale?
Or shall the Evil triumph, and robber Wrong pre-
vail?

Shall the broad land o'er which our flag in starry splendor waves,
Forego through us its freedom, and bear the tread of slaves?

The day is breaking in the East, of which the prophets told,
And brightens up the sky of Time the Christian Age of Gold:
Old Might to Right is yielding, battle blade to clerkly pen,
Earth's monarchs are her peoples, and her serfs stand up as men;
The isles rejoice together, in a day are nations born,
And the slave walks free in Tunis, and by Stamboul's Golden Horn!

Is this, O countrymen of mine! a day for us to sow
The soil of new-gained empire with slavery's seeds of woe?
To feed with our fresh life-blood the old world's cast-off crime,
Dropped, like some monstrous early birth, from the tired lap of Time?
To run anew the evil race the old lost nations ran,
And die like them of unbelief of God, and wrong of man?

Great Heaven! Is this our mission? End in this the prayers and tears,
The toil, the strife, the watchings of our younger, better years?
Still, as the old world rolls in light, shall ours in shadow turn,
A beamless Chaos, cursed of God, through outer darkness borne?
Where the far nations looked for light, a blackness in the air?

Where for words of hope they listened, the long
wail of despair?

The Crisis presses on us; face to face with us it
stands,
With solemn lips of question, like the Sphinx in
Egypt's sands!
This day we fashion Destiny, our web of Fate we
spin;
This day for all hereafter choose we holiness or sin;
Even now from starry Gerizim, or Ebal's cloudy
crown,
We call the dews of blessing or the bolts of cursing
down!

By all for which the martyrs bore their agony and
shame;
By all the warning words of truth with which the
prophets came;
By the Future which awaits us; by all the hopes
which cast
Their faint and trembling beams across the black-
ness of the Past;
And by the blessed thought of Him who for Earth's
freedom died,
O, my people! O, my brothers! let us choose the
righteous side.

So shall the Northern pioneer go joyful on his way;
To wed Penobscot's waters to San Francisco's bay;
To make the rugged places smooth, and sow the
vales with grain;
And bear, with Liberty and Law, the Bible in his
train:
The mighty West shall bless the East, and sea shall
answer sea,
And mountain unto mountain call: PRAISE GOD,
FOR WE ARE FREE!

MISCELLANEOUS.

MISCELLANEOUS.

THE KNIGHT OF ST. JOHN.

Ere down yon blue Carpathian hills
  The sun shall sink again!
Farewell to life and all its ills,
  Farewell to cell and chain.

These prison shades are dark and cold,—
  But, darker far than they,
The shadow of a sorrow old
  Is on my heart alway.

For since the day when Warkworth wood
  Closed o'er my steed and I,
An alien from my name and blood,
  A weed cast out to die,—

When, looking back in sunset light,
  I saw her turret gleam,
And from its casement, far and white,
  Her sign of farewell stream,

Like one who from some desert shore
  Doth home's green isles descry,
And, vainly longing, gazes o'er
  The waste of wave and sky;

So from the desert of my fate
  I gaze across the past;
Forever on life's dial-plate
  The shade is backward cast!

I've wandered wide from shore to shore,
  I've knelt at many a shrine;
And bowed me to the rocky floor
  Where Bethlehem's tapers shine;

And by the Holy Sepulchre
  I've pledged my knightly sword
To Christ, his blessed Church, and her,
  The Mother of our Lord.

Oh, vain the vow, and vain the strife!
  How vain do all things seem!
My soul is in the past, and life
  To-day is but a dream!

In vain the penance strange and long,
  And hard for flesh to bear;
The prayer, the fasting, and the thong,
  And sackcloth shirt of hair.

The eyes of memory will not sleep,—
  Its ears are open still;
And vigils with the past they keep
  Against my feeble will.

And still the loves and joys of old
  Do evermore uprise;
I see the flow of locks of gold,
  The shine of loving eyes!

Ah me! upon another's breast
  Those golden locks recline;
I see upon another rest
  The glance that once was mine

"O faithless Priest!—O perjured knight!"
  I hear the Master cry;
"Shut out the vision from thy sight,
  Let Earth and Nature die

"The Church of God is now thy spouse,
  And thou the bridegroom art;
Then let the burden of thy vows
  Crush down thy human heart!"

In vain! This heart its grief must know,
  Till life itself hath ceased,
And falls beneath the self-same blow,
  The lover and the priest!

O pitying Mother! souls of light,
  And saints, and martyrs old!
Pray for a weak and sinful knight,
  A suffering man uphold.

Then let the Paynim work his will,
  And death unbind my chain,
Ere down yon blue Carpathian hill
  The sun shall fall again.

THE HOLY LAND.

FROM LAMARTINE.

I HAVE not felt o'er seas of sand,
  The rocking of the desert bark;
Nor laved at Hebron's fount my hand,
  By Hebron's palm-trees cool and dark;
Nor pitched my tent at even-fall,
  On dust where Job of old has lain,
Nor dreamed beneath its canvas wall,
  The dream of Jacob o'er again.

One vast world-page remains unread;
  How shine the stars in Chaldea's sky,
How sounds the reverent pilgrim's tread,
  How beats the heart with God so nigh!—
How round gray arch and column lone
  The spirit of the old time broods,
And sighs in all the winds that moan
  Along the sandy solitudes!

In thy tall cedars, Lebanon,
  I have not heard the nations' cries,
Nor seen thy eagles stooping down
  Where buried Tyre in ruin lies.
The Christian's prayer I have not said,
  In Tadmor's temples of decay,
Nor startled with my dreary tread,
  The waste where Memnon's empire lay.

Nor have I, from thy hallowed tide,
  O, Jordan! heard the low lament,
Like that sad wail along thy side,
  Which Israel's mournful prophet sent!
Nor thrilled within that grotto lone,
  Where deep in night, the Bard of Kings
Felt hands of fire direct his own,
  And sweep for God the conscious strings.

I have not climbed to Olivet,
  Nor laid me where my Saviour lay,
And left his trace of tears as yet
  By angel eyes unwept away;
Nor watched at midnight's solemn time,
  The garden where his prayer and groan,
Wrung by his sorrow and our crime,
  Rose to One listening ear alone.

I have not kissed the rock-hewn grot,
  Where in his Mother's arms he lay,
Nor knelt upon the sacred spot
  Where last his footsteps pressed the clay;

Nor looked on that sad mountain head,
  Nor smote my sinful breast, where wide
His arms to fold the world he spread,
  And bowed his head to bless—and died!

PALESTINE.

Blest land of Judea! thrice hallowed of song,
Where the holiest of memories pilgrim-like throng;
In the shade of thy palms, by the shores of thy sea,
On the hills of thy beauty, my heart is with thee.

With the eye of a spirit I look on that shore,
Where pilgrim and prophet have lingered before;
With the glide of a spirit I traverse the sod
Made bright by the steps of the angels of God.

Blue sea of the hills!—in my spirit I hear
Thy waters, Genesaret, chime on my ear;
Where the Lowly and Just with the people sat down,
And thy spray on the dust of his sandals was thrown.

Beyond are Bethulia's mountains of green,
And the desolate hills of the wild Gadarene;
And I pause on the goat-crags of Tabor to see
The gleam of thy waters, O dark Galilee!

Hark, a sound in the valley! where, swollen and strong,
Thy river, O Kishon, is sweeping along;
Where the Canaanite strove with Jehovah in vain,
And thy torrent grew dark with the blood of the slain.

There down from his mountains stern Zebulon came,
And Napthali's stag, with his eye-balls of flame,
And the chariots of Jabin rolled harmlessly on,
For the arm of the Lord was Abinoam's son!

There sleep the still rocks and the caverns which rang
To the song which the beautiful prophetess sang,
When the princes of Issachar stood by her side,
And the shout of a host in its triumph replied.

Lo, Bethlehem's hill-site before me is seen,
With the mountains around, and the valleys between;
There rested the shepherds of Judah, and there
The song of the angels rose sweet on the air.

And Bethany's palm-trees in beauty still throw
Their shadows at noon on the ruins below;
But where are the sisters who hastened to greet
The lowly Redeemer, and sit at his feet?

I tread where the TWELVE in their way-faring trod;
I stand where they stood with the CHOSEN OF GOD—
Where his blessing was heard and his lessons were taught,
Where the blind were restored and the healing was wrought.

Oh, here with his flock the sad Wanderer came—
These hills he toiled over in grief, are the same—
The founts where he drank by the wayside still flow,
And the same airs are blowing which breathed on his brow!

And throned on her hills sits Jerusalem yet,
But with dust on her forehead, and chains on her feet;

For the crown of her pride to the mocker hath
gone,
And the holy Shechinah is dark where it shone.

But wherefore this dream of the earthly abode
Of Humanity clothed in the brightness of God?
Were my spirit but turned from the outward and
dim,
It could gaze, even now, on the presence of Him!

Not in clouds and in terrors, but gentle as when,
In love and in meekness, He moved among men;
And the voice which breathed peace to the waves
of the sea,
In the hush of my spirit would whisper to me!

And what if my feet may not tread where He stood,
Nor my ears hear the dashing of Galilee's flood,
Nor my eyes see the cross which He bowed him to
bear,
Nor my knees press Gethsemane's garden of prayer.

Yet loved of the Father, thy Spirit is near
To the meek, and the lowly, and penitent here;
And the voice of thy love is the same even now,
As at Bethany's tomb, or on Olivet's brow.

Oh, the outward hath gone!—but in glory and
power,
The SPIRIT surviveth the things of an hour;
Unchanged, undecaying, its Pentecost flame
On the heart's secret altar is burning the same!

EZEKIEL.

CHAPTER XXXIII. 30–33.

THEY hear thee not, O God! nor see•
Beneath thy rod they mock at thee;
The princes of our ancient line
Lie drunken with Assyrian wine;
The priests around thy altar speak
The false words which their hearers seek,
And hymns which Chaldea's wanton maids
Have sung in Dura's idol-shades,
Are with the Levites' chant ascending,
With Zion's holiest anthems blending!

On Israel's bleeding bosom set,
The heathen heel is crushing yet;
The towers upon our holy hill
Echo Chaldean footsteps still.
Our wasted shrines—who weeps for them?
Who mourneth for Jerusalem?
Who turneth from his gains away?
Whose knee with mine is bowed to pray?
Who, leaving feast and purpling cup,
Takes Zion's lamentation up?

A sad and thoughtful youth, I went
With Israel's early banishment;
And where the sullen Chebar crept,
The ritual of my fathers kept.
The water for the trench I drew,
The firstling of the flock I slew,
And, standing at the altar's side,
I shared the Levites' lingering pride,
That still amidst her mocking foes,
The smoke of Zion's offering rose.

In sudden whirlwind, cloud and flame,

The Spirit of the Highest came!
Before mine eyes a vision passed,
A glory terrible and vast;
With dreadful eyes of living things,
And sounding sweep of angel wings,
With circling light and sapphire throne,
And flame-like form of One thereon,
And voice of that dread Likeness sent
Down from the crystal firmament!

The burden of a prophet's power
Fell on me in that fearful hour;
From off unutterable woes
The curtain of the future rose;
I saw far down the coming time
The fiery chastisement of crime;
With noise of mingling hosts, and jar
Of falling towers and shouts of war,
I saw the nations rise and fall,
Like fire-gleams on my tent's white wall.

In dream and trance, I saw the slain
Of Egypt heaped like harvest grain;
I saw the walls of sea-born Tyre
Swept over by the spoiler's fire;
And heard the low, expiring moan
Of Edom on his rocky throne;
And, woe is me! the wild lament
From Zion's desolation sent;
And felt within my heart each blow
Which laid her holy places low.

In bonds and sorrow, day by day,
Before the pictured tile I lay;
And there, as in a mirror, saw
The coming of Assyria's war,—
Her swarthy lines of spearmen pass
Like locusts through Bethhoron's grass;
I saw them draw their stormy hem

Of battle round Jerusalem;
And, listening, heard the Hebrew wail
Blend with the victor-trump of Baal!

Who trembled at my warning word?
Who owned the prophet of the Lord?
How mocked the rude—how scoffed the vile—
How stung the Levites scornful smile,
As o'er my spirit, dark and slow,
The shadow crept of Israel's woe,
As if the angel's mournful roll
Had left its record on my soul,
And traced in lines of darkness there
The picture of its great despair!

Yet ever at the hour I feel
My lips in prophecy unseal.
Prince, priest, and Levite, gather near,
And Salem's daughters haste to hear,
On Chebar's waste and alien shore,
The harp of Judah swept once more.
They listen, as in Babel's throng
The Chaldeans to the dancer's song,
Or wild sabbeka's nightly play,
As careless and as vain as they.

And thus, oh Prophet-bard of old,
Hast thou thy tale of sorrow told!
The same which earth's unwelcome seers
Have felt in all succeeding years.
Sport of the changeful multitude,
Nor calmly heard nor understood,
Their song has seemed a trick of art,
Their warnings but the actor's part.
With bonds, and scorn, and evil will.
The world requites its prophets still.

So was it when the Holy One
The garments of the flesh put on!
Men followed where the Highest led
For common gifts of daily bread,
And gross of ear, of vision dim,
Owned not the God-like power of Him.
Vain as a dreamer's words to them
His wail above Jerusalem,
And meaningless the watch He kept
Through which his weak disciples slept.

Yet shrink not thou, whoe'er thou art,
For God's great purpose set apart,
Before whose far discerning eyes,
The Future as the Present lies!
Beyond a narrow-bounded age
Stretches thy prophet-heritage,
Through Heaven's dim spaces angel-trod,
Through arches round the throne of God!
Thy audience, worlds!—all Time to be
The witness of the Truth in thee!

THE WIFE OF MANOAH TO HER HUSBAND.

Against the sunset's glowing wall
The city towers rise black and tall,
Where Zorah on its rocky height,
Stands like an armed man in the light.

Down Eshtaol's vales of ripened grain
Falls like a cloud the night amain,
And up the hill-sides climbing slow
The barley reapers homeward go.

Look, dearest! how our fair child's head
The sunset light hath hallowed,
Where at this olive's foot he lies,
Uplooking to the tranquil skies.

Oh! while beneath the fervent heat
Thy sickle swept the bearded wheat,
I've watched with mingled joy and dread,
Our child upon his grassy bed.

Joy, which the mother feels alone
Whose morning hope like mine had flown,
When to her bosom, over blessed,
A dearer life than hers is pressed.

Dread, for the future dark and still,
Which shapes our dear one to its will;
Forever in his large calm eyes,
I read a tale of sacrifice.—

The same foreboding awe I felt
When at the altar's side we knelt,
And he, who as a pilgrim came,
Rose, winged and glorious, through the flame

I slept not, though the wild bees made
A dreamlike murmuring in the shade,
And on me the warm-fingered hours
Pressed with the drowsy smell of flowers.

Before me, in a vision, rose
The hosts of Israel's scornful foes,—
Rank over rank, helm, shield, and spear,
Glittered in noon's hot atmosphere.

I heard their boast, and bitter word,
Their mockery of the Hebrew's Lord,
I saw their hands his ark assail,
Their feet profane his holy veil.

No angel down the blue space spoke,
No thunder from the still sky broke,
But in their midst, in power and awe,
Like God's waked wrath, OUR CHILD I saw!

A child no more!—harsh-browed and strong,
He towered a giant in the throng,
And down his shoulders, broad and bare,
Swept the black terror of his hair.

He raised his arm—he smote amain,
As round the reaper falls the grain,
So the dark host around him fell,
So sank the foes of Israel!

Again I looked. In sunlight shone
The towers and domes of Askelon.
Priest, warrior, slave, a mighty crowd
Within her idol temple bowed.

Yet one knelt not; stark, gaunt, and blind,
His arms the massive pillars twined,—
An eyeless captive, strong with hate,
He stood there like an evil Fate.

The red shrines smoked—the trumpets pealed—
He stooped—the giant columns reeled—
Reeled tower and fane, sank arch and wall,
And the thick dust-cloud closed o'er all!

Above the shriek, the crash, the groan
Of the fallen pride of Askelon,
I heard, sheer down the echoing sky,
A voice as of an angel cry.—

The voice of him, who at our side
Sat through the golden eventide,
Of him, who on thy altar's blaze
Rose fire-winged, with his song of praise!

"Rejoice o'er Israel's broken chain,
Gray mother of the mighty slain!
Rejoice!" it cried, "He vanquisheth!
The strong in life is strong in death!

"To him shall Zorah's daughters raise
Through coming years their hymns of praise,
And gray old men, at evening tell
Of all he wrought for Israel.

"And they who sing and they who hear
Alike shall hold thy memory dear,
And pour their blessings on thy head,
Oh, mother of the mighty dead!"

It ceased: and though a sound I heard
As if great wings the still air stirred,
I only saw the barley sheaves,
And hills half hid by olive leaves.

I bowed my face, in awe and fear,
On the dear child who slumbered near,
"With me, as with my only son,
Oh God!" I said, "THY WILL BE DONE!"

THE CITIES OF THE PLAIN.

"GET ye up from the wrath of God's terrible day
Ungirded, unsandalled, arise and away!
'Tis the vintage of blood—'tis the fulness of time,
And vengeance shall gather the harvest of crime!"

The warning was spoken—the righteous had gone,
And the proud ones of Sodom were feasting alone;
All gay was the banquet—the revel was long,
With the pouring of wine and the breathing of song.

'Twas an evening of beauty; the air was perfume,
The earth was all greenness, the trees were all
bloom;
And softly the delicate viol was heard,
Like the murmur of love or the notes of a bird.

And beautiful maidens moved down in the dance,
With the magic of motion and sunshine of glance;
And white arms wreathed lightly, and tresses fell
free,
As the plumage of birds in some tropical tree.

Where the shrines of foul idols were lighted on high,
And wantonness tempted the lust of the eye;
Midst rites of obsceneness, strange, loathsome, ab-
horred,
The blasphemer scoffed at the name of the Lord.

Hark! the growl of the thunder—the quaking of
earth!
Woe—woe to the worship, and woe to the mirth!
The black sky has opened—there's flame in the
air—
The red arm of vengeance is lifted and bare!

Then the shriek of the dying rose wild where the
song
And the low tone of love had been whispered along;
For the fierce flames went lightly o'er palace and
bower,
Like the red tongues of demons, to blast and devour!

Down—down, on the fallen, the red ruin rained,
And the reveller sank with his wine-cup undrained;
The foot of the dancer, the music's loved thrill,
And the shout and the laughter grew suddenly still.

The last throb of anguish was fearfully given;
The last eye glared forth in its madness on Heaven!

The last groan of horror rose wildly and vain,
And death brooded over the pride of the Plain!

THE CRUCIFIXION.

Sunlight upon Judea's hills!
  And on the waves of Galilee—
On Jordan's stream, and on the rills
  That feed the dead and sleeping sea!
Most freshly from the green wood springs
The light breeze on its scented wings;
And gayly quiver in the sun
The cedar tops of Lebanon!

A few more hours—a change hath come!
  The sky is dark without a cloud!
The shouts of wrath and joy are dumb,
  And proud knees unto earth are bowed.
A change is on the hill of Death,
The helmed watchers pant for breath,
And turn with wild and maniac eyes
From the dark scene of sacrifice!

That Sacrifice!—the death of Him—
  The High and ever Holy One!
Well may the conscious Heaven grow dim,
  And blacken the beholding Sun
The wonted light hath fled away,
Night settles on the middle day,
And earthquake from his caverned bed
Is waking with a thrill of dread!

The dead are waking underneath!
  Their prison door is rent away!
And, ghastly with the seal of death,
  They wander in the eye of day!

The temple of the Cherubim,
The House of God is cold and dim;
A curse is on its trembling walls,
Its mighty veil asunder falls!

Well may the cavern-depths of Earth
  Be shaken, and her mountains nod;
Well may the sheeted dead come forth
  To gaze upon a suffering God!
Well may the temple-shrine grow dim,
And shadows veil the Cherubim,
When He, the chosen one of Heaven,
A sacrifice for guilt is given!

And shall the sinful heart, alone,
  Behold unmoved the atoning hour,
When Nature trembles on her throne,
  And Death resigns his iron power?
Oh, shall the heart—whose sinfulness
Gave keenness to his sore distress,
And added to his tears of blood—
Refuse its trembling gratitude!

THE STAR OF BETHLEHEM

WHERE Time the measure of his hours
  By changeful bud and blossom keeps,
And like a young bride crowned with flowers,
  Fair Shiraz in her garden sleeps;

Where, to her poet's turban stone,
  The Spring her gift of flowers imparts,
Less sweet than those his thoughts have sown
  In the warm soil of Persian hearts:

There sat the stranger, where the shade
  Of scattered date-trees thinly lay,
While in the hot clear heaven delayed
  The long, and still, and weary day.

Strange trees and fruits above him hung,
  Strange odors filled the sultry air,
Strange birds upon the branches swung,
  Strange insect voices murmured there.

And strange bright blossoms shone around,
  Turned sunward from the shadowy bowers,
As if the Gheber's soul had found
  A fitting home in Iran's flowers.

Whate'er he saw, whate'er he heard,
  Awakened feelings new and sad,—
No Christian garb, nor Christian word,
  Nor church with Sabbath bell chimes glad,

But Moslem graves, with turban stones,
  And mosque-spires gleaming white, in view,
And gray-beard Mollahs in low tones
  Chanting their Koran service through.

The flowers which smiled on either hand
  Like tempting fiends, were such as they
Which once, o'er all that Eastern land,
  As gifts on demon altars lay.

As if the burning eye of Baal
  The servant of his Conqueror knew,
From skies which knew no cloudy veil,
  The Sun's hot glances smote him through

"Ah me!" the lonely stranger said,
  "The hope which led my footsteps on,
And light from Heaven around them shed,
  O'er weary wave and waste, is gone!

"Where are the harvest fields all white,
For Truth to thrust her sickle in?
Where flock the souls, like doves in flight,
From the dark hiding-place of sin?

"A silent horror broods o'er all—
The burden of a hateful spell—
The very flowers around recall
The hoary magi's rites of hell!

"And what am I, o'er such a land
The banner of the Cross to bear?
Dear Lord, uphold me with thy hand,
Thy strength with human weakness share!"

He ceased; for at his very feet
In mild rebuke a floweret smiled—
How thrilled his sinking heart to greet
The Star-flower of the Virgin's child!

Sown by some wandering Frank, it drew
Its life from alien air and earth,
And told to Paynim sun and dew
The story of the Saviour's birth.

From scorching beams, in kindly mood,
The Persian plants its beauty screened,
And on its pagan sisterhood,
In love, the Christian floweret leaned.

With tears of joy the wanderer felt
The darkness of his long despair
Before that hallowed symbol melt,
Which God's dear love had nurtured there.

From Nature's face, that simple flower
The lines of sin and sadness swept;
And Magian pile and Paynim bower
In peace like that of Eden slept.

Each Moslem tomb, and cypress old,
  Looked holy through the sunset air;
And angel-like, the Muezzin told
  From tower and mosque the hour of prayer.

With cheerful steps, the morrow's dawn
  From Shiraz saw the stranger part;
The Star-flower of the Virgin-Born
  Still blooming in his hopeful heart!

HYMNS.

FROM THE FRENCH OF LAMARTINE.

One hymn more, O my lyre!
  Praise to the God above,
  Of joy and life and love,
Sweeping its strings of fire!

Oh! who the speed of bird and wind
  And sunbeam's glance will lend to me,
That, soaring upward, I may find
  My resting-place and home in Thee?—
Thou, whom my soul, midst doubt and gloom,
  Adoreth with a fervent flame—
Mysterious spirit! unto whom
  Pertain nor sign nor name!

Swiftly my lyre's soft murmurs go,
  Up from the cold and joyless earth,
Back to the God who bade them flow,
  Whose moving spirit sent them forth.
But as for me, O God! for me,
  The lowly creature of thy will,
Lingering and sad, I sigh to Thee,
  An earth-bound pilgrim still!

Was not my spirit born to shine
  Where yonder stars and suns are glowing?
To breathe with them the light divine,
  From God's own holy altar flowing?
To be, indeed, whate'er the soul
  In dreams hath thirsted for so long—
A portion of Heaven's glorious whole
  Of loveliness and song?

Oh! watchers of the stars at night,
  Who breathe their fire, as we the air—
Suns, thunders, stars, and rays of light,
  Oh! say, is He, the Eternal, there?
Bend there around his awful throne
  The seraph's glance, the angel's knee?
Or are thy inmost depths his own,
  O wild and mighty sea?

Thoughts of my soul, how swift ye go!
  Swift as the eagle's glance of fire,
Or arrows from the archer's bow,
  To the far aim of your desire!
Thought after thought, ye thronging rise,
  Like spring-doves from the startled wood,
Bearing like them your sacrifice
  Of music unto God!

And shall these thoughts of joy and love
  Come back again no more to me?—
Returning like the Patriarch's dove
  Wing-weary from the eternal sea,
To bear within my longing arms
  The promise-bough of kindlier skies,
Plucked from the green, immortal palms
  Which shadow Paradise?

All-moving spirit!—freely forth
  At thy command the strong wind goes;
Its errand to the passive earth,
  Nor art can stay, nor strength oppose,

Until it folds its weary wing
  Once more within the hand divine;
So, weary from its wandering,
  My spirit turns to thine!

Child of the sea, the mountain stream,
  From its dark caverns, hurries on,
Ceaseless, by night and morning's beam,
  By evening's star and noontide's sun,
Until at last it sinks to rest,
  O'erwearied, in the waiting sea,
And moans upon its mother's breast—
  So turns my soul to Thee!

O Thou who bidst the torrent flow,
  Who lendest wings unto the wind—
Mover of all things! where art thou?
  Oh, whither shall I go to find
The secret of thy resting-place?
  Is there no holy wing for me,
That, soaring, I may search the space
  Of highest heaven for Thee?

Oh, would I were as free to rise
  As leaves on Autumn's whirlwind borne—
The arrowy light of sunset skies,
  Or sound, or ray, or star of morn
Which melts in heaven at twilight's close,
  Or aught which soars unchecked and free
Through Earth and Heaven; that I might lose
  Myself in finding Thee!

When the breath divine is flowing,
Zephyr-like o'er all things going,
And as the touch of viewless fingers,
Softly on my soul it lingers,
Open to a breath the lightest,

Conscious of a touch the slightest—
As some calm still lake, whereon
Sinks the snowy-bosomed swan,
And the glistening water-rings
Circle round her moving wings:
When my upward gaze is turning
Where the stars of heaven are burning
Through the deep and dark abyss—
Flowers of midnight's wilderness,
Blowing with the evening's breath
Sweetly in their Maker's path:

When the breaking day is flushing
All the East, and light is gushing
Upward through the horizon's haze,
Sheaf-like, with its thousand rays
Spreading, until all above
Overflows with joy and love,
And below, on earth's green bosom,
All is changed to light and blossom:

When my waking fancies over
Forms of brightness flit and hover,
Holy as the seraphs are,
Who by Zion's fountains wear
On their foreheads, white and broad,
"HOLINESS UNTO THE LORD!"
When, inspired with rapture high,
It would seem a single sigh
Could a world of love create—
That my life could know no date,
And my eager thoughts could fill
Heaven and Earth, o'erflowing still!—

Then, O Father!—Thou alone,
From the shadow of Thy throne,
To the sighing of my breast
And its rapture answerest.
All my thoughts, which, upward winging,

Bathe where thy own light is springing—
All my yearnings to be free
Are as echoes answering Thee!

Seldom upon lips of mine
Father! rests that name of thine—
Deep within my inmost breast,
  In the secret place of mind,
  Like an awful presence shrined,
Doth the dread idea rest!
Hushed and holy dwells it there—
Prompter of the silent prayer,
Lifting up my spirit's eye
And its faint, but earnest cry,
From its dark and cold abode,
Unto thee, my Guide and God!

THE FEMALE MARTYR.

[Mary G——, aged 18, a "Sister of Charity," died in one of our Atlantic cities, during the prevalence of the Indian Cholera, while in voluntary attendance upon the sick.]

"Bring out your dead!" the midnight street
  Heard and gave back the hoarse, low call;
Harsh fell the tread of hasty feet—
Glanced through the dark the coarse white sheet—
  Her coffin and her pall.
  "What—only one!" The brutal hackman said,
  As, with an oath, he spurned away the dead.

How sunk the inmost hearts of all,
  As rolled that dead-cart slowly by,
With creaking wheel and harsh hoof-fall!
The dying turned him to the wall,
  To hear it and to die!—

Onward it rolled; while oft its driver stayed,
And hoarsely clamored, "Ho!—bring out your
dead."

It paused beside the burial-place;
"Toss in your load!"—and it was done.—
With quick hand and averted face,
Hastily to the grave's embrace
They cast them, one by one—
Stranger and friend—the evil and the just,
Together trodden in the churchyard dust!

And thou, young martyr!—thou wast there—
No white-robed sisters round thee trod—
Nor holy hymn, nor funeral prayer
Rose through the damp and noisome air,
Giving thee to thy God;
Nor flower, nor cross, nor hallowed taper gave
Grace to the dead, and beauty to the grave!

Yet, gentle sufferer!—there shall be,
In every heart of kindly feeling,
A rite as holy paid to thee
As if beneath the convent-tree
Thy sisterhood were kneeling,
At vesper hours, like sorrowing angels, keeping
Their tearful watch around thy place of sleeping

For thou wast one in whom the light
Of Heaven's own love was kindled well.
Enduring with a martyr's might,
Through weary day and wakeful night,
Far more than words may tell:
Gentle, and meek, and lowly, and unknown—
Thy mercies measured by thy God alone!

Where manly hearts were failing,—where
The throngful street grew foul with death,
O high-souled martyr!—thou wast there,

Inhaling from the loathsome air,
  Poison with every breath.
Yet shrinking not from offices of dread
For the wrung dying, and the unconscious dead.

And, where the sickly taper shed
  Its light through vapors, damp, confined,
Hushed as a seraph's fell thy tread—
A new Electra by the bed
  Of suffering human-kind!
Pointing the spirit, in its dark dismay,
To that pure hope which fadeth not away.

Innocent teacher of the high
  And holy mysteries of Heaven!
How turned to thee each glazing eye,
In mute and awful sympathy,
  As thy low prayers were given;
And the o'er-hovering Spoiler wore, the while,
An angel's features—a deliverer's smile!

A blessed task!—and worthy one
  Who, turning from the world, as thou,
Before life's pathway had begun
To leave its spring-time flower and sun,
  Had sealed her early vow;
Giving to God her beauty and her youth,
Her pure affections and her guileless truth.

Earth may not claim thee. Nothing here
  Could be for thee a meet reward;
Thine is a treasure far more dear—
Eye hath not seen it, nor the ear
  Of living mortal heard,—
The joys prepared—the promised bliss above—
The holy presence of Eternal Love!

Sleep on in peace. The earth has not
  A nobler name than thine shall be.

The deeds by martial manhood wrought,
The lofty energies of thought,
  The fire of poesy—
These have but frail and fading honors ;—thine
Shall Time unto Eternity consign.

Yea, and when thrones shall crumble down,
  And human pride and grandeur fall,—
The herald's line of long renown—
The mitre and the kingly crown—
  Perishing glories all!
The pure devotion of thy generous heart
Shall live in Heaven, of which it was a part

THE FROST SPIRIT.

He comes—he comes—the Frost Spirit comes!
    You may trace his footsteps now
On the naked woods and the blasted fields and the
    brown hill's withered brow.
He has smitten the leaves of the gray old trees
    where their pleasant green came forth,
And the winds, which follow wherever he goes,
    have shaken them down to earth.

He comes—he comes—the Frost Spirit comes!—
    from the frozen Labrador—
From the icy bridge of the Northern seas, which
    the white bear wanders o'er—
Where the fisherman's sail is stiff with ice, and
    the luckless forms below
In the sunless cold of the lingering night into
    marble statues grow!

He comes—he comes—the Frost Spirit comes!—on
    the rushing Northern blast,

And the dark Norwegian pines have bowed as his fearful breath went past.
With an unscorched wing he has hurried on, where the fires of Hecla glow
On the darkly beautiful sky above and the ancient ice below.

He comes—he comes—the Frost Spirit comes!—and the quiet lake shall feel
The torpid touch of his glazing breath, and ring to the skater's heel;
And the streams which danced on the broken rocks, or sang to the leaning grass,
Shall bow again to their winter chain, and in mournful silence pass.

He comes—he comes—the Frost Spirit comes!—let us meet him as we may,
And turn with the light of the parlor-fire his evil power away;
And gather closer the circle round, when that fire-light dances high,
And laugh at the shriek of the baffled Fiend as his sounding wing goes by!

THE VAUDOIS TEACHER.[38]

"Oh, lady fair, these silks of mine are beautiful and rare—
The richest web of the Indian loom, which beauty's queen might wear;
And my pearls are pure as thy own fair neck, with whose radiant light they vie;
I have brought them with me a weary way,—will my gentle lady buy?"

And the lady smiled on the worn old man through the dark and clustering curls,
Which veiled her brow as she bent to view his silks and glittering pearls;
And she placed their price in the old man's hand, and lightly turned away,
But she paused at the wanderer's earnest call—"My gentle lady, stay!"

"Oh, lady fair, I have yet a gem which a purer lustre flings,
Than the diamond flash of the jewelled crown on the lofty brow of kings—
A wonderful pearl of exceeding price, whose virtue shall not decay,
Whose light shall be as a spell to thee and a blessing on thy way!"

The lady glanced at the mirroring steel where her form of grace was seen,
Where her eye shone clear, and her dark locks waved their clasping pearls between;—
Bring forth thy pearl of exceeding worth, thou traveller gray and old—
And name the price of thy precious gem, and my page shall count thy gold.

The cloud went off from the pilgrim's brow, as a small and meagre book,
Unchased with gold or gem of cost, from his folding robe he took!
"Here, lady fair, is the pearl of price, may it prove as such to thee!
Nay—keep thy gold—I ask it not, for the word of God is free!"

The hoary traveller went his way, but the gift he left behind
Hath had its pure and perfect work on that high-born maiden's mind,

And she hath turned from the pride of sin to the
lowliness of truth,
And given her human heart to God in its beautiful
hour of youth!

And she hath left the gray old halls, where an evil
faith had power,
The courtly knights of her father's train, and the
maidens of her bower;
And she hath gone to the Vaudois vales by lordly
feet untrod,
Where the poor and needy of earth are rich in the
perfect love of God!

THE CALL OF THE CHRISTIAN.

Not always as the whirlwind's rush
On Horeb's mount of fear,
Not always as the burning bush
To Midian's shepherd seer,
Nor as the awful voice which came
To Israel's prophet bards,
Nor as the tongues of cloven flame,
Nor gift of fearful words—

Not always thus, with outward sign
Of fire or voice from Heaven,
The message of a truth divine,
The call of God is given!
Awaking in the human heart
Love for the true and right—
Zeal for the Christian's "better part,"
Strength for the Christian's fight.

Nor unto manhood's heart alone
The holy influence steals:

Warm with a rapture not its own,
  The heart of woman feels!
As she who by Samaria's wall
  The Saviour's errand sought—
As those who with the fervent Paul
  And meek Aquila wrought:

Or those meek ones whose martyrdom
  Rome's gathered grandeur saw:
Or those who in their Alpine home
  Braved the Crusader's war,
When the green Vaudois, trembling, heard,
  Through all its vales of death,
The martyr's song of triumph poured
  From woman's failing breath.

And gently, by a thousand things
  Which o'er our spirits pass,
Like breezes o'er the harp's fine strings,
  Or vapors o'er a glass,
Leaving their token strange and new
  Of music or of shade,
The summons to the right and true
  And merciful is made.

Oh, then, if gleams of truth and light
  Flash o'er thy waiting mind,
Unfolding to thy mental sight
  The wants of human kind;
If brooding over human grief,
  The earnest wish is known
To soothe and gladden with relief
  An anguish not thine own;

Though heralded with nought of fear,
  Or outward sign or show:
Though only to the inward ear
  It whispers soft and low;

Though dropping, as the manna fell,
Unseen, yet from above,
Noiseless as dew-fall, heed it well—
Thy Father's call of love!

MY SOUL AND I.

Stand still, my soul, in the silent dark
I would question thee,
Alone in the shadow drear and stark
With God and me!

What, my soul, was thy errand here?
Was it mirth or ease,
Or heaping up dust from year to year?
"Nay, none of these!"

Speak, soul, aright in his holy sight
Whose eye looks still
And steadily on thee through the night:
"To do his will!"

What hast thou done, oh soul of mine,
That thou tremblest so?—
Hast thou wrought his task, and kept the line
He bade thee go?

What, silent all!—art sad of cheer?
Art fearful now?
When God seemed far and men were near
How brave wert thou?

Aha! thou tremblest!—well I see
Thou'rt craven grown.
Is it so hard with God and me
To stand alone?—

Summon thy sunshine bravery back
    Oh, wretched sprite!
Let me hear thy voice through this deep and black
    Abysmal night.

What hast thou wrought for Right and Truth,
    For God and Man,
From the golden hours of bright-eyed youth
    To life's mid span?

Ah, soul of mine, thy tones I hear,
    But weak and low,
Like far sad murmurs on my ear
    They come and go.

"I have wrestled stoutly with the Wrong,
    And borne the Right
From beneath the footfall of the throng
    To life and light.

"Wherever Freedom shivered a chain,
    God speed, quoth I;
To Error amidst her shouting train
    I gave the lie."

Ah, soul of mine! ah, soul of mine!
    Thy deeds are well:
Were they wrought for Truth's sake or for thine?
    My soul, pray tell.

"Of all the work my hand hath wrought
    Beneath the sky,
Save a place in kindly human thought,
    No gain have I."

Go to, go to!—for thy very self
    Thy deeds were done:
Thou for fame, the miser for pelf,
    Your end is one!

And where art thou going, soul of mine?
    Canst see the end?
And whither this troubled life of thine
    Evermore doth tend?

What daunts thee now?—what shakes thee so?
    My sad soul say.
"I see a cloud like a curtain low
    Hang o'er my way.

"Whither I go I cannot tell:
    That cloud hangs black,
High as the heaven and deep as hell,
    Across my track.

"I see its shadow coldly enwrap
    The souls before.
Sadly they enter it, step by step,
    To return no more.

"They shrink, they shudder, dear God! they kneel,
    To thee in prayer.
They shut their eyes on the cloud, but feel
    That it still is there.

"In vain they turn from the dread Before
    To the Known and Gone;
For while gazing behind them evermore
    Their feet glide on.

"Yet, at times, I see upon sweet pale faces
    A light begin
To tremble, as if from holy places
    And shrines within.

"And at times methinks their cold lips move
    With hymn and prayer,
As if somewhat of awe, but more of love
    And hope were there.

"I call on the souls who have left the light
To reveal their lot;
I bend mine ear to that wall of night,
And they answer not.

"But I hear around me sighs of pain
And the cry of fear,
And a sound like the slow sad dropping of rain,
Each drop a tear!

"Ah, the cloud is dark, and day by day,
I am moving thither:
I must pass beneath it on my way—
God pity me!—WHITHER?"

Ah, soul of mine! so brave and wise
In the life-storm loud,
Fronting so calmly all human eyes
In the sunlit crowd!

Now standing apart with God and me
Thou art weakness all,
Gazing vainly after the things to be
Through Death's dread wall.

But never for this, never for this
Was thy being lent;
For the craven's fear is but selfishness,
Like his merriment.

Folly and Fear are sisters twain:
One closing her eyes,
The other peopling the dark inane
With spectral lies.

Know well, my soul, God's hand controls
Whate'er thou fearest;
Round Him in calmest music rolls
Whate'er thou hearest.

What to thee is shadow, to Him is day,
And the end He knoweth,
And not on a blind and aimless way
The spirit goeth.

Man sees no future—a phantom show
Is alone before him;
Past Time is dead, and the grasses grow,
And flowers bloom o'er him.

Nothing before, nothing behind:
The steps of Faith
Fall on the seeming void, and find
The rock beneath.

The Present, the Present is all thou hast
For thy sure possessing;
Like the patriarch's angel hold it fast
Till it gives its blessing.

Why fear the night? why shrink from Death,
That phantom wan?
There is nothing in Heaven or earth beneath
Save God and man.

Peopling the shadows we turn from Him
And from one another;
All is spectral and vague and dim
Save God and our brother!

Like warp and woof all destinies
Are woven fast,
Linked in sympathy like the keys
Of an organ vast.

Pluck one thread, and the web ye mar;
Break but one
Of a thousand keys, and the paining jar
Through all will run.

Oh, restless spirit! wherefore strain
Beyond thy sphere?—
Heaven and hell, with their joy and pain,
Are now and here.

Back to thyself is measured well
All thou hast given;
Thy neighbor's wrong is thy present hell,
His bliss, thy heaven.

And in life, in death, in dark and light,
All are in God's care;
Sound the black abyss, pierce the deep of night,
And He is there!

All which is real now remaineth,
And fadeth never:
The hand which upholds it now, sustaineth
The soul forever.

Leaning on him, make with reverent meekness
His own thy will,
And with strength from Him shall thy utter weakness
Life's task fulfil;

And that cloud itself, which now before thee
Lies dark in view,
Shall with beams of light from the inner glory
Be stricken through.

And like meadow mist through Autumn's dawn
Uprolling thin,
Its thickest folds when about thee drawn
Let sunlight in.

Then of what is to be, and of what is done,
Why queriest thou?—
The past and the time to be are one,
And both are NOW!

TO A FRIEND,

ON HER RETURN FROM EUROPE.

How smiled the land of France
Under thy blue eye's glance,
Light-hearted rover!
Old walls of chateaux gray,
Towers of an early day,
Which the Three Colors play
Flauntingly over.

Now midst the brilliant train
Thronging the banks of Seine:
Now midst the splendor
Of the wild Alpine range,
Waking with change on change
Thoughts in thy young heart strange,
Lovely, and tender.

Vales, soft Elysian,
Like those in the vision
Of Mirza, when, dreaming,
He saw the long hollow dell,
Touched by the prophet's spell,
Into an ocean swell
With its isles teeming.

Cliffs wrapped in snows of years,
Splintering with icy spears
Autumn's blue heaven:
Loose rock and frozen slide,
Hung on the mountain side,
Waiting their hour to glide
Downward, storm-driven!

Rhine stream, by castle old,
Baron's and robber's hold,
Peacefully flowing;
Sweeping through vineyards green,
Or where the cliffs are seen
O'er the broad wave between
Grim shadows throwing.

Or, where St. Peter's dome
Swells o'er eternal Rome,
Vast, dim, and solemn,—
Hymns ever chanting low—
Censers swung to and fro—
Sable stoles sweeping slow
Cornice and column!

Oh, as from each and all
Will there not voices call
Evermore back again?
In the mind's gallery
Wilt thou not always see
Dim phantoms beckon thee
O'er that old track again?

New forms thy presence haunt—
New voices softly chant—
New faces greet thee!—
Pilgrims from many a shrine
Hallowed by poet's line,
At memory's magic sign,
Rising to meet thee

And when such visions come
Unto thy olden home,
Will they not waken
Deep thoughts of Him whose hand
Led thee o'er sea and land
Back to the household band
Whence thou wast taken?

While, at the sunset time,
Swells the cathedral's chime,
Yet, in thy dreaming,
While to thy spirit's eye
Yet the vast mountains lie
Piled in the Switzer's sky,
Icy and gleaming:

Prompter of silent prayer,
Be the wild picture there
In the mind's chamber,
And, through each coming day
Him, who, as staff and stay,
Watched o'er thy wandering way,
Freshly remember.

So, when the call shall be
Soon or late unto thee,
As to all given,
Still may that picture live,
All its fair forms survive,
And to thy spirit give
Gladness in Heaven!

THE ANGEL OF PATIENCE.

A FREE PARAPHRASE OF THE GERMAN.

To weary hearts, to mourning homes,
God's meekest Angel gently comes:
No power has he to banish pain,
Or give us back our lost again;
And yet in tenderest love, our dear
And Heavenly Father sends him here.

There's quiet in that Angel's glance,
There's rest in his still countenance!

He mocks no grief with idle cheer,
Nor wounds with words the mourner's ear;
But ills and woes he may not cure
He kindly trains us to endure.

Angel of Patience! sent to calm
Our feverish brows with cooling palm;
To lay the storms of hope and fear,
And reconcile life's smile and tear;
The throbs of wounded pride to still,
And make our own our Father's will!

Oh! thou who mournest on thy way,
With longings for the close of day;
He walks with thee, that Angel kind,
And gently whispers "Be resigned:
Bear up, bear on, the end shall tell
The dear Lord ordereth all things well!"

FOLLEN.

ON READING HIS ESSAY ON THE "FUTURE STATE."

Friend of my soul!—as with moist eye
I look up from this page of thine,
Is it a dream that thou art nigh,
Thy mild face gazing into mine?

That presence seems before me now,
A placid heaven of sweet moonrise,
When dew-like, on the earth below
Descends the quiet of the skies.

The calm brow through the parted hair,
The gentle lips which knew no guile,
Softening the blue eye's thoughtful care
With the bland beauty of their smile.

Ah me!—at times that last dread scene
Of Frost and Fire and moaning Sea,
Will cast its shade of doubt between
The failing eyes of Faith and thee.

Yet, lingering o'er thy charmed page,
Where through the twilight air of earth,
Alike enthusiast and sage,
Prophet and bard, thou gazest forth;

Lifting the Future's solemn veil;
The reaching of a mortal hand
To put aside the cold and pale
Cloud-curtains of the Unseen Land;

In thoughts which answer to my own,
In words which reach my inward ear,
Like whispers from the void Unknown,
I feel thy living presence here.

The waves which lull thy body's rest,
The dust thy pilgrim footsteps trod,
Unwasted, through each change, attest
The fixed economy of God.

Shall these poor elements outlive
The mind whose kingly will they wrought?
Their gross unconsciousness survive
Thy Godlike energy of thought?

THOU LIVEST, FOLLEN!—not in vain
Hath thy fine spirit meekly borne
The burthen of Life's cross of pain,
And the thorned crown of suffering worn.

Oh! while Life's solemn mystery glooms
Around us like a dungeon's wall—
Silent earth's pale and crowded tombs,
Silent the heaven which bends o'er all!—

While day by day our loved ones glide
  In spectral silence, hushed and lone,
To the cold shadows which divide
  The living from the dread Unknown;

While even on the closing eye,
  And on the lip which moves in vain,
The seals of that stern mystery
  Their undiscovered trust retain;—

And only midst the gloom of death,
  Its mournful doubts and haunting fears,
Two pale, sweet angels, Hope and Faith,
  Smile dimly on us through their tears;

'T is something to a heart like mine
  To think of thee as living yet;
To feel that such a light as thine
  Could not in utter darkness set.

Less dreary seems the untried way
  Since thou hast left thy footprints there,
And beams of mournful beauty play
  Round the sad Angel's sable hair.

Oh!—at this hour when half the sky
  Is glorious with its evening light,
And fair broad fields of summer lie
  Hung o'er with greenness in my sight;

While through these elm boughs wet with rain
  The sunset's golden walls are seen,
With clover bloom and yellow grain
  And wood-draped hill and stream between;

I long to know if scenes like this
  Are hidden from an angel's eyes;
If earth's familiar loveliness
  Haunts not thy heaven's serener skies.

For sweetly here upon thee grew
  The lesson which that beauty gave,
The ideal of the Pure and True
  In earth and sky and gliding wave.

And it may be that all which lends
  The soul an upward impulse here,
With a diviner beauty blends,
  And greets us in a holier sphere.

Through groves where blighting never fell
  The humbler flowers of earth may twine;
And simple draughts from childhood's well
  Blend with the angel-tasted wine.

But be the prying vision veiled,
  And let the seeking lips be dumb,—
Where even seraph eyes have failed
  Shall mortal blindness seek to come?

We only know that thou hast gone,
  And that the same returnless tide
Which bore thee from us still glides on,
  And we who mourn thee with it glide.

On all thou lookest we shall look,
  And to our gaze ere long shall turn
That page of God's mysterious book
  We so much wish, yet dread to learn.

With Him, before whose awful power
  Thy spirit bent its trembling knee;—
Who, in the silent greeting flower,
  And forest leaf, looked out on thee,—

We leave thee, with a trust serene,
  Which Time, nor Change, nor Death can move,
While with thy childlike faith we lean
  On Him whose dearest name is Love!

TO THE REFORMERS OF ENGLAND

God bless ye, brothers!—in the fight
 Ye're waging now, ye cannot fail,
For better is your sense of right
 Than king-craft's triple mail.

Than tyrant's law, or bigot's ban
 More mighty is your simplest word;
The free heart of an honest man
 Than crosier or the sword.

Go—let your bloated Church rehearse
 The lesson it has learned so well;
It moves not with its prayer or curse
 The gates of Heaven or hell.

Let the State scaffold rise again—
 Did Freedom die when Russel died?
Forget ye how the blood of Vane
 From earth's green bosom cried?

The great hearts of your olden time
 Are beating with you, full and strong
All holy memories and sublime
 And glorious round ye throng.

The bluff, bold men of Runnymede
 Are with ye still in times like these;
The shades of England's mighty dead,
 Your cloud of witnesses!

The truths ye urge are borne abroad
 By every wind and every tide;
The voice of Nature and of God
 Speaks out upon your side.

The weapons which your hands have found
 Are those which Heaven itself has wrought,
Light, Truth, and Love ;—your battle ground
 The free, broad field of Thought.

No partial, selfish purpose breaks
 The simple beauty of your plan,
Nor lie from throne or altar shakes
 Your steady faith in man.

The languid pulse of England starts
 And bounds beneath your words of power,
The beating of her million hearts
 Is with you at this hour!

Oh, ye who, with undoubting eyes,
 Through present cloud and gathering storm,
Behold the span of Freedom's skies,
 And sunshine soft and warm,—

Press bravely onward!—not in vain
 Your generous trust in human kind;
The good which bloodshed could not gain
 Your peaceful zeal shall find.

Press on!—the triumph shall be won
 Of common rights and equal laws,
The glorious dream of Harrington,
 And Sidney's good old cause.

Blessing the cotter and the crown,
 Sweetening worn Labor's bitter cup,
And, plucking not the highest down,
 Lifting the lowest up.

Press on!—and we who may not share
 The toil or glory of your fight,
May ask, at least, in earnest prayer,
 God's blessing on the right!

THE QUAKER OF THE OLDEN TIME.

THE Quaker of the olden time!—
How calm and firm and true,
Unspotted by its wrong and crime,
He walked the dark earth through
The lust of power, the love of gain,
The thousand lures of sin
Around him, had no power to stain
The purity within.

With that deep insight which detects
All great things in the small,
And knows how each man's life affects
The spiritual life of all,
He walked by faith and not by sight,
By love and not by law;
The presence of the wrong or right
He rather felt than saw.

He felt that wrong with wrong partakes,
That nothing stands alone,
That whoso gives the motive, makes
His brother's sin his own.
And, pausing not for doubtful choice
Of evils great or small,
He listened to that inward voice
Which called away from all.

Oh! Spirit of that early day,
So pure and strong and true,
Be with us in the narrow way
Our faithful fathers knew.
Give strength the evil to forsake,
The cross of Truth to bear,
And love and reverent fear to make
Our daily lives a prayer!

THE REFORMER.

All grim and soiled and brown with tan,
  I saw a Strong One, in his wrath,
Smiting the godless shrines of man
    Along his path.

The Church beneath her trembling dome
  Essayed in vain her ghostly charm:
Wealth shook within his gilded home
    With strange alarm.

Fraud from his secret chambers fled
  Before the sunlight bursting in:
Sloth drew her pillow o'er her head
    To drown the din.

"Spare," Art, implored, "yon holy pile;
  That grand, old, time-worn turret spare;
Meek Reverence, kneeling in the aisle,
    Cried out, "Forbear!"

Gray-bearded Use, who, deaf and blind,
  Groped for his old accustomed stone,
Leaned on his staff, and wept, to find
    His seat o'erthrown.

Young Romance raised his dreamy eyes,
  O'erhung with paly locks of gold:
"Why smite," he asked in sad surprise,
    "The fair, the old?"

Yet louder rang the Strong One's stroke,
  Yet nearer flashed his axe's gleam;
Shuddering and sick of heart I woke,
    As from a dream.

I looked: aside the dust-cloud rolled—
  The Waster seemed the Builder too;
Up springing from the ruined Old
    I saw the New.

'Twas but the ruin of the bad—
  The wasting of the wrong and ill;
Whate'er of good the old time had
    Was living still.

Calm grew the brows of him I feared;
  The frown which awed me passed away,
And left behind a smile which cheered
    Like breaking day.

The grain grew green on battle-plains,
  O'er swarded war-mounds grazed the cow;
The slave stood forging from his chains
    The spade and plough.

Where frowned the fort, pavilions gay
  And cottage windows, flower-entwined,
Looked out upon the peaceful bay
    And hills behind.

Through vine-wreathed cups with wine once red,
  The lights on brimming crystal fell,
Drawn, sparkling, from the rivulet head
    And mossy well.

Through prison walls, like Heaven-sent hope,
  Fresh breezes blew, and sunbeams strayed,
And with the idle gallows-rope
    The young child played.

Where the doomed victim in his cell
  Had counted o'er the weary hours,
Glad school-girls, answering to the bell,
    Came crowned with flowers.

Grown wiser for the lesson given,
  I fear no longer, for I know
That, where the share is deepest driven,
    The best fruits grow.

The outworn rite, the old abuse,
  The pious fraud transparent grown,
The good held captive in the use
    Of wrong alone—

These wait their doom, from that great law
  Which makes the past time serve to-day;
And fresher life the world shall draw
    From their decay.

Oh! backward-looking son of time!—
  The new is old, the old is new,
The cycle of a change sublime
    Still sweeping through.

So wisely taught the Indian seer;
  Destroying Seva, forming Brahm,
Who wake by turns Earth's love and fear,
    Are one, the same.

As idly as, in that old day,
  Thou mournest, did thy sires repine,
So, in his time, thy child grown gray,
    Shall sigh for thine.

Yet, not the less for them or thou
  The eternal step of Progress beats
To that great anthem, calm and slow,
    Which God repeats!

Take heart!—the Waster builds again—
  A charmed life old goodness hath;
The tares may perish—but the grain
    Is not for death.

God works in all things; all obey
  His first propulsion from the night:
Ho, wake and watch!—the world is gray
    With morning light!

THE PRISONER FOR DEBT.

Look on him!—through his dungeon grate
  Feebly and cold, the morning light
Comes stealing round him, dim and late,
  As if it loathed the sight.
Reclining on his strawy bed,
His hand upholds his drooping head—
His bloodless cheek is seamed and hard,
Unshorn his gray, neglected beard;
And o'er his bony fingers flow
His long, dishevelled locks of snow.

No grateful fire before him glows,
  And yet the winter's breath is chill;
And o'er his half-clad person goes
  The frequent ague thrill!
Silent, save ever and anon,
A sound, half murmur and half groan,
Forces apart the painful grip
Of the old sufferer's bearded lip;
O sad and crushing is the fate
Of old age chained and desolate!

Just God! why lies that old man there?
  A murderer shares his prison bed,
Whose eye-balls, through his horrid hair,
  Gleam on him, fierce and red;
And the rude oath and heartless jeer
Fall ever on his loathing ear,
And, or in wakefulness or sleep,
Nerve, flesh, and pulses thrill and creep

Whene'er that ruffian's tossing limb,
Crimson with murder, touches him!

What has the gray-haired prisoner done?
Has murder stained his hands with gore?
Not so; his crime's a fouler one;
GOD MADE THE OLD MAN POOR!
For this he shares a felon's cell—
The fittest earthly type of hell!
For this, the boon for which he poured
His young blood on the invader's sword,
And counted light the fearful cost—
His blood-gained liberty is lost!

And so, for such a place of rest,
Old prisoner, dropped thy blood as rain
On Concord's field, and Bunker's crest,
And Saratoga's plain?
Look forth, thou man of many scars,
Through thy dim dungeon's iron bars;
It must be joy, in sooth, to see
Yon monument upreared to thee—
Piled granite and a prison cell—
The land repays thy service well!

Go, ring the bells and fire the guns,
And fling the starry banner out;
Shout "Freedom!" till your lisping ones
Give back their cradle-shout:
Let boastful eloquence declaim
Of honor, liberty, and fame;
Still let the poet's strain be heard,
With glory for each second word,
And every thing with breath agree
To praise "our glorious liberty!"

But when the patron cannon jars,
That prison's cold and gloomy wall
And through its grates the stripes and stars
Rise on the wind and fall—

Think ye that prisoner's aged ear
Rejoices in the general cheer?
Think ye his dim and failing eye
Is kindled at your pageantry?
Sorrowing of soul, and chained of limb,
What is your carnival to him?

Down with the LAW that binds him thus!
  Unworthy freemen, let it find
No refuge from the withering curse
  Of God and human kind!
Open the prison's living tomb,
And usher from its brooding gloom
The victims of your savage code,
To the free sun and air of God;
No longer dare as crime to brand
The chastening of the Almighty's hand.

LINES,

WRITTEN ON READING PAMPHLETS PUBLISHED BY CLERGYMEN AGAINST THE ABOLITION OF THE GALLOWS.

I.

THE suns of eighteen centuries have shone
  Since the Redeemer walked with man, and made
The fisher's boat, the cavern's floor of stone,
  And mountain moss, a pillow for his head;
And He, who wandered with the peasant Jew,
  And broke with publicans the bread of shame,
  And drank, with blessings in his Father's name,
The water which Samaria's outcast drew,
Hath now his temples upon every shore,
  Altar and shrine and priest,—and incense dim
  Evermore rising, with low prayer and hymn,
From lips which press the temple's marble floor,
Or kiss the gilded sign of the dread Cross He bore

II.

Yet as of old, when, meekly "doing good,"
He fed a blind and selfish multitude,
And even the poor companions of his lot
With their dim earthly vision knew him not,
  How ill are his high teachings understood!
Where He hath spoken Liberty, the priest
  At his own altar binds the chain anew;
Where He hath bidden to Life's equal feast,
  The starving many wait upon the few;
Where He hath spoken Peace, his name hath been
The loudest war-cry of contending men;
Priests, pale with vigils, in his name have blessed
The unsheathed sword, and laid the spear in rest,
Wet the war-banner with their sacred wine,
And crossed its blazon with the holy sign;
Yea, in his name who bade the erring live,
And daily taught his lesson—to forgive!—
  Twisted the cord and edged the murderous steel;
And, with his words of mercy on their lips,
Hung gloating o'er the pincer's burning grips,
  And the grim horror of the straining wheel;
Fed the slow flame which gnawed the victim's limb,
Who saw before his searing eye-balls swim
  The image of *their* Christ in cruel zeal,
Through the black torment-smoke, held mockingly
    to him!

III.

The blood which mingled with the desert sand,
  And beaded with its red and ghastly dew
The vines and olives of the Holy Land—
  The shrieking curses of the hunted Jew—
The white-sown bones of heretics, where'er
They sank beneath the Crusade's holy spear—
Goa's dark dungeons—Malta's sea-washed cell,
  Where with the hymns the ghostly fathers sung
  Mingled the groans by subtle torture wrung,

Heaven's anthem blending with the shriek of hell!
The midnight of Bartholomew—the stake
  Of Smithfield, and that thrice-accursed flame
Which Calvin kindled by Geneva's lake—
New England's scaffold, and the priestly sneer
Which mocked its victims in that hour of fear,
  When guilt itself a human tear might claim,—
Bear witness, O Thou wronged and merciful One!
That Earth's most hateful crimes have in thy name
    been done!

IV.

Thank God! that I have lived to see the time
  When the great truth begins at last to find
  An utterance from the deep heart of mankind,
Earnest and clear, that ALL REVENGE IS CRIME!
That man is holier than a creed,—that all
  Restraint upon him must consult his good,
Hope's sunshine linger on his prison wall,
  And Love look in upon his solitude.
The beautiful lesson which our Saviour taught
Through long, dark centuries its way hath wrought
Into the common mind and popular thought;
And words, to which by Galilee's lake shore
The humble fishers listened with hushed oar,
Have found an echo in the general heart,
And of the public faith become a living part.

V.

Who shall arrest this tendency?—Bring back
The cells of Venice and the bigot's rack?
Harden the softening human heart again
To cold indifference to a brother's pain?
Ye most unhappy men!—who, turned away
From the mild sunshine of the Gospel day,
  Grope in the shadows of Man's twilight time,
What mean ye, that with ghoul-like zest ye brood,
O'er those foul altars streaming with warm blood,
  Permitted in another age and clime?

Why cite that law with which the bigot Jew
Rebuked the Pagan's mercy, when he knew
No evil in the Just One?—Wherefore turn
To the dark cruel past?—Can ye not learn
From the pure Teacher's life, how mildly free
Is the great Gospel of Humanity?
The Flamen's knife is bloodless, and no more
Mexitli's altars soak with human gore,
No more the ghastly sacrifices smoke
Through the green arches of the Druid's oak;
And ye of milder faith, with your high claim
Of prophet-utterance in the Holiest name,
Will ye become the Druids of *our* time?
  Set up your scaffold-altars in *our* land,
And, consecrators of Law's darkest crime,
  Urge to its loathsome work the hangman's hand?
Beware—lest human nature, roused at last,
From its peeled shoulder your incumbrance cast,
  And, sick to loathing of your cry for blood,
Rank ye with those who led their victims round
The Celt's red altar and the Indian's mound,
  Abhorred of Earth and Heaven—a pagan brother-
      hood!

THE HUMAN SACRIFICE.

I.

Far from his close and noisome cell,
  By grassy lane and sunny stream,
Blown clover field and strawberry dell,
And green and meadow freshness, fell
  The footsteps of his dream.
Again from careless feet the dew
  Of summer's misty morn he shook;
Again with merry heart he threw
  His light line in the rippling brook.

Back crowded all his school-day joys—
  He urged the ball and quoit again,
And heard the shout of laughing boys
  Come ringing down the walnut glen.
Again he felt the western breeze,
  With scent of flowers and crisping hay;
And down again through wind-stirred trees
He saw the quivering sunlight play.
An angel in home's vine-hung door,
He saw his sister smile once more;
Once more the truant's brown-locked head
Upon his mother's knees was laid,
And sweetly lulled to slumber there,
With evening's holy hymn and prayer!

II.

He woke. At once on heart and brain
The present Terror rushed again—
Clanked on his limbs the felon's chain!
He woke, to hear the church-tower tell
Time's footfall on the conscious bell,
And, shuddering, feel that clanging din
His life's LAST HOUR had ushered in;
To see within his prison yard,
Through the small window, iron barred,
The gallows shadow rising dim
Between the sunrise heaven and him,—
A horror in God's blessed air—
  A blackness in his morning light—
Like some foul devil-altar there
  Built up by demon hands at night.
  And, maddened by that evil sight,
Dark, horrible, confused, and strange,
A chaos of wild, weltering change,
All power of check and guidance gone,
Dizzy and blind, his mind swept on.
In vain he strove to breathe a prayer,
  In vain he turned the Holy Book,

He only heard the gallows-stair
  Creek as the wind its timbers shook.
No dream for him of sin forgiven,
  While still that baleful spectre stood,
  With its hoarse murmur, "*Blood for Blood!*"
Between him and the pitying Heaven!

III.

Low on his dungeon floor he knelt,
  And smote his breast, and on his chain,
Whose iron clasp he always felt,
  His hot tears fell like rain;
And near him, with the cold, calm look
  And tone of one whose formal part,
  Unwarmed, unsoftened of the heart,
Is measured out by rule and book,
With placid lip and tranquil blood,
The hangman's ghostly ally stood,
Blessing with solemn text and word
The gallows-drop and strangling cord;
Lending the sacred Gospel's awe
And sanction to the crime of Law.

IV.

He saw the victim's tortured brow—
  The sweat of anguish starting there—
The record of a nameless woe
  In the dim eye's imploring stare,
  Seen hideous through the long, damp hair—
Fingers of ghastly skin and bone
Working and writhing on the stone!—
And heard, by mortal terror wrung
From heaving breast and stiffened tongue,
  The choking sob and low hoarse prayer;
As o'er his half-crazed fancy came
A vision of the eternal flame—
Its smoking cloud of agonies—
Its demon-worm that never dies—
The everlasting rise and fall

Of fire-waves round the infernal wall;
While high above that dark red flood,
Black, giant-like, the gallows stood:
Two busy fiends attending there;
One with cold mocking rite and prayer,
The other with impatient grasp,
Tightening the death-rope's strangling clasp

V.

The unfelt rite at length was done—
  The prayer unheard at length was said—
An hour had passed:—the noon-day sun
  Smote on the features of the dead!
And he who stood the doomed beside,
Calm gauger of the swelling tide
Of mortal agony and fear,
Heeding with curious eye and ear
Whate'er revealed the keen excess
Of man's extremest wretchedness:
And who in that dark anguish saw
  An earnest of the victim's fate,
The vengeful terrors of God's law,
  The kindlings of Eternal hate—
The first drops of that fiery rain
Which beats the dark red realm of pain,—
Did he uplift his earnest cries
  Against the crime of Law, which gave
  His brother to that fearful grave,
Whereon Hope's moonlight never lies,
  And Faith's white blossoms never wave
To the soft breath of Memory's sighs;—
Which sent a spirit marred and stained,
By fiends of sin possessed, profaned,
In madness and in blindness stark,
Into the silent, unknown dark?
No—from the wild and shrinking dread
With which he saw the victim led
  Beneath the dark veil which divides

Ever the living from the dead,
 And Nature's solemn secret hides,
The man of prayer can only draw
New reasons for his bloody law;
New faith in staying Murder's hand
By murder at that Law's command;
New reverence for the gallows-rope,
As human nature's latest hope;
Last relic of the good old time,
When Power found license for its crime,
And held a writhing world in check
By that fell cord about its neck;
Stifled Sedition's rising shout,
Choked the young breath of Freedom out,
And timely checked the words which sprung
From Heresy's forbidden tongue;
While in its noose of terror bound,
The Church its cherished union found,
Conforming, on the Moslem plan,
The motley-colored mind of man,
Not by the Koran and the Sword,
But by the Bible and the Cord!

VI.

Oh, Thou! at whose rebuke the grave
Back to warm life its sleeper gave,
Beneath whose sad and tearful glance
The cold and changed countenance
Broke the still horror of its trance,
And waking, saw with joy above,
A brother's face of tenderest love;
Thou, unto whom the blind and lame,
The sorrowing and the sin-sick came,
And from thy very garment's hem
Drew life and healing unto them,
The burden of thy holy faith
Was love and life, not hate and death,
Man's demon ministers of pain,

The fiends of his revenge were sent
  From thy pure Gospel's element
To their dark home again.
Thy name is Love! What, then, is he,
  Who in that name the gallows rears,
An awful altar built to Thee,
  With sacrifice of blood and tears?
Oh, once again thy healing lay
  On the blind eyes which knew Thee not
And let the light of thy pure day
  Melt in upon his darkened thought.
Soften his hard, cold heart, and show
  The power which in forbearance lies,
And let him feel that mercy now
  Is better than old sacrifice!

VII.

As on the White Sea's charmed shore,
  The Parsee sees his holy hill
With dunnest smoke-clouds curtained o'er,
Yet knows beneath them, evermore,
  The low, pale fire is quivering still;
So underneath its clouds of sin,
  The heart of man retaineth yet
Gleams of its holy origin;
  And half-quenched stars that never set,
Dim colors of its faded bow,
  And early beauty, linger there,
And o'er its wasted desert blow
  Faint breathings of its morning air,
Oh! never yet upon the scroll
Of the sin-stained, but priceless soul,
  Hath Heaven inscribed "DESPAIR!"
Cast not the clouded gem away,
Quench not the dim but living ray—
  My brother man, Beware!
With that deep voice which from the skies
Forbade the Patriarch's sacrifice,
  God's angel cries, FORBEAR!

RANDOLPH OF ROANOKE.

Oh, Mother Earth! upon thy lap
  Thy weary ones receiving,
And o'er them, silent as a dream,
  Thy grassy mantle weaving,
Fold softly in thy long embrace
  That heart so worn and broken,
And cool its pulse of fire beneath
  Thy shadows old and oaken.

Shut out from him the bitter word
  And serpent hiss of scorning;
Nor let the storms of yesterday
  Disturb his quiet morning.
Breathe over him forgetfulness
  Of all save deeds of kindness,
And, save to smiles of grateful eyes,
  Press down his lids in blindness.

There, where with living ear and eye
  He heard Potomac's flowing,
And, through his tall ancestral trees,
  Saw Autumn's sunset glowing,
He sleeps—still looking to the West,
  Beneath the dark wood shadow,
As if he still would see the sun
  Sink down on wave and meadow.

Bard, Sage, and Tribune!—in himself
  All moods of mind contrasting—
The tenderest wail of human woe,
  The scorn-like lightning blasting;
The pathos which from rival eyes
  Unwilling tears could summon,
The stinging taunt, the fiery burst
  Of hatred scarcely human!

Mirth, sparkling like a diamond shower,
  From lips of life-long sadness;
Clear picturings of majestic thought
  Upon a ground of madness;
And over all Romance and Song
  A classic beauty throwing,
And laurelled Clio at his side
  Her storied pages showing.

All parties feared him: each in turn
  Beheld its schemes disjointed,
As right or left his fatal glance
  And spectral finger pointed.
Sworn foe of Cant, he smote it down
  With trenchant wit unsparing,
And, mocking, rent with ruthless hand
  The robe Pretence was wearing.

Too honest or too proud to feign
  A love he never cherished,
Beyond Virginia's border line
  His patriotism perished.
While others hailed in distant skies
  Our eagle's dusky pinion,
He only saw the mountain bird
  Stoop o'er his Old Dominion!

Still through each change of fortune strange,
  Racked nerve, and brain all burning,
His loving faith in Mother-land
  Knew never shade of turning;
By Britain's lakes, by Neva's wave,
  Whatever sky was o'er him,
He heard her rivers' rushing sound,
  Her blue peaks rose before him.

He held his slaves, yet made withal
  No false and vain pretences,
Nor paid a lying priest to seek
  For scriptural defences

His harshest words of proud rebuke,
  His bitterest taunt and scorning,
Fell fire-like on the Northern brow
  That bent to him in fawning.

He held his slaves: yet kept the while
  His reverence for the Human;
In the dark vassals of his will
  He saw but Man and Woman!
No hunter of God's outraged poor
  His Roanoke valley entered;
No trader in the souls of men
  Across his threshhold ventured.

And when the old and wearied man
  Laid down for his last sleeping,
And at his side, a slave no more,
  His brother man stood weeping,
His latest thought, his latest breath,
  To Freedom's duty giving,
With failing tongue and trembling hand
  The dying blest the living.

Oh! never bore his ancient State
  A truer son or braver!
None trampling with a calmer scorn
  On foreign hate or favor.
He knew her faults, yet never stooped
  His proud and manly feeling
To poor excuses of the wrong
  Or meanness of concealing.

But none beheld with clearer eye
  The plague-spot o'er her spreading,
None heard more sure the steps of Doom
  Along her future treading.
For her as for himself he spake,
  When, his gaunt frame upbracing,
He traced with dying hand "REMORSE!"
  And perished in the tracing.

As from the grave where Henry sleeps,
  From Vernon's weeping willow,
And from the grassy pall which hides
  The Sage of Monticello,
So from the leaf-strewn burial-stone
  Of Randolph's lowly dwelling,
Virginia! o'er thy land of slaves
  A warning voice is swelling!

And hark! from thy deserted fields
  Are sadder warnings spoken,
From quenched hearths, where thy exiled sons
  Their household gods have broken.
The curse is on thee—wolves for men,
  And briars for corn-sheaves giving!
Oh! more than all thy dead renown
  Were now one hero living!

DEMOCRACY.

All things whatsoever ye would that men should do to you, do ye even so to them.—*Matthew* vii. 12.

Bearer of Freedom's holy light,
  Breaker of Slavery's chain and rod,
The foe of all which pains the sight,
  Or wounds the generous ear of God!

Beautiful yet thy temples rise,
  Though there profaning gifts are thrown;
And fires unkindled of the skies
  Are glaring round thy altar-stone.

Still sacred—though thy name be breathed
  By those whose hearts thy truth deride;
And garlands, plucked from thee, are wreathed
  Around the haughty brows of Pride.

O, ideal of my boyhood's time!
  The faith in which my father stood,
Even when the sons of Lust and Crime
  Had stained thy peaceful courts with blood!

Still to those courts my footsteps turn,
  For through the mists which darken there,
I see the flame of Freedom burn—
  The Kebla of the patriot's prayer!

The generous feeling, pure and warm,
  Which owns the rights of *all* divine—
The pitying heart—the helping arm—
  The prompt self-sacrifice—are thine.

Beneath thy broad, impartial eye,
  How fade the lines of caste and birth!
How equal in their suffering lie
  The groaning multitudes of earth!

Still to a stricken brother true,
  Whatever clime hath nurtured him;
As stooped to heal the wounded Jew
  The worshipper of Gerizim.

By misery unrepelled, unawed
  By pomp or power, thou see'st a MAN
In prince or peasant—slave or lord—
  Pale priest, or swarthy artisan.

Through all disguise, form, place, or name,
  Beneath the flaunting robes of sin,
Through poverty and squalid shame,
  Thou lookest on *the man* within.

On man, as man, retaining yet,
  Howe'er debased, and soiled, and dim,
The crown upon his forehead set—
  The immortal gift of God to him.

And tnere is reverence in thy look;
For that frail form which mortals wear
The Spirit of the Holiest took,
And veiled his perfect brightness there.

Not from the shallow babbling fount
Of vain philosophy thou art;
He who of old on Syria's mount
Thrilled, warmed, by turns, the listener's heart,

In holy words which cannot die,
In thoughts which angels leaned to know,
Proclaimed thy message from on high—
Thy mission to a world of woe.

That voice's echo hath not died!
From the blue lake of Galilee,
And Tabor's lonely mountain side,
It calls a struggling world to thee.

Thy name and watchword o'er this land
I hear in every breeze that stirs
And round a thousand altars stand
Thy banded party worshippers.

Not to these altars of a day,
At party's call, my gift I bring;
But on thy olden shrine I lay
A freeman's dearest offering:—

The voiceless utterance of his will—
His pledge to Freedom and to Tiuth,
That manhood's heart remembers still
The homage of his generous youth.

Election Day, 1843.

TO RONGE.

STRIKE home, strong-hearted man! Down to the root
Of old oppression sink the Saxon steel.
Thy work is to hew down. In God's name then
Put nerve into thy task. Let other men
Plant, as they may, that better tree, whose fruit
The wounded bosom of the Church shall heal.
Be thou the image-breaker. Let thy blows
Fall heavy as the Suabian's iron hand,
On crown or crosier, which shall interpose
Between thee and the weal of Father-land.
Leave creeds to closet idlers. First of all,
Shake thou all German dream-land with the fall
Of that accursed tree, whose evil trunk
Was spared of old by Erfurt's stalwart monk.
Fight not with ghosts and shadows. Let us hear
The snap of chain-links. Let our gladdened ear
Catch the pale prisoner's welcome, as the light
Follows thy axe-stroke, through his cell of night.
Be faithful to both worlds; nor think to feed
Earth's starving millions with the husks of creed.
Servant of Him whose mission high and holy
Was to the wronged, the sorrowing, and the lowly,
Thrust not his Eden promise from our sphere,
Distant and dim beyond the blue sky's span;
Like him of Patmos, see it, now and here,—
The New Jerusalem comes down to man!
Be warned by Luther's error. Nor like him,
When the roused Teuton dashes from his limb
The rusted chain of ages, help to bind
His hands, for whom thou claim'st the freedom of the mind!

CHALKLEY HALL.[39]

How bland and sweet the greeting of this breeze
    To him who flies
From crowded street and red wall's weary gleam,
Till far behind him like a hideous dream
    The close dark city lies!—

Here, while the market murmurs, while men throng
    The marble floor
Of Mammon's altar, from the crush and din
Of the world's madness let me gather in
    My better thoughts once more.

Oh! once again revive, while on my ear
    The cry of Gain
And low hoarse hum of Traffic die away,
Ye blessed memories of my early day
    Like sere grass wet with rain!—

Once more let God's green earth and sunset air
    Old feelings waken;
Through weary years of toil and strife and ill,
Oh, let me feel that my good angel still
    Hath not his trust forsaken.

And well do time and place befit my mood:
    Beneath the arms
Of this embracing wood, a good man made
His home, like Abraham resting in the shade
    Of Mamre's lonely palms.

Here, rich with autumn gifts of countless years,
    The virgin soil
Turned from the share he guided, and in rain
And summer sunshine throve the fruits and grain
    Which blessed his honest toil.

Here, from his voyages on the stormy seas,
Weary and worn,
He came to meet his children and to bless
The Giver of all good in thankfulness
And praise for his return.

And here his neighbors gathered in to greet
Their friend again,
Safe from the wave and the destroying gales,
Which reap untimely green Bermuda's vales,
And vex the Carib main.

To hear the good man tell of simple truth,
Sown in an hour
Of weakness in some far-off Indian isle,
From the parched bosom of a barren soil,
Raised up in life and power:

How at those gatherings in Barbadian vales,
A tendering love
Came o'er him, like the gentle rain from heaven,
And words of fitness to his lips were given,
And strength as from above:

How the sad captive listened to the Word,
Until his chain
Grew lighter, and his wounded spirit felt
The healing balm of consolation melt
Upon its life-long pain:

How the armed warrior sate him down to hear
Of Peace and Truth,
And the proud ruler and his Creole dame,
Jewelled and gorgeous in her beauty came,
And fair and bright-eyed youth.

Oh, far away beneath New England's sky,
Even when a boy,
Following my plough by Merrimack's green shore,

His simple record I have pondered o'er
    With deep and quiet joy.

And hence this scene, in sunset glory warm—
    Its woods around,
Its still stream winding on in light and shade,
Its soft, green meadows and its upland glade—
    To me is holy ground.

And dearer far than haunts where Genius keeps
    His vigils still;
Than that where Avon's son of song is laid,
Or Vaucluse hallowed by its Petrarch's shade,
    Or Virgil's laurelled hill.

To the gray walls of fallen Paraclete,
    To Juliet's urn,
Fair Arno and Sorrento's orange grove,
Where Tasso sang, let young Romance and Love
    Like brother pilgrims turn.

But here a deeper and serener charm
    To all is given;
And blessed memories of the faithful dead
O'er wood and vale and meadow-stream have shed
    The holy hues of Heaven!

TO J. P.

Not as a poor requital of the joy
    With which my childhood heard that lay of thine,
    Which, like an echo of the song divine
At Bethlehem breathed above the Holy Boy,
    Bore to my ear the Airs of Palestine,—
Not to the poet, but the man I bring
In friendship's fearless trust my offering:

How much it lacks I feel, and thou wilt see,
Yet well I know that thou hast deemed with me
Life all too earnest, and its time too short
For dreamy ease and Fancy's graceful sport;
And girded for thy constant strife with wrong
Like Nehemiah fighting while he wrought
The broken walls of Zion, even thy song
Hath a rude martial tone, a blow in every thought!

THE CYPRESS-TREE OF CEYLON.

[IBN BATUTA, the celebrated Mussulman traveller of the fourteenth century, speaks of a Cypress-tree in Ceylon, universally held sacred by the natives, the leaves of which were said to fall only at certain intervals, and he who had the happiness to find and eat one of them, was restored, at once, to youth and vigor The traveller saw several venerable JOGEES, or saints, sitting silent and motionless under the tree, patiently awaiting the falling of a leaf.]

THEY sat in silent watchfulness
The sacred cypress-tree about,
And, from beneath old wrinkled brows
Their failing eyes looked out.

Gray Age and Sickness waiting there
Through weary night and lingering day—
Grim as the idols at their side
And motionless as they.

Unheeded in the boughs above
The song of Ceylon's birds was sweet;
Unseen of them the island flowers
Bloomed brightly at their feet.

O'er them the tropic night-storm swept,
The thunder crashed on rock and hill;
The cloud-fire on their eye-balls blazed,
Yet there they waited still!

What was the world without to them?
  The Moslem's sunset-call—the dance
Of Ceylon's maids—the passing gleam
  Of battle-flag and lance?

They waited for that falling leaf,
  Of which the wandering Jogees sing:
Which lends once more to wintry age
  The greenness of its spring.

Oh!—if these poor and blinded ones
  In trustful patience wait to feel
O'er torpid pulse and failing limb
  A youthful freshness steal;

Shall we, who sit beneath that Tree,
  Whose healing leaves of life are shed
In answer to the breath of prayer
  Upon the waiting head:

Not to restore our failing forms,
  And build the spirit's broken shrine,
But, on the fainting SOUL to shed
  A light and life divine:

Shall we grow weary in our watch,
  And murmur at the long delay?
Impatient of our Father's time
  And his appointed way?

Or, shall the stir of outward things
  Allure and claim the Christian's eye,
When on the heathen watcher's ear
  Their powerless murmurs die?

Alas! a deeper test of faith
  Than prison cell or martyr's stake,
The self-abasing watchfulness
  Of silent prayer may make.

We gird us bravely to rebuke
  Our erring brother in the wrong:
And in the ear of Pride and Power
  Our warning voice is strong.

Easier to smite with Peter's sword,
  Than "watch one hour" in humbling prayer
Life's "great things," like the Syrian lord,
  Our hearts can do and dare.

But oh! we shrink from Jordan's side,
  From waters which alone can save:
And murmur for Abana's banks
  And Pharpar's brighter wave.

Oh, Thou, who in the garden's shade
  Didst wake thy weary ones again,
Who slumbered at that fearful hour
  Forgetful of thy pain;

Bend o'er us now, as over them,
  And set our sleep-bound spirits free,
Nor leave us slumbering in the watch
  Our souls should keep with Thee!

A DREAM OF SUMMER.

Bland as the morning breath of June
  The southwest breezes play;
And, through its haze, the winter noon
  Seems warm as summer's day
The snow-plumed Angel of the North
  Has dropped his icy spear;
Again the mossy earth looks forth,
  Again the streams gush clear.

The fox his hill-side cell forsakes,
  The muskrat leaves his nook,
The bluebird in the meadow brakes
  Is singing with the brook.
"Bear up, oh mother Nature!" cry
  Bird, breeze, and streamlet free;
"Our winter voices prophesy
  Of summer days to thee!"

So, in those winters of the soul,
  By bitter blasts and drear
O'erswept from Memory's frozen pole,
  Will sunny days appear.
Reviving Hope and Faith, they show
  The soul its living powers,
And how beneath the winter's snow
  Lie germs of summer flowers!

The Night is mother of the Day,
  The Winter of the Spring,
And ever upon old Decay
  The greenest mosses cling.
Behind the cloud the starlight lurks,
  Through showers the sunbeams fall;
For God, who loveth all his works,
  Has left his Hope with all!

4th 1st month, 1847.

TO ——,

WITH A COPY OF WOOLMAN'S JOURNAL.

Get the writings of John Woolman by heart."—*Essays of Elia*

MAIDEN! with the fair brown tresses
  Shading o'er thy dreamy eye,
Floating on thy thoughtful forehead
  Cloud wreaths of its sky.

Youthful years and maiden beauty,
Joy with them should still abide—
Instinct take the place of Duty—
Love, not Reason, guide.

Ever in the New rejoicing,
Kindly beckoning back the Old,
Turning, with the gift of Midas,
All things into gold.

And the passing shades of sadness
Wearing even a welcome guise,
As when some bright lake lies open
To the sunny skies;

Every wing of bird above it,
Every light cloud floating on,
Glitters like that flashing mirror
In the self-same sun.

But, upon thy youthful forehead
Something like a shadow lies;
And a serious soul is looking
From thy earnest eyes.

With an early introversion,
Through the forms of outward things,
Seeking for the subtle essence,
And the hidden springs.

Deeper than the gilded surface
Hath thy wakeful vision seen,
Farther than the narrow present
Have thy journeyings been.

Thou hast midst Life's empty noises
Heard the solemn steps of Time,
And the low mysterious voices
Of another clime.

All the mystery of Being
  Hath upon thy spirit pressed—
Thoughts which, like the Deluge wanderer,
  Find no place of rest:

That which mystic Plato pondered,
  That which Zeno heard with awe,
And the star-rapt Zoroaster
  In his night-watch saw.

From the doubt and darkness springing
  Of the dim, uncertain Past,
Moving to the dark still shadows
  O'er the Future cast,

Early hath Life's mighty question
  Thrilled within thy heart of youth
With a deep and strong beseeching:
  WHAT and WHERE IS TRUTH?

Hollow creed and ceremonial,
  Whence the ancient life hath fled,
Idle faith unknown to action,
  Dull and cold and dead.

Oracles, whose wire-worked meanings
  Only wake a quiet scorn,—
Not from these thy seeking spirit
  Hath its answer drawn.

But, like some tired child at even,
  On thy mother Nature's breast,
Thou methinks, art vainly seeking
  Truth, and peace, and rest.

O'er that mother's rugged features
  Thou art throwing Fancy's veil,
Light and soft as woven moonbeams,
  Beautiful and frail!

O'er the rough chart of Existence,
Rocks of sin and wastes of woe,
Soft airs breathe, and green leaves tremble,
And cool fountains flow.

And to thee an answer cometh
From the earth and from the sky,
And to thee the hills and waters
And the stars reply.

But a soul-sufficing answer
Hath no outward origin;
More than Nature's many voices
May be heard within.

Even as the great Augustine
Questioned earth and sea and sky,
And the dusty tomes of learning
And old poesy.

But his earnest spirit needed
More than outward Nature taught—
More than blest the poet's vision
Or the sage's thought.

Only in the gathered silence
Of a calm and waiting frame
Light and wisdom as from Heaven
To the seeker came.

Not to case and aimless quiet
Doth that inward answer tend,
But to works of love and duty
As our being's end,—

Not to idle dreams and trances,
Length of face, and solemn tone,
But to Faith, in daily striving
And performance shown.

Earnest toil and strong endeavor
  Of a spirit which within
Wrestles with familiar evil
  And besetting sin;

And without, with tireless vigor,
  Steady heart, and weapon strong,
In the power of truth assailing
  Every form of wrong.

Guided thus, how passing lovely
  Is the track of WOOLMAN'S feet!
And his brief and simple record
  How serenely sweet!

O'er life's humblest duties throwing
  Light the earthling never knew,
Freshening all its dark waste places
  As with Hermon's dew.

All which glows in Pascal's pages—
  All which sainted Guion sought,
Or the blue-eyed German Rahel
  Half-unconscious taught:—

Beauty, such as Goethe pictured,
  Such as Shelley dreamed of, shed
Living warmth and starry brightness
  Round that poor man's head.

Not a vain and cold ideal,
  Not a poet's dream alone,
But a presence warm and real,
  Seen and felt and known.

When the red right hand of slaughter
  Moulders with the steel it swung,
When the name of seer and poet
  Dies on Memory's tongue,

All bright thoughts and pure shall gather
  Round that meek and suffering one—
Glorious, like the seer-seen angel
  Standing in the sun!

Take the good man's book and ponder
  What its pages say to thee—
Blessed as the hand of healing
  May its lesson be.

If it only serves to strengthen
  Yearnings for a higher good,
For the fount of living waters
  And diviner food;

If the pride of human reason
  Feels its meek and still rebuke,
Quailing like the eye of Peter
  From the Just One's look!—

If with readier ear thou heedest
  What the Inward Teacher saith,
Listening with a willing spirit
  And a child-like faith,—

Thou mayest live to bless the giver,
  Who himself but frail and weak,
Would at least the highest welfare
  Of another seek;

And his gift, though poor and lowly
  It may seem to other eyes,
Yet may prove an angel holy
  In a pilgrim's guise.

LEGGETT'S MONUMENT.

"Ye build the tombs of the prophets."—Holy Writ.

Yes—pile the marble o'er him! It is well
  That ye who mocked him in his long stern strife,
  And planted in the pathway of his life
The ploughshares of your hatred hot from hell,
  Who clamored down the bold reformer when
  He pleaded for his captive fellow-men,
Who spurned him in the market-place, and sought
  Within thy walls, St. Tammany, to bind
In party chains the free and honest thought,
  The angel utterance of an upright mind,—
Well is it now that o'er his grave ye raise
The stony tribute of your tardy praise,
For not alone that pile shall tell to Fame
Of the brave heart beneath, but of the builders' shame!

IN WAR TIME.

TO

SAMUEL E. SEWALL

AND

HARRIET W. SEWALL,

OF MELROSE.

OLOR ISCANUS queries: "Why should we
Vex at the land's ridiculous miserie?"
So on his Usk banks, in the blood-red dawn
Of England's civil strife, did careless Vaughan
Bemock his times. O friends of many years!
Though faith and trust are stronger than our fears,
And the signs promise peace with liberty,
Not thus we trifle with our country's tears
And sweat of agony. The future's gain
Is certain as God's truth; but, meanwhile, pain
Is bitter and tears are salt: our voices take
A sober tone; our very household songs
Are heavy with a nation's griefs and wrongs;
And innocent mirth is chastened for the sake
Of the brave hearts that nevermore shall beat,
The eyes that smile no more, the unreturning feet

IN WAR TIME.

THY WILL BE DONE.

WE see not, know not; all our way
Is night,—with Thee alone is day:
From out the torrent's troubled drift,
Above the storm our prayers we lift,
    Thy will be done!

The flesh may fail, the heart may faint,
But who are we to make complaint,
Or dare to plead, in times like these,
The weakness of our love of ease?
    Thy will be done!

We take with solemn thankfulness
Our burden up, nor ask it less,
And count it joy that even we
May suffer, serve, or wait, for Thee,
    Whose will be done!

Though dim as yet in tint and line,
We trace Thy picture's wise design,
And thank Thee that our age supplies
Its dark relief of sacrifice.
    Thy will be done!

And if, in our unworthiness,
Thy sacrificial wine we press;
If from Thy ordeal's heated bars

Our feet are seamed with crimson scars,
 Thy will be done!

If, for the age to come, this hour
Of trial hath vicarious power,
And, blest by Thee, our present pain
Be Liberty's eternal gain,
 Thy will be done!

Strike, Thou the Master, we Thy keys,
The anthem of the destinies!
The minor of Thy loftier strain,
Our hearts shall breathe the old refrain,
 Thy will be done!

A WORD FOR THE HOUR.

The firmament breaks up. In black eclipse
Light after light goes out. One evil star,
Luridly glaring through the smoke of war,
As in the dream of the Apocalypse,
Drags others down. Let us not weakly weep
Nor rashly threaten. Give us grace to keep
Our faith and patience; wherefore should we leap
On one hand into fratricidal fight,
Or, on the other, yield eternal right,
Frame lies of law, and good and ill confound?
What fear we? Safe on freedom's vantage-ground
Our feet are planted: let us there remain
In unrevengeful calm, no means untried
Which truth can sanction, no just claim denied,
The sad spectators of a suicide!
They break the links of Union: shall we light
The fires of hell to weld anew the chain
On that red anvil where each blow is pain?
Draw we not even now a freer breath,

As from our shoulders falls a load of death
Loathsome as that the Tuscan's victim bore
When keen with life to a dead horror bound?
Why take we up the accursed thing again?
Pity, forgive, but urge them back no more
Who, drunk with passion, flaunt disunion's rag
With its vile reptile-blazon. Let us press
The golden cluster on our brave old flag
In closer union, and, if numbering less,
Brighter shall shine the stars which still remain.

16th, 1st month, 1861.

"EIN FESTE BURG IST UNSER GOTT"

(LUTHER'S HYMN.)

WE wait beneath the furnace-blast
  The pangs of transformation;
Not painlessly doth God recast
  And mould anew the nation.
    Hot burns the fire
    Where wrongs expire;
    Nor spares the hand
    That from the land
  Uproots the ancient evil.

The hand-breadth cloud the sages feared
  Its bloody rain is dropping;
The poison plant the fathers spared
  All else is overtopping.
    East, West, South, North,
    It curses the earth;
    All justice dies,
    And fraud and lies
  Live only in its shadow.

What gives the wheat-field blades of steel?
  What points the rebel cannon?
What sets the roaring rabble's heel
  On the old star-spangled pennon?
    What breaks the oath
    Of the men o' the South?
    What whets the knife
    For the Union's life?—
  Hark to the answer: Slavery!

Then waste no blows on lesser foes
  In strife unworthy freemen.
God lifts to-day the veil, and shows
  The features of the demon!
    O North and South,
    Its victims both,
    Can ye not cry,
    "Let slavery die!"
  And union find in freedom?

What though the cast-out spirit tear
  The nation in his going?
We who have shared the guilt must share
  The pang of his o'erthrowing!
    Whate'er the loss,
    Whate'er the cross,
    Shall they complain
    Of present pain
  Who trust in God's hereafter?

For who that leans on His right arm
  Was ever yet forsaken?
What righteous cause can suffer harm
  If He its part has taken?
    Though wild and loud
    And dark the cloud,
    Behind its folds
    His hand upholds
  The calm sky of to-morrow!

Above the maddening cry for blood,
  Above the wild war-drumming,
Let Freedom's voice be heard, with good
  The evil overcoming.
    Give prayer and purse
    To stay the Curse
    Whose wrong we share,
    Whose shame we bear,
  Whose end shall gladden Heaven!

In vain the bells of war shall ring
  Of triumphs and revenges,
While still is spared the evil thing
  That severs and estranges.
    But blest the ear
    That yet shall hear
    The jubilant bell
    That rings the knell
  Of Slavery forever!

Then let the selfish lip be dumb,
  And hushed the breath ot sighing;
Before the joy of peace must come
  The pains of purifying.
    God give us grace
    Each in his place
    To bear his lot,
    And, murmuring not,
  Endure and wait and labor!

TO JOHN C. FREMONT.

THY error, Fremont, simply was to act
A brave man's part, without the statesman's tact,
And, taking counsel but of common sense,

To strike at cause as well as consequence.
O, never yet since Roland wound his horn
At Roncesvalles, has a blast been blown
Far-heard, wide-echoed, startling as thine own,
Heard from the van of freedom's hope forlorn!
It had been safer, doubtless, for the time,
To flatter treason, and avoid offence
To that Dark Power whose underlying crime
Heaves upward its perpetual turbulence.
But, if thine be the fate of all who break
The ground for truth's seed, or forerun their years
Till lost in distance, or with stout hearts make
A lane for freedom through the level spears,
Still take thou courage! God has spoken through thee,
Irrevocable, the mighty words, Be free!
The land shakes with them, and the slave's dull ear
Turns from the rice-swamp stealthily to hear.
Who would recall them now must first arrest
The winds that blow down from the free Northwest,
Ruffling the Gulf; or like a scroll roll back
The Mississippi to its upper springs.
Such words fulfil their prophecy, and lack
But the full time to harden into things.

THE WATCHERS.

BESIDE a stricken field I stood;
On the torn turf, on grass and wood,
Hung heavily the dew of blood.

Still in their fresh mounds lay the slain,
But all the air was quick with pain
And gusty sighs and tearful rain.

Two angels, each with drooping head
And folded wings and noiseless tread,
Watched by that valley of the dead.

The one, with forehead saintly bland
And lips of blessing, not command,
Leaned, weeping, on her olive wand.

The other's brows were scarred and knit,
His restless eyes were watch-fires lit,
His hands for battle-gauntlets fit.

"How long!"—I knew the voice of Peace,—
"Is there no respite?—no release?—
When shall the hopeless quarrel cease?

"O Lord, how long!—One human soul
Is more than any parchment scroll,
Or any flag thy winds unroll.

"What price was Ellsworth's, young and brave?
How weigh the gift that Lyon gave,
Or count the cost of Winthrop's grave?

"O brother! if thine eye can see,
Tell how and when the end shall be,
What hope remains for thee and me."

Then Freedom sternly said: "I shun
No strife nor pang beneath the sun,
When human rights are staked and won.

"I knelt with Ziska's hunted flock,
I watched in Toussaint's cell of rock,
I walked with Sidney to the block.

"The moor of Marston felt my tread,
Through Jersey snows the march I led,
My voice Magenta's charges sped.

"But now, through weary day and night,
I watch a vague and aimless fight
For leave to strike one blow aright.

"On either side my foe they own:
One guards through love his ghastly throne,
And one through fear to reverence grown.

"Why wait we longer, mocked, betrayed,
By open foes, or those afraid
To speed thy coming through my aid?

"Why watch to see who win or fall?—
I shake the dust against them all,
I leave them to their senseless brawl."

"Nay," Peace implored: "yet longer wait;
The doom is near, the stake is great:
God knoweth if it be too late.

"Still wait and watch; the way prepare
Where I with folded wings of prayer
May follow, weaponless and bare."

"Too late!" the stern, sad voice replied,
"Too late!" its mournful echo sighed,
In low lament the answer died.

A rustling as of wings in flight,
An upward gleam of lessening white,
So passed the vision, sound and sight.

But round me, like a silver bell
Rung down the listening sky to tell
Of holy help, a sweet voice fell.

"Still hope and trust," it sang; "the rod
Must fall, the wine-press must be trod,
But all is possible with God!"

TO ENGLISHMEN.

You flung your taunt across the wave;
We bore it as became us,
Well knowing that the fettered slave
Left friendly lips no option save
To pity or to blame us.

You scoffed our plea. "Mere lack of will,
Not lack of power," you told us:
We showed our free-state records; still
You mocked, confounding good and ill,
Slave-haters and slaveholders.

We struck at Slavery; to the verge
Of power and means we checked it;
Lo!—presto, change! its claims you urge,
Send greetings to it o'er the surge,
And comfort and protect it.

But yesterday you scarce could shake,
In slave-abhorring rigor,
Our Northern palms for conscience' sake:
To-day you clasp the hands that ache
With "walloping the nigger!"[41]

O Englishmen!—in hope and creed,
In blood and tongue our brothers!
We too are heirs of Runnymede;
And Shakspeare's fame and Cromwell's deed
Are not alone our mother's.

"Thicker than water," in one rill
Through centuries of story
Our Saxon blood has flowed, and still
We share with you its good and ill,
The shadow and the glory.

Joint heirs and kinfolk, leagues of wave
  Nor length of years can part us:
Your right is ours to shrine and grave,
The common freehold of the brave,
  The gift of saints and martyrs.

Our very sins and follies teach
  Our kindred frail and human:
We carp at faults with bitter speech,
The while for one unshared by each,
  We have a score in common.

We bowed the heart, if not the knee,
  To England's Queen, God bless her!
We praised you when your slaves went free:
We seek to unchain ours. Will ye
  Join hands with the oppressor?

And is it Christian England cheers
  The bruiser, not the bruisèd?
And must she run, despite the tears
And prayers of eighteen hundred years,
  Amuck in Slavery's crusade?

O black disgrace! O shame and loss
  Too deep for tongue to phrase on!
Tear from your flag its holy cross,
And in your van of battle toss
  The pirate's skull-bone blazon!

ASTRÆA AT THE CAPITOL.

ABOLITION OF SLAVERY IN THE DISTRICT OF COLUMBIA, 1862.

When first I saw our banner wave
  Above the nation's council-hall,
  I heard beneath its marble wall
The clanking fetters of the slave!

In the foul market-place I stood,
  And saw the Christian mother sold,
  And childhood with its locks of gold,
Blue-eyed and fair with Saxon blood.

I shut my eyes, I held my breath,
  And, smothering down the wrath and shame
  That set my Northern blood aflame,
Stood silent—where to speak was death.

Beside me gloomed the prison-cell
  Where wasted one in slow decline
  For uttering simple words of mine,
And loving freedom all too well.

The flag that floated from the dome
  Flapped menace in the morning air;
  I stood a perilled stranger where
The human broker made his home.

For crime was virtue: Gown and Sword
  And Law their threefold sanction gave,
  And to the quarry of the slave
Went hawking with our symbol-bird.

On the oppressor's side was power;
  And yet I knew that every wrong,
  However old, however strong,
But waited God's avenging hour.

I knew that truth would crush the lie,—
  Somehow, sometime, the end would be;
  Yet scarcely dared I hope to see
The triumph with my mortal eye.

But now I see it! In the sun
  A free flag floats from yonder dome,
  And at the nation's hearth and home
The justice long delayed is done.

Not as we hoped, in calm of prayer,
  The message of deliverance comes,
  But heralded by roll of drums
On waves of battle-troubled air!—

Midst sounds that madden and appall,
  The song that Bethlehem's shepherds knew!
  The harp of David melting through
The demon-agonies of Saul!

Not as we hoped;—but what are we?
  Above our broken dreams and plans
  God lays, with wiser hand than man's,
The corner-stones of liberty.

I cavil not with Him: the voice
  That freedom's blessed gospel tells
  Is sweet to me as silver bells,
Rejoicing!—yea, I will rejoice!

Dear friends still toiling in the sun,—
  Ye dearer ones who, gone before,
  Are watching from the eternal shore
The slow work by your hands begun,—

Rejoice with me! The chastening rod
  Blossoms with love; the furnace heat
  Grows cool beneath His blessed feet
Whose form is as the Son of God!

Rejoice! Our Marah's bitter springs
  Are sweetened; on our ground of grief
  Rise day by day in strong relief
The prophecies of better things.

Rejoice in hope! The day and night
  Are one with God, and one with them
  Who see by faith the cloudy hem
Of Judgment fringed with Mercy's light!

THE BATTLE AUTUMN OF 1862.

THE flags of war like storm-birds fly,
  The charging trumpets blow;
Yet rolls no thunder in the sky,
  No earthquake strives below.

And, calm and patient, Nature keeps
  Her ancient promise well,
Though o'er her bloom and greenness sweeps
  The battle's breath of hell.

And still she walks in golden hours
  Through harvest-happy farms,
And still she wears her fruits and flowers
  Like jewels on her arms.

What mean the gladness of the plain,
  This joy of eve and morn,
The mirth that shakes the beard of grain
  And yellow locks of corn?

Ah! eyes may well be full of tears,
  And hearts with hate are hot;
But even-paced come round the years,
  And Nature changes not.

She meets with smiles our bitter grief,
  With songs our groans of pain;
She mocks with tint of flower and leaf
  The war-field's crimson stain.

Still, in the cannon's pause, we hear
  Her sweet thanksgiving-psalm;
Too near to God for doubt or fear,
  She shares th' eternal calm.

She knows the seed lies safe below
The fires that blast and burn;
For all the tears of blood we sow
She waits the rich return.

She sees with clearer eye than ours
The good of suffering born,—
The hearts that blossom like her flowers,
And ripen like her corn.

O, give to us, in times like these,
The vision of her eyes;
And make her fields and fruited trees
Our golden prophecies!

O, give to us her finer ear!
Above this stormy din,
We too would hear the bells of cheer
Ring peace and freedom in!

MITHRIDATES AT CHIOS.[42]

Know'st thou, O slave-cursed land!
How, when the Chian's cup of guilt
Was full to overflow, there came
God's justice in the sword of flame
That, red with slaughter to its hilt,
Blazed in the Cappadocian victor's hand?

The heavens are still and far;
But, not unheard of awful Jove,
The sighing of the island slave
Was answered, when the Ægean wave
The keels of Mithridates clove,
And the vines shrivelled in the breath of war.

"Robbers of Chios! hark,"
The victor cried, "to Heaven's decree!
Pluck your last cluster from the vine,
Drain your last cup of Chian wine;
Slaves of your slaves, your doom shall be,
In Colchian mines by Phasis rolling dark."

Then rose the long lament
From the hoar sea-god's dusky caves:
The priestess rent her hair and cried,
"Woe! woe! The gods are sleepless-eyed!"
And, chained and scourged, the slaves of slaves,
The lords of Chios into exile went.

"The gods at last pay well,"
So Hellas sang her taunting song,
"The fisher in his net is caught,
The Chian hath his master bought;"
And isle from isle, with laughter long,
Took up and sped the mocking parable.

Once more the slow, dumb years
Bring their avenging cycle round,
And, more than Hellas taught of old,
Our wiser lesson shall be told,
Of slaves uprising, freedom-crowned,
To break, not wield, the scourge wet with their blood and tears.

THE PROCLAMATION.

Saint Patrick, slave to Milcho of the herds
Of Ballymena, wakened with these words:
"Arise, and flee
Out from the land of bondage, and be free!"

Glad as a soul in pain, who hears from heaven
The angels singing of his sins forgiven,
And, wondering, sees
His prison opening to their golden keys,

He rose a man who laid him down a slave,
Shook from his locks the ashes of the grave,
And outward trod
Into the glorious liberty of God.

He cast the symbols of his shame away;
And, passing where the sleeping Milcho lay,
Though back and limb
Smarted with wrong, he prayed, "God pardon him!"

So went he forth: but in God's time he came
To light on Uilline's hills a holy flame;
And, dying, gave
The land a saint that lost him as a slave.

O dark, sad millions, patiently and dumb
Waiting for God, your hour, at last, has come,
And freedom's song
Breaks the long silence of your night of wrong!

Arise and flee! shake off the vile restraint
Of ages; but, like Ballymena's saint,
The oppressor spare,
Heap only on his head the coals of prayer.

Go forth, like him! like him return again,
To bless the land whereon in bitter pain
Ye toiled at first,
And heal with freedom what your slavery cursed.

ANNIVERSARY POEM.

[Read before the Alumni of the Friends' Yearly Meeting School, at the Annual Meeting at Newport, R. I., 15th 6th Mo., 1863.]

Once more, dear friends, you meet beneath
A clouded sky:
Not yet the sword has found its sheath,
And on the sweet spring airs the breath
Of war floats by.

Yet trouble springs not from the ground,
Nor pain from chance;
The Eternal order circles round,
And wave and storm find mete and bound
In Providence.

Full long our feet the flowery ways
Of peace have trod,
Content with creed and garb and phrase:
A harder path in earlier days
Led up to God.

Too cheaply truths, once purchased dear,
Are made our own;
Too long the world has smiled to hear
Our boast of full corn in the ear
By others sown;

To see us stir the martyr fires
Of long ago,
And wrap our satisfied desires
In the singed mantles that our sires
Have dropped below.

But now the cross our worthies bore
On us is laid;

Profession's quiet sleep is o'er,
And in the scale of truth once more
Our faith is weighed.

The cry of innocent blood at last
Is calling down
An answer in the whirlwind-blast,
The thunder and the shadow cast
From Heaven's dark frown.

The land is red with judgments. Who
Stands guiltless forth ?
Have *we* been faithful as we knew,
To God and to our brother true,
To Heaven and Earth ?

How faint, through din of merchandise
And count of gain,
Have seemed to us the captive's cries !
How far away the tears and sighs
Of souls in pain !

This day the fearful reckoning comes
To each and all ;
We hear amidst our peaceful homes
The summons of the conscript drums,
The bugle's call.

Our path is plain ; the war-net draws
Round us in vain,
While, faithful to the Higher Cause,
We keep our fealty to the laws
Through patient pain.

The levelled gun, the battle-brand,
We may not take ;
But, calmly loyal, we can stand
And suffer with our suffering land
For conscience' sake.

Why ask for ease where all is pain?
Shall *we* alone
Be left to add our gain to gain,
When over Armageddon's plain
The trump is blown?

To suffer well is well to serve;
Safe in our Lord
The rigid lines of law shall curve
To spare us; from our heads shall swerve
Its smiting sword.

And light is mingled with the gloom,
And joy with grief;
Divinest compensations come,
Through thorns of judgment mercies bloom
In sweet relief.

Thanks for our privilege to bless,
By word and deed,
The widow in her keen distress,
The childless and the fatherless,
The hearts that bleed!

For fields of duty, opening wide,
Where all our powers
Are tasked the eager steps to guide
Of millions on a path untried:
THE SLAVE IS OURS!

Ours by traditions dear and old,
Which make the race
Our wards to cherish and uphold,
And cast their freedom in the mould
Of Christian grace.

And we may tread the sick-bed floors
Where strong men pine,
And, down the groaning corridors,

Pour freely from our liberal stores
The oil and wine.

Who murmurs that in these dark days
His lot is cast?
God's hand within the shadow lays
The stones whereon His gates of praise
Shall rise at last.

Turn and o'erturn, O outstretched Hand!
Nor stint, nor stay;
The years have never dropped their sand
On mortal issue vast and grand
As ours to-day.

Already, on the sable ground
Of man's despair
Is Freedom's glorious picture found
With all its dusky hands unbound
Upraised in prayer.

O, small shall seem all sacrifice
And pain and loss,
When God shall wipe the weeping eyes,
For suffering give the victor's prize,
The crown for cross!

AT PORT ROYAL.

The tent-lights glimmer on the land,
The ship-lights on the sea;
The night-wind smooths with drifting sand
Our track on lone Tybee.

At last our grating keels outslide,
Our good boats forward swing;

And while we ride the land-locked tide,
  Our negroes row and sing.

For dear the bondman holds his gifts
  Of music and of song:
The gold that kindly Nature sifts
  Among his sands of wrong;

The power to make his toiling days
  And poor home-comforts please;
The quaint relief of mirth that plays
  With sorrow's minor keys.

Another glow than sunset's fire
  Has filled the West with light,
Where field and garner, barn and byre
  Are blazing through the night.

The land is wild with fear and hate,
  The rout runs mad and fast;
From hand to hand, from gate to gate.
  The flaming brand is passed.

The lurid glow falls strong across
  Dark faces broad with smiles:
Not theirs the terror, hate, and loss
  That fire yon blazing piles.

With oar-strokes timing to their song,
  They weave in simple lays
The pathos of remembered wrong,
  The hope of better days,—

The triumph-note that Miriam sung,
  The joy of uncaged birds:
Softening with Afric's mellow tongue
  Their broken Saxon words.

SONG OF THE NEGRO BOATMEN.

O, praise an' tanks! De Lord he come
  To set de people free;
An' massa tink it day ob doom,
  An' we ob jubilee.
De Lord dat heap de Red-Sea waves
  He jus' as 'trong as den;
He say de word: we las' night slaves;
  To-day, de Lord's freemen.
    De yam will grow, de cotton blow,
      We'll hab de rice an' corn;
    O nebber you fear, if nebber you hear
      De driver blow his horn!

Ole massa on he trabbels gone;
  He leaf de land behind:
De Lord's breff blow him furder on,
  Like corn-shuck in de wind.
We own de hoe, we own de plough,
  We own de hands dat hold;
We sell de pig, we sell de cow,
  But nebber chile be sold.
    De yam will grow, de cotton blow,
      We'll hab de rice an' corn:
    O nebber you fear, if nebber you hear
      De driver blow his horn!

We pray de Lord: he gib us signs
  Dat some day we be free;
De Norf-wind tell it to de pines,
  De wild-duck to de sea;
We tink it when de church-bell ring,
  We dream it in de dream;
De rice-bird mean it when he sing,
  De eagle when he scream.
    De yam will grow, de cotton blow,
      We'll hab de rice an' corn:

O nebber you fear, if nebber you hear
De driver blow his horn!

We know de promise nebber fail,
An' nebber lie de word;
So like de 'postles in de jail,
We waited for de Lord:
An' now he open ebery door,
An' trow away de key;
He tink we lub him so before,
We lub him better free.
De yam will grow, de cotton blow,
He'll gib de rice an' corn:
O nebber you fear, if nebber you hear
De driver blow his horn!

So sing our dusky gondoliers;
And with a secret pain,
And smiles that seem akin to tears,
We hear the wild refrain.

We dare not share the negro's trust,
Nor yet his hope deny;
We only know that God is just,
And every wrong shall die.

Rude seems the song; each swarthy face,
Flame-lighted, ruder still:
We start to think that hapless race
Must shape our good or ill;

That laws of changless justice bind
Oppressor with oppressed;
And, close as sin and suffering joined,
We march to Fate abreast.

Sing on, poor hearts! your chant shall be
Our sign of blight or bloom,—
The Vala-song of Liberty,
Or death-rune of our doom!

BARBARA FRIETCHIE.

Up from the meadows rich with corn,
Clear in the cool September morn,

The clustered spires of Frederick stand
Green-walled by the hills of Maryland.

Round about them orchards sweep,
Apple- and peach-tree fruited deep,

Fair as a garden of the Lord
To the eyes of the famished rebel horde,

On that pleasant morn of the early fall
When Lee marched over the mountain-wall,—

Over the mountains winding down,
Horse and foot, into Frederick town.

Forty flags with their silver stars,
Forty flags with their crimson bars,

Flapped in the morning wind: the sun
Of noon looked down, and saw not one.

Up rose old Barbara Frietchie then,
Bowed with her fourscore years and ten;

Bravest of all in Frederick town,
She took up the flag the men hauled down;

In her attic-window the staff she set,
To show that one heart was loyal yet.

Up the street came the rebel tread,
Stonewall Jackson riding ahead.

Under his slouched hat left and right
He glanced; the old flag met his sight.

"Halt!"—the dust-brown ranks stood fast.
"Fire!"—out blazed the rifle-blast.

It shivered the window, pane and sash;
It rent the banner with seam and gash.

Quick, as it fell, from the broken staff
Dame Barbara snatched the silken scarf;

She leaned far out on the window-sill,
And shook it forth with a royal will.

"Shoot, if you must, this old gray head,
But spare your country's flag," she said.

A shade of sadness, a blush of shame,
Over the face of the leader came;

The nobler nature within him stirred
To life at that woman's deed and word:

"Who touches a hair of yon gray head
Dies like a dog! March on!" he said.

All day long through Frederick street
Sounded the tread of marching feet:

All day long that free flag tost
Over the heads of the rebel host.

Ever its torn folds rose and fell
On the loyal winds that loved it well;

And through the hill-gaps sunset light
Shone over it with a warm good-night.

Barbara Frietchie's work is o'er,
And the Rebel rides on his raids no more.

Honor to her! and let a tear
Fall, for her sake, on Stonewall's bier.

Over Barbara Frietchie's grave
Flag of Freedom and Union, wave!

Peace and order and beauty draw
Round thy symbol of light and law;

And ever the stars above look down
On thy stars below in Frederick town!

HOME BALLADS.

HOME BALLADS.

COBBLER KEEZAR'S VISION.[43]

THE beaver cut his timber
  With patient teeth that day,
The minks were fish-wards, and the crows
  Surveyors of highway,—

When Keezar sat on the hill-side
  Upon his cobbler's form,
With a pan of coals on either hand
  To keep his waxed-ends warm.

And there, in the golden weather,
  He stitched and hammered and sung;
In the brook he moistened his leather,
  In the pewter mug his tongue.

Well knew the tough old Teuton
  Who brewed the stoutest ale,
And he paid the good-wife's reckoning
  In the coin of song and tale.

The songs they still are singing
  Who dress the hills of vine,
The tales that haunt the Brocken
  And whisper down the Rhine.

Woodsy and wild and lonesome,
  The swift stream wound away,
Through birches and scarlet maples
  Flashing in foam and spray,—

Down on the sharp-horned ledges
  Plunging in steep cascade,
Tossing its white-maned waters
  Against the hemlock's shade.

Woodsy and wild and lonesome,
  East and west and north and south;
Only the village of fishers
  Down at the river's mouth;

Only here and there a clearing,
  With its farm-house rude and new,
And tree-stumps, swart as Indians,
  Where the scanty harvest grew.

No shout of home-bound reapers,
  No vintage-song he heard,
And on the green no dancing feet
  The merry violin stirred.

"Why should folk be glum," said Keezar,
  "When Nature herself is glad,
And the painted woods are laughing
  At the faces so sour and sad?"

Small heed had the careless cobbler
  What sorrow of heart was theirs
Who travailed in pain with the births of God,
  And planted a state with prayers,—

Hunting of witches and warlocks,
  Smiting the heathen horde,—
One hand on the mason's trowel,
  And one on the soldier's sword!

But give him his ale and cider,
  Give him his pipe and song,
Little he cared for church or state,
  Or the balance of right and wrong.

"'Tis work, work, work," he muttered,—
  "And for rest a snuffle of psalms!"
He smote on his leathern apron
  With his brown and waxen palms.

"O for the purple harvests
  Of the days when I was young!
For the merry grape-stained maidens,
  And the pleasant songs they sung!

"O for the breath of vineyards,
  Of apples and nuts and wine!
For an oar to row and a breeze to blow
  Down the grand old river Rhine!"

A tear in his blue eye glistened,
  And dropped on his beard so gray.
"Old, old am I," said Keezar,
  "And the Rhine flows far away!"

But a cunning man was the cobbler;
  He could call the birds from the trees,
Charm the black snake out of the ledges,
  And bring back the swarming bees.

All the virtues of herbs and metals,
  All the lore of the woods, he knew,
And the arts of the Old World mingled
  With the marvels of the New.

Well he knew the tricks of magic,
  And the lapstone on his knee
Had the gift of the Mormon's goggles
  Or the stone of Doctor Dee.

For the mighty master Agrippa
  Wrought it with spell and rhyme
From a fragment of mystic moonstone
  In the tower of Nettesheim.

To a cobbler Minnesinger
  The marvellous stone gave he,—
And he gave it, in turn, to Keezar,
  Who brought it over the sea.

He held up that mystic lapstone,
  He held it up like a lens,
And he counted the long years coming
  By twenties and by tens.

"One hundred years," quoth Keezar,
  "And fifty have I told:
Now open the new before me,
  And shut me out the old!"

Like a cloud of mist, the blackness
  Rolled from the magic stone,
And a marvellous picture mingled
  The unknown and the known.

Still ran the stream to the river,
  And river and ocean joined;
And there were the bluffs and the blue sea-line,
  And cold north hills behind.

But the mighty forest was broken
  By many a steepled town,
By many a white-walled farm-house,
  And many a garner brown.

Turning a score of mill-wheels,
  The stream no more ran free;
White sails on the winding river,
  White sails on the far-off sea.

Below in the noisy village
  The flags were floating gay,
And shone on a thousand faces
  The light of a holiday.

Swiftly the rival ploughmen
  Turned the brown earth from their shares;
Here were the farmer's treasures,
  There were the craftsman's wares.

Golden the good-wife's butter,
  Ruby her currant-wine;
Grand were the strutting turkeys,
  Fat were the beeves and swine.

Yellow and red were the apples,
  And the ripe pears russet-brown,
And the peaches had stolen blushes
  From the girls who shook them down.

And with blooms of hill and wild-wood,
  That shame the toil of art,
Mingled the gorgeous blossoms
  Of the garden's tropic heart.

" What is it I see ? " said Keezar:
  " Am I here, or am I there ?
Is it a fête at Bingen ?
  Do I look on Frankfort fair ?

" But where are the clowns and puppets,
  And imps with horns and tail ?
And where are the Rhenish flagons ?
  And where is the foaming ale ?

" Strange things, I know, will happen,—
  Strange things the Lord permits;
But that droughty folk should be jolly
  Puzzles my poor old wits.

" Here are smiling manly faces,
  And the maiden's step is gay;
Nor sad by thinking, nor mad by drinking,
  Nor mopes, nor fools, are they.

"Here's pleasure without regretting,
  And good without abuse,
The holiday and the bridal
  Of beauty and of use.

"Here's a priest and there is a Quaker,—
  Do the cat and the dog agree?
Have they burned the stocks for oven-wood?
  Have they cut down the gallows-tree?

"Would the old folk know their children?
  Would they own the graceless town,
With never a ranter to worry
  And never a witch to drown?"

Loud laughed the cobbler Keezar,
  Laughed like a school-boy gay;
Tossing his arms above him,
  The lapstone rolled away.

It rolled down the rugged hill-side,
  It spun like a wheel bewitched,
It plunged through the leaning willows,
  And into the river pitched.

There, in the deep, dark water,
  The magic stone lies still,
Under the leaning willows
  In the shadow of the hill.

But oft the idle fisher
  Sits on the shadowy bank,
And his dreams make marvellous pictures
  Where the wizard's lapstone sank.

And still, in the summer twilights,
  When the river seems to run
Out from the inner glory,
  Warm with the melted sun,

The weary mill-girl lingers
  Beside the charmèd stream,
And the sky and the golden water
  Shape and color her dream.

Fair wave the sunset gardens,
  The rosy signals fly;
Her homestead beckons from the cloud,
  And love goes sailing by!

AMY WENTWORTH.

TO W. B.

As they who watch by sick-beds find relief
Unwittingly from the great stress of grief
And anxious care in fantasies outwrought
From the hearth's embers flickering low, or caught
From whispering wind, or tread of passing feet,
Or vagrant memory calling up some sweet
Snatch of old song or romance, whence or why
They scarcely know or ask,—so, thou and I,
Nursed in the faith that Truth alone is strong
In the endurance which outwearies Wrong,
With meek persistence baffling brutal force,
And trusting God against the universe,—
We, doomed to watch a strife we may not share
With other weapons than the patriot's prayer,
Yet owning, with full hearts and moistened eyes,
The awful beauty of self-sacrifice,
And wrung by keenest sympathy for all
Who give their loved ones for the living wall
'Twixt law and treason,—in this evil day
May haply find, through automatic play
Of pen and pencil, solace to our pain,
And hearten others with the strength we gain.

I know it has been said our times require
No play of art, nor dalliance with the lyre,
No weak essay with Fancy's chloroform
To calm the hot, mad pulses of the storm,
But the stern war-blast rather, such as sets
The battle's teeth of serried bayonets,
And pictures grim as Vernet's. Yet with these
Some softer tints may blend, and milder keys
Relieve the storm-stunned ear. Let us keep sweet,
If so we may, our hearts, even while we eat
The bitter harvest of our own device
And half a century's moral cowardice.
As Nürnberg sang while Wittenberg defied,
And Kranach painted by his Luther's side,
And through the war-march of the Puritan
The silver stream of Marvell's music ran,
So let the household melodies be sung,
The pleasant pictures on the wall be hung,—
So let us hold against the hosts of night
And slavery all our vantage-ground of light.
Let Treason boast its savagery, and shake
From its flag-folds its symbol rattlesnake,
Nurse its fine arts, lay human skins in tan,
And carve its pipe-bowls from the bones of man,
And make the tale of Fijian banquets dull
By drinking whiskey from a loyal skull,—
But let us guard, till this sad war shall cease,
(God grant it soon!) the graceful arts of peace:
No foes are conquered who the victors teach
Their vandal manners and barbaric speech.

And while, with hearts of thankfulness, we bear
Of the great common burden our full share,
Let none upbraid us that the waves entice
Thy sea-dipped pencil, or some quaint device,
Rhythmic and sweet, beguiles my pen away
From the sharp strifes and sorrows of to-day.
Thus, while the east-wind keen from Labrador
Sings in the leafless elms, and from the shore

Of the great sea comes the monotonous roar
Of the long-breaking surf, and all the sky
Is gray with cloud, home-bound and dull, I try
To time a simple legend to the sounds
Of winds in the woods, and waves on pebbled
bounds,—
A song for oars to chime with, such as might
Be sung by tired sea-painters, who at night
Look from their hemlock camps, by quiet cove
Or beach, moon-lighted, on the waves they love.
(So hast thou looked, when level sunset lay
On the calm bosom of some Eastern bay,
And all the spray-moist rocks and waves that rolled
Up the white sand-slopes flashed with ruddy gold.)
Something it has—a flavor of the sea,
And the sea's freedom—which reminds of thee.
Its faded picture, dimly smiling down
From the blurred fresco of the ancient town,
I have not touched with warmer tints in vain,
If, in this dark, sad year, it steals one thought
from pain.

HER fingers shame the ivory keys
They dance so light along;
The bloom upon her parted lips
Is sweeter than the song.

O perfumed suitor, spare thy smiles!
Her thoughts are not of thee;
She better loves the salted wind,
The voices of the sea.

Her heart is like an outbound ship
That at its anchor swings;
The murmur of the stranded shell
Is in the song she sings.

She sings, and, smiling, hears her praise,
  But dreams the while of one
Who watches from his sea-blown deck
  The icebergs in the sun.

She questions all the winds that blow,
  And every fog-wreath dim,
And bids the sea-birds flying north
  Bear messages to him.

She speeds them with the thanks of men
  He perilled life to save,
And grateful prayers like holy oil
  To smooth for him the wave.

Brown Viking of the fishing-smack!
  Fair toast of all the town!—
The skipper's jerkin ill beseems
  The lady's silken gown!

But ne'er shall Amy Wentworth wear
  For him the blush of shame
Who dares to set his manly gifts
  Against her ancient name.

The stream is brightest at its spring,
  And blood is not like wine;
Nor honored less than he who heirs
  Is he who founds a line.

Full lightly shall the prize be won,
  If love be Fortune's spur;
And never maiden stoops to him
  Who lifts himself to her.

Her home is brave in Jaffrey Street,
  With stately stairways worn
By feet of old Colonial knights
  And ladies gentle-born.

Still green about its ample porch
  The English ivy twines,
Trained back to show in English oak
  The herald's carven signs.

And on her, from the wainscot old,
  Ancestral faces frown,—
And this has worn the soldier's sword,
  And that the judge's gown.

But, strong of will and proud as they,
  She walks the gallery floor
As if she trod her sailor's deck
  By stormy Labrador!

The sweetbrier blooms on Kittery-side,
  And green are Elliot's bowers;
Her garden is the pebbled beach,
  The mosses are her flowers.

She looks across the harbor-bar
  To see the white gulls fly;
His greeting from the Northern sea
  Is in their clanging cry.

She hums a song, and dreams that he,
  As in its romance old,
Shall homeward ride with silken sails
  And masts of beaten gold!

O rank is good, and gold is fair,
  And high and low mate ill;
But love has never known a law
  Beyond its own sweet will!

THE COUNTESS.

TO E. W.

I KNOW not, Time and Space so intervene,
Whether, still waiting with a trust serene,
Thou bearest up thy fourscore years and ten,
Or, called at last, art now Heaven's citizen;
But, here or there, a pleasant thought of thee,
Like an old friend, all day has been with me.
The shy, still boy, for whom thy kindly hand
Smoothed his hard pathway to the wonder-land
Of thought and fancy, in gray manhood yet
Keeps green the memory of his early debt.
To-day, when truth and falsehood speak their words
Through hot-lipped cannon and the teeth of swords,
Listening with quickened heart and ear intent
To each sharp clause of that stern argument,
I still can hear at times a softer note
Of the old pastoral music round me float,
While through the hot gleam of our civil strife
Looms the green mirage of a simpler life.
As, at his alien post, the sentinel
Drops the old bucket in the homestead well,
And hears old voices in the winds that toss
Above his head the live-oak's beard of moss,
So, in our trial-time, and under skies
Shadowed by swords like Islam's paradise,
I wait and watch, and let my fancy stray
To milder scenes and youth's Arcadian day;
And howsoe'er the pencil dipped in dreams
Shades the brown woods or tints the sunset streams,
The country doctor in the foreground seems,
Whose ancient sulky down the village lanes
Dragged, like a war-car, captive ills and pains.
I could not paint the scenery of my song,
Mindless of one who looked thereon so long·

Who, night and day, on duty's lonely round,
Made friends o' the woods and rocks, and knew
the sound
Of each small brook, and what the hill-side trees
Said to the winds that touched their leafy keys;
Who saw so keenly and so well could paint
The village-folk, with all their humors quaint,—
The parson ambling on his wall-eyed roan,
Grave and erect, with white hair backward blown;
The tough old boatman, half amphibious grown;
The muttering witch-wife of the gossip's tale,
And the loud straggler levying his black-mail,—
Old customs, habits, superstitions, fears,
All that lies buried under fifty years.
To thee, as is most fit, I bring my lay,
And, grateful, own the debt I cannot pay.

OVER the wooded northern ridge,
Between its houses brown,
To the dark tunnel of the bridge
The street comes straggling down.

You catch a glimpse through birch and pine
Of gable, roof, and porch,
The tavern with its swinging sign,
The sharp horn of the church.

The river's steel-blue crescent curves
To meet, in ebb and flow,
The single broken wharf that serves
For sloop and gundelow.

With salt sea-scents along its shores
The heavy hay-boats crawl,
The long antennæ of their oars
In lazy rise and fall.

Along the gray abutment's wall
The idle shad-net dries;
The toll-man in his cobbler's stall
Sits smoking with closed eyes.

You hear the pier's low undertone
Of waves that chafe and gnaw;
You start,—a skipper's horn is blown
To raise the creaking draw.

At times a blacksmith's anvil sounds
With slow and sluggard beat,
Or stage-coach on its dusty rounds
Wakes up the staring street.

A place for idle eyes and ears,
A cobwebbed nook of dreams;
Left by the stream whose waves are years
The stranded village seems.

And there, like other moss and rust,
The native dweller clings,
And keeps, in uninquiring trust,
The old, dull round of things.

The fisher drops his patient lines,
The farmer sows his grain,
Content to hear the murmuring pines
Instead of railroad-train.

Go where, along the tangled steep
That slopes against the west,
The hamlet's buried idlers sleep
In still profounder rest.

Throw back the locust's flowery plume,
The birch's pale-green scarf,
And break the web of brier and bloom
From name and epitaph.

A simple muster-roll of death,
  Of pomp and romance shorn,
The dry, old names that common breath
  Has cheapened and outworn.

Yet pause by one low mound, and part
  The wild vines o'er it laced,
And read the words by rustic art
  Upon its headstone traced.

Haply yon white-haired villager
  Of fourscore years can say
What means the noble name of her
  Who sleeps with common clay.

An exile from the Gascon land
  Found refuge here and rest,
And loved, of all the village band,
  Its fairest and its best.

He knelt with her on Sabbath morn,
  He worshipped through her eyes,
And on the pride that doubts and scorns
  Stole in her faith's surprise.

Her simple daily life he saw
  By homeliest duties tried,
In all things by an untaught law
  Of fitness justified.

For her his rank aside he laid;
  He took the hue and tone
Of lowly life and toil, and made
  Her simple ways his own.

Yet still, in gay and careless ease,
  To harvest-field or dance
He brought the gentle courtesies,
  The nameless grace of France.

And she who taught him love not less
From him she loved in turn
Caught in her sweet unconsciousness
What love is quick to learn.

Each grew to each in pleased accord,
Nor knew the gazing town
If she looked upward to her lord
Or he to her looked down.

How sweet, when summer's day was o'er,
His violin's mirth and wail,
The walk on pleasant Newbury's shore,
The river's moonlit sail!

Ah! life is brief, though love be long;
The altar and the bier,
The burial hymn and bridal song,
Were both in one short year!

Her rest is quiet on the hill,
Beneath the locust's bloom;
Far off her lover sleeps as still
Within his scutcheoned tomb.

The Gascon lord, the village maid,
In death still clasp their hands;
The love that levels rank and grade
Unites their severed lands.

What matter whose the hill-side grave,
Or whose the blazoned stone?
Forever to her western wave
Shall whisper blue Garonne!

O Love!—so hallowing every soil
That gives thy sweet flower room,
Wherever, nursed by ease or toil,
The human heart takes bloom!—

Plant of lost Eden, from the sod
  Of sinful earth unriven,
White blossom of the trees of God
  Dropped down to us from heaven !—

This tangled waste of mound and stone
  Is holy for thy sake ;
A sweetness which is all thy own
  Breathes out from fern and brake.

And while ancestral pride shall twine
  The Gascon's tomb with flowers,
Fall sweetly here, O song of mine,
  With summer's bloom and showers !

And let the lines that severed seem
  Unite again in thee,
As western wave and Gallic stream
  Are mingled in one sea !

OCCASIONAL POEMS.

OCCASIONAL POEMS.

NAPLES.—1860.

INSCRIBED TO ROBERT C. WATERSTON, OF BOSTON.

I GIVE thee joy!—I know to thee
The dearest spot on earth must be
Where sleeps thy loved one by the summer sea;

Where, near her sweetest poet's tomb,
The land of Virgil gave thee room
To lay thy flower with her perpetual bloom.

I know that when the sky shut down
Behind thee on the gleaming town,
On Baiæ's baths and Posilippo's crown;

And, through thy tears, the mocking day
Burned Ischia's mountain lines away,
And Capri melted in its sunny bay,—

Through thy great farewell sorrow shot
The sharp pang of a bitter thought
That slaves must tread around that holy spot.

Thou knewest not the land was blest
In giving thy beloved rest,
Holding the fond hope closer to her breast

That every sweet and saintly grave
Was freedom's prophecy, and gave
The pledge of Heaven to sanctify and save.

That pledge is answered. To thy ear
The unchained city sends its cheer,
And, tuned to joy, the muffled bells of fear

Ring Victor in. The land sits free
And happy by the summer sea,
And Bourbon Naples now is Italy!

She smiles above her broken chain
The languid smile that follows pain,
Stretching her cramped limbs to the sun again.

O, joy for all, who hear her call
From Camaldoli's convent-wall
And Elmo's towers to freedom's carnival!

A new life breathes among her vines
And olives, like the breath of pines
Blown downward from the breezy Apennines.

Lean, O my friend, to meet that breath,
Rejoice as one who witnesseth
Beauty from ashes rise, and life from death!

Thy sorrow shall no more be pain,
Its tears shall fall in sunlit rain,
Writing the grave with flowers: "Arisen again!"

THE SUMMONS.

My ear is full of summer sounds,
Of summer sights my languid eye;
Beyond the dusty village bounds
I loiter in my daily rounds,
And in the noon-time shadows lie.

I hear the wild bee wind his horn,
 The bird swings on the ripened wheat,
The long green lances of the corn
Are tilting in the winds of morn,
 The locust shrills his song of heat.

Another sound my spirit hears,
 A deeper sound that drowns them all,—
A voice of pleading choked with tears,
The call of human hopes and fears,
 The Macedonian cry to Paul!

The storm-bell rings, the trumpet blows;
 I know the word and countersign;
Wherever Freedom's vanguard goes,
Where stand or fall her friends or foes,
 I know the place that should be mine.

Shamed be the hands that idly fold,
 And lips that woo the reed's accord,
When laggard Time the hour has tolled
For true with false and new with old
 To fight the battles of the Lord!

O brothers! blest by partial Fate
 With power to match the will and deed,
To him your summons comes too late
Who sinks beneath his armor's weight,
 And has no answer but God-speed!

THE WAITING.

I WAIT and watch: before my eyes
 Methinks the night grows thin and gray;
I wait and watch the eastern skies

To see the golden spears uprise
  Beneath the oriflamme of day!

Like one whose limbs are bound in trance
  I hear the day-sounds swell and grow,
And see across the twilight glance,
Troop after troop, in swift advance,
  The shining ones with plumes of snow!

I know the errand of their feet,
  I know what mighty work is theirs;
I can but lift up hands unmeet,
The threshing-floors of God to beat,
  And speed them with unworthy prayers.

I will not dream in vain despair
  The steps of progress wait for me:
The puny leverage of a hair
The planet's impulse well may spare,
  A drop of dew the tided sea.

The loss, if loss there be, is mine,
  And yet not mine if understood;
For one shall grasp and one resign,
One drink life's rue, and one its wine,
  And God shall make the balance good.

O power to do! O baffled will!
  O prayer and action! ye are one
Who may not strive, may yet fulfil
The harder task of standing still,
  And good but wished with God is done!

MOUNTAIN PICTURES.

I.

FRANCONIA FROM THE PEMIGEWASSET.

ONCE more, O Mountains of the North, unveil
  Your brows, and lay your cloudy mantles by!
And once more, ere the eyes that seek ye fail,
  Uplift against the blue walls of the sky
Your mighty shapes, and let the sunshine weave
  Its golden net-work in your belting woods,
  Smile down in rainbows from your falling floods,
And on your kingly brows at morn and eve
  Set crowns of fire! So shall my soul receive
Haply the secret of your calm and strength,
  Your unforgotten beauty interfuse
  My common life, your glorious shapes and hues
  And sun-dropped splendors at my bidding come,
  Loom vast through dreams, and stretch in billowy length
From the sea-level of my lowland home!

They rise before me! Last night's thunder-gust
Roared not in vain: for where its lightnings thrust
Their tongues of fire, the great peaks seem so near,
Burned clean of mist, so starkly bold and clear,
I almost pause the wind in the pines to hear,
The loose rock's fall, the steps of browsing deer.
The clouds that shattered on yon slide-worn walls
  And splintered on the rocks their spears of rain
Have set in play a thousand waterfalls,
Making the dusk and silence of the woods
Glad with the laughter of the chasing floods,
And luminous with blown spray and silver gleams,
While, in the vales below, the dry-lipped streams
  Sing to the freshened meadow-lands again.

So, let me hope, the battle-storm that beats
 The land with hail and fire may pass away
 With its spent thunders at the break of day,
Like last night's clouds, and leave, as it retreats,
 A greener earth and fairer sky behind,
 Blown crystal-clear by Freedom's Northern wind!

II.

MONADNOCK FROM WACHUSET.

I WOULD I were a painter, for the sake
 Of a sweet picture, and of her who led,
 A fitting guide, with reverential tread,
Into that mountain mystery. First a lake
 Tinted with sunset; next the wavy lines
  Of far receding hills; and yet more far,
 Monadnock lifting from his night of pines
  His rosy forehead to the evening star.
Beside us, purple-zoned, Wachuset laid
His head against the West, whose warm light made
  His aureole; and o'er him, sharp and clear,
Like a shaft of lightning in mid-launching stayed,
 A single level cloud-line, shone upon
 By the fierce glances of the sunken sun,
  Menaced the darkness with its golden spear!

So twilight deepened round us. Still and black
The great woods climbed the mountain at our back;
And on their skirts, where yet the lingering day
On the shorn greenness of the clearing lay,
 The brown old farm-house like a bird's nest hung.
With home-life sounds the desert air was stirred:
The bleat of sheep along the hill we heard,
The bucket plashing in the cool, sweet well,
The pasture-bars that clattered as they fell;
Dogs barked, fowls fluttered, cattle lowed; the gate

Of the barn-yard creaked beneath the merry weight
Of sun-brown children, listening, while they swung,
The welcome sound of supper-call to hear;
And down the shadowy lane, in tinklings clear,
The pastoral curfew of the cow-bell rung.
Thus soothed and pleased, our backward path we took,
Praising the farmer's home. He only spake,
Looking into the sunset o'er the lake,
Like one to whom the far-off is most near:
"Yes, most folks think it has a pleasant look;
I love it for my good old mother's sake,
Who lived and died here in the peace of God!"
The lesson of his words we pondered o'er,
As silently we turned the eastern flank
Of the mountain, where its shadow deepest sank,
Doubling the night along our rugged road:
We felt that man was more than his abode,—
The inward life than Nature's raiment more;
And the warm sky, the sundown-tinted hill,
The forest and the lake, seemed dwarfed and dim
Before the saintly soul, whose human will
Meekly in the Eternal footsteps trod,
Making her homely toil and household ways
An earthly echo of the song of praise
Swelling from angel lips and harps of seraphim

OUR RIVER.

FOR A SUMMER FESTIVAL AT "THE LAURELS" ON THE MERRIMACK.

Once more on yonder laurelled height
The summer flowers have budded;
Once more with summer's golden light

The vales of home are flooded;
And once more, by the grace of Him
Of every good the Giver,
We sing upon its wooded rim
The praises of our river:

Its pines above, its waves below,
The west wind down it blowing,
As fair as when the young Brissot
Beheld it seaward flowing,—
And bore its memory o'er the deep,
To soothe a martyr's sadness,
And fresco, in his troubled sleep,
His prison-walls with gladness.

We know the world is rich with streams
Renowned in song and story,
Whose music murmurs through our dreams
Of human love and glory:
We know that Arno's banks are fair,
And Rhine has castled shadows,
And, poet-tuned, the Doon and Ayr
Go singing down their meadows.

But while, unpictured and unsung
By painter or by poet,
Our river waits the tuneful tongue
And cunning hand to show it,—
We only know the fond skies lean
Above it, warm with blessing,
And the sweet soul of our Undine
Awakes to our caressing.

No fickle Sun-God holds the flocks
That graze its shores in keeping;
No icy kiss of Dian mocks
The youth beside it sleeping:
Our Christian river loveth most
The beautiful and human;

The heathen streams of Naiads boast,
  But ours of man and woman.

The miner in his cabin hears
  The ripple we are hearing;
It whispers soft to homesick ears
  Around the settler's clearing:
In Sacramento's vales of corn,
  Or Santee's bloom of cotton,
Our river by its valley-born
  Was never yet forgotten.

The drum rolls loud,—the bugle fills
  The summer air with clangor;
The war-storm shakes the solid hills
  Beneath its tread of anger:
Young eyes that last year smiled in ours
  Now point the rifle's barrel,
And hands then stained with fruits and flowers
  Bear redder stains of quarrel.

But blue skies smile, and flowers bloom on,
  And rivers still keep flowing,—
The dear God still his rain and sun
  On good and ill bestowing.
His pine-trees whisper, "Trust and wait!"
  His flowers are prophesying
That all we dread of change or fate
  His love is underlying.

And thou, O Mountain-born!—no more
  We ask the wise Allotter
Than for the firmness of thy shore,
  The calmness of thy water,
The cheerful lights that overlay
  Thy rugged slopes with beauty,
To match our spirits to our day
  And make a joy of duty.

ANDREW RYKMAN'S PRAYER.

ANDREW RYKMAN's dead and gone:
You can see his leaning slate
In the graveyard, and thereon
Read his name and date.

"*Trust is truer than our fears,*"
Runs the legend through the moss,
"*Gain is not in added years,*
Nor in death is loss."

Still the feet that thither trod,
All the friendly eyes are dim;
Only Nature, now, and God
Have a care for him.

There the dews of quiet fall,
Singing birds and soft winds stray;
Shall the tender Heart of all
Be less kind than they?

What he was and what he is
They who ask may haply find,
If they read this prayer of his
Which he left behind.

Pardon, Lord, the lips that dare
Shape in words a mortal's prayer!
Prayer, that, when my day is done,
And I see its setting sun,
Shorn and beamless, cold and dim,
Sink beneath the horizon's rim,—
When this ball of rock and clay

Crumbles from my feet away,
And the solid shores of sense
Melt into the vague immense,
Father! I may come to Thee
Even with the beggar's plea,
As the poorest of Thy poor,
With my needs, and nothing more.

Not as one who seeks his home
With a step assured I come;
Still behind the tread I hear
Of my life-companion, Fear;
Still a shadow deep and vast
From my westering feet is cast,
Wavering, doubtful, undefined,
Never shapen nor outlined:
From myself the fear has grown,
And the shadow is my own.
Yet, O Lord, through all a sense
Of Thy tender providence
Stays my failing heart on Thee,
And confirms the feeble knee;
And, at times, my worn feet press
Spaces of cool quietness,
Lilied whiteness shone upon
Not by light of moon or sun.
Hours there be of inmost calm,
Broken but by grateful psalm,
When I love Thee more than fear Thee,
And Thy blessed Christ seems near me,
With forgiving look, as when
He beheld the Magdalen.
Well I know that all things move
To the spheral rhythm of love,—
That to Thee, O Lord of all!
Nothing can of chance befall:
Child and seraph, mote and star,
Well Thou knowest what we are;
Through Thy vast creative plan

Looking, from the worm to man,
There is pity in Thine eyes,
But no hatred nor surprise.
Not in blind caprice of will,
Not in cunning sleight of skill,
Not for show of power, was wrought
Nature's marvel in Thy thought.
Never careless hand and vain
Smites these chords of joy and pain;
No immortal selfishness
Plays the game of curse and bless:
Heaven and earth are witnesses
That Thy glory goodness is.
Not for sport of mind and force
Hast Thou made Thy universe,
But as atmosphere and zone
Of Thy loving heart alone.
Man, who walketh in a show,
Sees before him, to and fro,
Shadow and illusion go;
All things flow and fluctuate,
Now contract and now dilate.
In the welter of this sea,
Nothing stable is but Thee;
In this whirl of swooning trance,
Thou alone art permanence;
All without Thee only seems,
All beside is choice of dreams.
Never yet in darkest mood
Doubted I that Thou wast good,
Nor mistook my will for fate,
Pain of sin for heavenly hate,—
Never dreamed the gates of pearl
Rise from out the burning marl,
Or that good can only live
Of the bad conservative,
And through counterpoise of hell
Heaven alone be possible.

For myself alone I doubt;
All is well, I know, without;
I alone the beauty mar,
I alone the music jar.
Yet, with hands by evil stained,
And an ear by discord pained,
I am groping for the keys
Of the heavenly harmonies;
Still within my heart I bear
Love for all things good and fair.
Hands of want or souls in pain
Have not sought my door in vain;
I have kept my fealty good
To the human brotherhood;
Scarcely have I asked in prayer
That which others might not share.
I, who hear with secret shame
Praise that paineth more than blame,
Rich alone in favors lent,
Virtuous by accident,
Doubtful where I fain would rest,
Frailest where I seem the best,
Only strong for lack of test,—
What am I, that I should press
Special pleas of selfishness,
Coolly mounting into heaven
On my neighbor unforgiven?
Ne'er to me, howe'er disguised,
Comes a saint unrecognized;
Never fails my heart to greet
Noble deed with warmer beat;
Halt and maimed, I own not less
All the grace of holiness;
Nor, through shame or self-distrust,
Less I love the pure and just.
Lord, forgive these words of mine:
What have I that is not Thine?—
Whatsoe'er I fain would boast
Needs Thy pitying pardon most.

Thou, O Elder Brother! who
In Thy flesh our trial knew,
Thou, who hast been touched by these
Our most sad infirmities,
Thou alone the gulf canst span
In the dual heart of man,
And between the soul and sense
Reconcile all difference,
Change the dream of me and mine
For the truth of Thee and Thine,
And, through chaos, doubt, and strife,
Interfuse Thy calm of life.
Haply, thus by Thee renewed,
In Thy borrowed goodness good,
Some sweet morning yet in God's
Dim, æonian periods,
Joyful I shall wake to see
Those I love who rest in Thee,
And to them in Thee allied
Shall my soul be satisfied.

Scarcely Hope hath shaped for me
What the future life may be.
Other lips may well be bold;
Like the publican of old,
I can only urge the plea,
"Lord, be merciful to me!"
Nothing of desert I claim,
Unto me belongeth shame.
Not for me the crowns of gold,
Palms, and harpings manifold;
Not for erring eye and feet
Jasper wall and golden street.
What Thou wilt, O Father, give!
All is gain that I receive.
If my voice I may not raise
In the elders' song of praise,
If I may not, sin-defiled,
Claim my birthright as a child,

Suffer it that I to Thee
As an hired servant be;
Let the lowliest task be mine,
Grateful, so the work be Thine;
Let me find the humblest place
In the shadow of Thy grace:
Blest to me were any spot
Where temptation whispers not.
If there be some weaker one,
Give me strength to help him on;
If a blinder soul there be,
Let me guide him nearer Thee.
Make my mortal dreams come true
With the work I fain would do;
Clothe with life the weak intent,
Let me be the thing I meant;
Let me find in Thy employ
Peace that dearer is than joy;
Out of self to love be led
And to heaven acclimated,
Until all things sweet and good
Seem my natural habitude.

So we read the prayer of him
Who, with John of Labadie,
Trod, of old, the oozy rim
Of the Zuyder Zee.

Thus did Andrew Rykman pray.
Are we wiser, better grown,
That we may not, in our day,
Make his prayer our own?

THE CRY OF A LOST SOUL.[44]

In that black forest, where, when day is done,
With a snake's stillness glides the Amazon
Darkly from sunset to the rising sun,

A cry, as of the pained heart of the wood,
The long, despairing moan of solitude
And darkness and the absence of all good,

Startles the traveller, with a sound so drear,
So full of hopeless agony and fear,
His heart stands still and listens like his ear.

The guide, as if he heard a dead-bell toll,
Starts, drops his oar against the gunwale's thole,
Crosses himself, and whispers, "A lost soul!"

"No, Señor, not a bird. I know it well,—
It is the pained soul of some infidel
Or cursèd heretic that cries from hell.

"Poor fool! with hope still mocking his despair,
He wanders, shrieking on the midnight air
For human pity and for Christian prayer.

"Saints strike him dumb! Our Holy Mother hath
No prayer for him who, sinning unto death,
Burns always in the furnace of God's wrath!"

Thus to the baptized pagan's cruel lie,
Lending new horror to that mournful cry,
The voyager listens, making no reply.

Dim burns the boat-lamp: shadows deepen round,
From giant trees with snake-like creepers wound,
And the black water glides without a sound.

But in the traveller's heart a secret sense
Of nature plastic to benign intents,
And an eternal good in Providence,

Lifts to the starry calm of heaven his eyes;
And lo! rebuking all earth's ominous cries,
The Cross of pardon lights the tropic skies!

"Father of all!" he urges his strong plea,
"Thou lovest all: thy erring child may be
Lost to himself, but never lost to Thee!

"All souls are Thine; the wings of morning bear
None from that Presence which is everywhere,
Nor hell itself can hide, for Thou art there.

"Through sins of sense, perversities of will,
Through doubt and pain, through guilt and shame
and ill,
Thy pitying eye is on Thy creature still.

"Wilt thou not make, Eternal Source and Goal!
In Thy long years, life's broken circle whole,
And change to praise the cry of a lost soul?"

ITALY.

Across the sea I heard the groans
Of nations in the intervals
Of wind and wave. Their blood and bones
Cried out in torture, crushed by thrones,
And sucked by priestly cannibals.

I dreamed of freedom slowly gained
By martyr meekness, patience, faith.
And lo! an athlete grimly stained,

With corded muscles battle-strained,
Shouting it from the fields of death!

I turn me, awe-struck, from the sight,
Among the clamoring thousands mute,
I only know that God is right,
And that the children of the light
Shall tread the darkness under foot.

I know the pent fire heaves its crust,
That sultry skies the bolt will form
To smite them clear; that Nature must
The balance of her powers adjust,
Though with the earthquake and the storm.

God reigns, and let the earth rejoice!
I bow before His sterner plan.
Dumb are the organs of my choice;
He speaks in battle's stormy voice,
His praise is in the wrath of man!

Yet, surely as He lives, the day
Of peace He promised shall be ours,
To fold the flags of war, and lay
Its sword and spear to rust away,
And sow its ghastly fields with flowers!

THE RIVER PATH

No bird-song floated down the hill,
The tangled bank below was still;

No rustle from the birchen stem,
No ripple from the water's hem.

The dusk of twilight round us grew,
We felt the falling of the dew;

For, from us, ere the day was done,
The wooded hills shut out the sun.

But on the river's farther side
We saw the hill-tops glorified,—

A tender glow, exceeding fair,
A dream of day without its glare.

With us the damp, the chill, the gloom:
With them the sunset's rosy bloom;

While dark, through willowy vistas seen,
The river rolled in shade between.

From out the darkness where we trod
We gazed upon those hills of God,

Whose light seemed not of moon or sun.
We spake not, but our thought was one.

We paused, as if from that bright shore
Beckoned our dear ones gone before;

And stilled our beating hearts to hear
The voices lost to mortal ear!

Sudden our pathway turned from night;
The hills swung open to the light;

Through their green gates the sunshine showed
A long, slant splendor downward flowed.

Down glade and glen and bank it rolled;
It bridged the shaded stream with gold;

And, borne on piers of mist, allied
The shadowy with the sunlit side!

"So," prayed we, "when our feet draw near
The river dark, with mortal fear,

"And the night cometh chill with dew,
O Father!—let thy light break through!

"So let the hills of doubt divide,
So bridge with faith the sunless tide!

"So let the eyes that fail on earth
On thy eternal hills look forth;

"And in thy beckoning angels know
The dear ones whom we loved below!"

A MEMORIAL.

M. A. C.

O THICKER, deeper, darker growing,
The solemn vista to the tomb
Must know henceforth another shadow,
And give another cypress room.

In love surpassing that of brothers,
We walked, O friend, from childhood's day;
And, looking back o'er fifty summers,
Our footprints track a common way.

One in our faith, and one our longing
To make the world within our reach
Somewhat the better for our living,
And gladder for our human speech.

Thou heardst with me the far-off voices,
The old beguiling song of fame,
But life to thee was warm and present,
And love was better than a name.

To homely joys and loves and friendships
  Thy genial nature fondly clung;
And so the shadow on the dial
  Ran back and left thee always young.

And who could blame the generous weakness
  Which, only to thyself unjust,
So overprized the worth of others,
  And dwarfed thy own with self-distrust?

All hearts grew warmer in the presence
  Of one who, seeking not his own,
Gave freely for the love of giving,
  Nor reaped for self the harvest sown.

Thy greeting smile was pledge and prelude
  Of generous deeds and kindly words;
In thy large heart were fair guest-chambers,
  Open to sunrise and the birds!

The task was thine to mould and fashion
  Life's plastic newness into grace;
To make the boyish heart heroic,
  And light with thought the maiden's face.

O'er all the land, in town and prairie,
  With bended heads of mourning, stand
The living forms that owe their beauty
  And fitness to thy shaping hand.

Thy call has come in ripened manhood,
  The noonday calm of heart and mind,
While I, who dreamed of thy remaining
  To mourn me, linger still behind:

Live on, to own, with self-upbraiding,
  A debt of love still due from me,—
The vain remembrance of occasions,
  Forever lost, of serving thee.

It was not mine among thy kindred
  To join the silent funeral prayers,
But all that long sad day of summer
  My tears of mourning dropped with theirs.

All day the sea-waves sobbed with sorrow,
  The birds forgot their merry trills;
All day I heard the pines lamenting
  With thine upon thy homestead hills.

Green be those hill-side pines forever,
  And green the meadowy lowlands be,
And green the old memorial beeches,
  Name-carven in the woods of Lee!

Still let them greet thy life companions
  Who thither turn their pilgrim feet,
In every mossy line recalling
  A tender memory sadly sweet.

O friend! if thought and sense avail not
  To know thee henceforth as thou art,
That all is well with thee forever
  I trust the instincts of my heart.

Thine be the quiet habitations,
  Thine the green pastures, blossom-sown,
And smiles of saintly recognition,
  As sweet and tender as thy own.

Thou com'st not from the hush and shadow
  To meet us, but to thee we come;
With thee we never can be strangers,
  And where thou art must still be home

HYMN.

SUNG AT CHRISTMAS BY THE SCHOLARS OF ST. HELENA'S ISLAND, S. C.

O NONE in all the world before
  Were ever glad as we!
We're free on Carolina's shore,
  We're all at home and free.

Thou Friend and Helper of the poor,
  Who suffered for our sake,
To open every prison door,
  And every yoke to break!

Bend low thy pitying face and mild,
  And help us sing and pray;
The hand that blessed the little child,
  Upon our foreheads lay.

We hear no more the driver's horn,
  No more the whip we fear,
This holy day that saw thee born
  Was never half so dear.

The very oaks are greener clad,
  The waters brighter smile;
O never shone a day so glad,
  On sweet St. Helen's Isle.

We praise thee in our songs to-day,
  To thee in prayer we call,
Make swift the feet and straight the way
  Of freedom unto all.

Come once again, O blessed Lord!
  Come walking on the sea!
And let the mainlands hear the word
  That sets the islands free!

NOTES.

Note 1, page 5.

Winnepurkit, otherwise called George, Sachem of Saugus, married a daughter of Passaconaway, the great Pennacook chieftain, in 1662. The wedding took place at Pennacook (now Concord, N. H.), and the ceremonies closed with a great feast. According to the usages of the chiefs, Passaconaway ordered a select number of his men to accompany the newly-married couple to the dwelling of the husband, where in turn there was another great feast. Some time after, the wife of Winnepurkit expressing a desire to visit her father's house, was permitted to go accompanied by a brave escort of her husband's chief men. But when she wished to return, her father sent a messenger to Saugus, informing her husband, and asking him to come and take her away. He returned for answer that he had escorted his wife to her father's house in a style that became a chief, and that now if she wished to return, her father must send her back in the same way. This Passaconaway refused to do, and it is said that here terminated the connection of his daughter with the Saugus chief.—*Vide Morton's New Canaan.*

Note 2, page 11.

This was the name which the Indians of New England gave to two or three of their principal chiefs, to whom all their inferior sagamores acknowledged allegiance. Passaconaway seems to have been one of these chiefs. His residence was at Pennacook.—*Mass. Hist. Coll.*, vol. iii., pp. 21, 22. "He was regarded," says Hubbard, "as a great sorcerer, and his fame was widely spread. It was said of him that he could cause a green leaf to grow in winter, trees to dance, water to burn, &c. He was, undoubtedly, one of those shrewd and powerful men whose achievements are always regarded by a barbarous people as the result of supernatural aid. The Indians gave to such the names of Powahs or Panisees."

"The Panisees are men of great courage and wisdom, and to these the Devill appeareth more familiarly than to others."—*Winslow's Relation.*

NOTE 3, page 16.

"The Indians," says Roger Williams, "have a god whom they call Wetuomanit, who presides over the household."

NOTE 4, page 19.

There are rocks in the River at the Falls of Amoskeag, in the cavities of which, tradition says the Indians formerly stored and concealed their corn.

NOTE 5, page 23.

The Spring God.—*See Roger Williams's Key,* &c.

NOTE 6, page 27.

"Mat wonck kunna-monee." We shall see thee or her no more.—*Vide Roger Williams's* "*Key to the Indian Language.*"

NOTE 7, page 28.

"The Great South West God."—*See Roger Williams's* "*Observations,*" &c.

NOTE 8, page 31.

MOGG MEGONE, or Hegone, was a leader among the Saco Indians, in the bloody war of 1677. He attacked and captured the garrison at Black Point, October 12th of that year; and cut off, at the same time, a party of Englishmen near Saco River. From a deed signed by this Indian in 1664, and from other circumstances, it seems that, previous to the war, he had mingled much with the colonists. On this account, he was probably selected by the principal sachems as their agent, in the treaty signed in November, 1676.

NOTE 9, page 32.

Baron de St. Castine came to Canada in 1644. Leaving his civilized companions, he plunged into the great wilderness, and settled among the Penobscot Indians, near the mouth of their noble river. He here took for his wives the daughters of the great Modocawando—the most powerful sachem of the east. His castle was plundered by Governor Andros, during his reckless administration; and the enraged Baron is supposed to have excited the Indians into open hostility to the English.

Note 10, page 32.

The owner and commander of the garrison at Black Point, which Mogg attacked and plundered. He was an old man at the period to which the tale relates.

Note 11, page 32.

Major Phillips, one of the principal men of the Colony. His garrison sustained a long and terrible siege by the savages. As a magistrate and a gentleman, he exacted of his plebeian neighbors a remarkable degree of deference. The Court Records of the settlement inform us that an individual was fined for the heinous offence of saying that "Major Phillips' mare was as lean as an Indian dog."

Note 12, page 33.

Captain Harmon, of Georgeana, now York, was, for many years, the terror of the Eastern Indians. In one of his expeditions up the Kennebec River, at the head of a party of rangers, he discovered twenty of the savages asleep by a large fire. Cautiously creeping towards them until he was certain of his aim, he ordered his men to single out their objects. The first discharge killed or mortally wounded the whole number of the unconscious sleepers.

Note 13, page 33.

Wood Island, near the mouth of the Saco. It was visited by the Sieur de Monts and Champlain, in 1603. The following extract, from the journal of the latter, relates to it. "Having left the Kennebec, we ran along the coast to the westward, and cast anchor under a small island, near the main-land, were we saw twenty or more natives. I here visited an island, beautifully clothed with a fine growth of forest trees, particularly of the oak and walnut; and overspread with vines, that, in their season.

produce excellent grapes. We named it the island of Bacchus."—*Les voyages de Sieur Champlain, Liv.* 2, c. 8.

NOTE 14, page 33.

John Bonython was the son of Richard Bonython, Gent., one of the most efficient and able magistrates of the Colony. John proved to be "a degenerate plant." In 1635, we find, by the Court Records, that, for some offence, he was fined 40*s*. In 1640, he was fined for abuse toward R. Gibson, the minister, and Mary, his wife. Soon after, he was fined for disorderly conduct in the house of his father. In 1645, the "Great and General Court" adjudged "John Bonython outlawed, and incapable of any of his majesty's laws, and proclaimed him a rebel." [Court Records of the Province, 1645.] In 1651, he bade defiance to the laws of Massachusetts, and was again outlawed. He acted independently of all law and authority; and hence, doubtless, his burlesque title of "The Sagamore of Saco, which has come down to the present generation in the following epitaph:

"Here lies Bonython; the Sagamore of Saco,
He lived a rogue, and died a knave, and went to Hobomoko."

By some means or other, he obtained a large estate. In this poem, I have taken some liberties with him, not strictly warranted by historical facts, although the conduct imputed to him is in keeping with his general character. Over the last years of his life lingers a deep obscurity. Even the manner of his death is uncertain. He was supposed to have been killed by the Indians; but this is doubted by the able and indefatigable author of the history of Saco and Biddeford.—*Part. I.* p. 115.

NOTE 15, page 33.

Foxwell's Brook flows from a marsh or bog, called the "Heath," in Saco, containing thirteen hundred acres. On this brook, and surrounded by wild and romantic scenery, is a beautiful waterfall, of more than sixty feet.

NOTE 16, page 36.

Hiacoomes, the first Christian preacher on Martha's Vineyard; for a biography of whom the reader is referred to Increase Mayhew's account of the Praying Indians,

1726. The following is related of him: "One Lord's day after meeting, where Hiacoomes had been preaching, there came in a Powwaw very angry, and said, 'I know all the meeting Indians are liars. You say you don't care for the Powwaws;'—then, calling two or three of them by name, he railed at them, and told them they were deceived, for the Powwaws could kill all the meeting Indians, if they set about it. But Hiacoomes told him that he would be in the midst of all the Powwaws in the island, and they should do the utmost they could against him; and when they should do their worst by their witchcraft to kill him, he would without fear set himself against them, by remembering Jehovah. He told them also he did put all the Powwaws under his heel. Such was the faith of this good man. Nor were these Powwaws ever able to do these Christian Indians any hurt, though others were frequently hurt and killed by them."—*Mayhew*, pp. 6, 7, c. 1.

NOTE 17, page 39.

"The tooth-ache," says Roger Williams in his observations upon the language and customs of the New England tribes, "is the only paine which will force their stoute nearts to cry." He afterwards remarks that even the Indian women never cry as he has heard "some of their men in this paine."

NOTE 18, page 41.

Wuttamuttata, "Let us drink." *Weekan*, "It is sweet." *Vide* Roger Williams's Key to the Indian Language, "in that parte of America called New England." London, 1643, p. 35.

NOTE 19, page 42.

Wetuomanit—a house god, or demon. "They—the Indians—have given me the names of thirty-seven gods, which I have, all which in their solemne Worships they invocate!" R. Williams's Briefe Observations of the Customs, Manners, Worships, &c., of the Natives, in Peace and Warre, in Life and Death: on all which is added Spiritual Observations, General and Particular, of Chiefe and Special use—upon all occasions—to all the English inhabiting these parts; yet Pleasant and Profitable to the view of all Mene. p. 110, c. 21.

Note 20, page 45.

Mt. Desert Island, the Bald Mountain upon which overlooks Frenchman's and Penobscot Bay. It was upon this island that the Jesuits made their earliest settlement.

Note 21, page 47.

Father Hennepin, a missionary among the Iroquois, mentions that the Indians believed him to be a conjuror, and that they were particularly afraid of a bright silver chalice which he had in his possession. "The Indians," says Pere Jerome Lallamant, "fear us as the greatest sorcerers on earth."

Note 22, page 49.

Bomazeen is spoken of by Penhallow, as "the famous warrior and chieftain of Norridgewock." He was killed in the attack of the English upon Norridgewock, in 1724.

Note 23, page 49.

Pere Ralle, or Rasles, was one of the most zealous and indefatigable of that band of Jesuit missionaries who, at the beginning of the seventeenth century, penetrated the forests of America, with the avowed object of converting the heathen. The first religious mission of the Jesuits, to the savages in North America, was in 1611. The zeal of the fathers for the conversion of the Indians to the Catholic faith, knew no bounds. For this, they plunged into the depths of the wilderness; habituated themselves to all the hardships and privations of the natives; suffered cold, hunger, and some of them death itself, by the extremest tortures. Pere Brebeuf, after laboring in the cause of his mission for twenty years, together with his companion, Pere Lallamant, was burned alive. To these might be added the names of those Jesuits who were put to death by the Iroquois—Daniel, Garnier, Buteaux, La Riborerde, Goupil, Constantin, and Liegeouis. "For bed," says Father Lallamant, in his *Relation de ce qui s'est dans le pays des Hurons*, 1640, c. 3, "we have nothing but a miserable piece of bark of a tree; for nourishment, a handful or two of corn, either roasted or soaked in water, which seldom satisfies our hunger; and after all, not venturing to perform even the ceremonies of our religion, without being considered as sorcerers." Their success among the natives, however, by no means equalled their exertions. Pere Lallamant says—"With respect to adult persons, in good health, there is little apparent success; on the contrary, there have been nothing but storms and whirlwinds from that quarter."

Sebastian Ralle established himself, sometime about the year 1670, at Norridgewock, where he continued more than forty years. He was accused, and perhaps not without justice, of exciting his praying Indians against the English, whom he looked upon as the enemies not only of his king, but also of the Catholic religion. He was killed by the English, in 1724, at the foot of the cross, which his own hands had planted. This Indian church was broken up, and its members either killed outright or dispersed.

In a letter written by Ralle to his nephew, he gives the following account of his church, and his own labors. "All my converts repair to the church regularly twice every day; first, very early in the morning, to attend mass, and again in the evening, to assist in the prayers at sunset. As it is necessary to fix the imagination of savages, whose attention is easily distracted, I have composed prayers, calculated to inspire them with just sentiments of the august sacrifice of our altars: they chant, or at least recite them aloud, during mass. Besides preaching to them on Sundays and saint's days, I seldom let a working day pass, without making a concise exhortation, for the purpose of inspiring them with horror at those vices to which they are most addicted, or to confirm them in the practice of some particular virtue." Vide *Lettres Edifiantes et Cur.*, vol. 6, page 127.

Note 24, page 58.

The character of Ralle has probably never been correctly delineated. By his brethren of the Romish Church, he has been nearly apotheosized. On the other hand, our Puritan historians have represented him as a demon in human form. He was undoubtedly sincere in his devotion to the interests of his church, and not over-scrupulous as to the means of advancing those interests. "The French," says the author of the History of Saco and Biddeford, "after the peace of 1713, secretly promised to supply the Indians with arms and ammunition, if they would renew hostilities. Their principal agent was the celebrated Ralle, the French Jesuit." p. 215.

NOTE 25, page 61.

Hertel de Rouville was an active and unsparing enemy of the English. He was the leader of the combined French and Indian forces which destroyed Deerfield and massacred its inhabitants, in 1703. He was afterwards killed in the attack upon Haverhill. Tradition says that on examining his dead body, his head and face were found to be perfectly smooth, without the slightest appearance of hair or beard.

NOTE 26, page 62.

Cowesass?—tawhich wessaseen? Are you afraid?—why fear you?

NOTE 27, page 72.

The celebrated Captain Smith, after resigning the government of the colony in Virginia, in his capacity of Admiral of New England," made a careful survey of the coast from Penobscot to Cape Cod, in the summer of 1614.

NOTE 28, page 72.

Lake Winnipiseogee—*The Smile of the Great Spirit*—the source of one of the branches of the Merrimack.

NOTE 29, page 72.

Capt. Smith gave to the promontory, now called Cape Ann, the name of Tragabizanda, in memory of his young and beautiful mistress of that name, who, while he was a captive at Constantinople, like Desdemona, "loved him for the dangers he had passed."

NOTE 30, page 74.

Some three or four years since, a fragment of a statue, rudely chiselled from dark gray stone, was found in the town of Bradford, on the Merrimack. Its origin must be left entirely to conjecture. The fact that the ancient Northmen visited New England, some centuries before the discoveries of Columbus, is now very generally admitted.

NOTE 31, page 99.

De Soto, in the sixteenth century, penetrated into the

wilds of the new world in search of gold and the fountain of perpetual youth.

NOTE 32, page 117.

TOUSSAINT L'OUVERTURE, the black chieftain of Hayti, was a slave on the plantation "de Libertas," belonging to M. BAYOU. When the rising of the negroes took place, in 1791, TOUSSAINT refused to join them until he had aided M. BAYOU and his family to escape to Baltimore. The white man had discovered in Toussaint many noble qualities, and had instructed him in some of the first branches of education; and the preservation of his life was owing to the negro's gratitude for this kindness.

In 1797, Toussaint L'Ouverture was appointed, by the French government, General-in-Chief of the armies of St. Domingo, and, as such, signed the Convention with General Maitland, for the evacuation of the island by the British. From this period, until 1801, the island, under the government of Toussaint, was happy, tranquil, and prosperous. The miserable attempt of Napoleon to re-establish slavery in St. Domingo, although it failed of its intended object, proved fatal to the negro chieftain. Treacherously seized by Leclerc, he was hurried on board a vessel by night, and conveyed to France, where he was confined in a cold subterranean dungeon, at Besancon, where, in April, 1803, he died. The treatment of Toussaint finds a parallel only in the murder of the Duke D'Enghein. It was the remark of Godwin, in his Lectures, that the West India Islands, since their first discovery by Columbus, could not boast of a single name which deserves comparison with that of Toussaint L'Ouverture.

NOTE 33, page 123.

The reader may, perhaps, call to mind the beautiful sonnet of William Wordsworth, addressed to Toussaint L'Ouverture, during his confinement in France.

"Toussaint!—thou most unhappy man of men!
Whether the whistling rustic tends his plough
Within thy hearing, or thou liest now
Buried in some deep dungeon's earless den;
Oh, miserable chieftain!—where and when
Wilt thou find patience?—Yet, die not, do thou
Wear rather in thy bonds a cheerful brow:
Though fallen thyself, never to rise again,

Live and take comfort. Thou hast left behind
  Powers that will work for thee; air, earth, and skies,—
There's not a breathing of the common wind
  That will forget thee: thou hast great allies.
Thy friends are exultations, agonies,
  And love, and man's unconquerable mind."

NOTE 84, page 124.

The French ship LE RODEUR, with a crew of twenty-two men, and with one hundred and sixty negro slaves, sailed from Bonny, in Africa, April, 1819. On approaching the line, a terrible malady broke out—an obstinate disease of the eyes—contagious, and altogether beyond the resources of medicine. It was aggravated by the scarcity of water among the slaves (only half a wine glass per day being allowed to an individual), and by the extreme impurity of the air in which they breathed. By the advice of the physician, they were brought upon deck occasionally; but some of the poor wretches, locking themselves in each other's arms, leaped overboard, in the hope, which so universally prevails among them, of being swiftly transported to their own homes in Africa. To check this, the captain ordered several, who were stopped in the attempt, to be shot, or hanged, before their companions. The disease extended to the crew; and one after another were smitten with it, until only *one* remained unaffected. Yet even this dreadful condition did not preclude calculation: to save the expense of supporting slaves rendered unsalable, and to obtain grounds for a claim against the underwriters, *thirty-six of the negroes, having become blind, were thrown into the sea and drowned!*

In the midst of their dreadful fears lest the solitary individual, whose sight remained unaffected, should also be seized with the malady, a sail was discovered. It was the Spanish slaver, Leon. The same disease had been there; and, horrible to tell, all the crew had become blind! Unable to assist each other, the vessels parted. The Spanish ship has never since been heard of. The Rodeur reached Guadaloupe on the 21st of June; the only man who had escaped the disease, and had thus been enabled to steer the slaver into port, caught it in three days after its arrival.—*Speech of M. Benjamin Constant, in the French Chamber of Deputies*, June 17, 1820.

NOTE 85, page 168.

The Northern Author of the Congressional rule against receiving petitions of the people on the subject of Slavery.

NOTE 36, page 195.

Dr. Thacher, surgeon in Scammel's regiment, in his description of the siege of Yorktown, says: "The labor on the Virginia plantations is performed altogether by a species of the human race cruelly wrested from their native country, and doomed to perpetual bondage, while their masters are manfully contending for freedom and the natural rights of man. Such is the inconsistency of human nature." Eighteen hundred slaves were found at Yorktown, after its surrender, and restored to their masters. Well was it said by Dr. Barnes, in his late work on Slavery: "No slave was any nearer his freedom after the surrender of Yorktown, than when Patrick Henry first taught the notes of liberty to echo among the hills and vales of Virginia."

NOTE 37, page 211.

The rights and liberties affirmed by MAGNA CHARTA were deemed of such importance, in the 13th century, that the Bishops, twice a year, with tapers burning, and in their pontifical robes, pronounced, in the presence of the king and the representatives of the estates of England the greater excommunication against the infringer of that instrument. The imposing ceremony took place in the great Hall of Westminster. A copy of the curse, as pronounced in 1253, declares that, "By the authority of Almighty God, and the blessed Apostles and Martyrs, and all the saints in heaven, all those who violate the English liberties, and secretly or openly, by deed, word, or counsel, do make statutes, *or observe them being made*, against said liberties, are accursed and sequestered from the company of heaven and the sacraments of the Holy Church."

WILLIAM PENN, in his admirable political pamphlet, "*England's Present Interest Considered*," alluding to the curse of the Charter-breakers, says: "I am no Roman Catholic, and little value their other curses; yet I declare I would not for the world incur this curse, as every man deservedly doth, who offers violence to the fundamental freedom thereby repeated and confirmed."

NOTE 38, page 252.

"The manner in which the Waldenses and heretics disseminated their principles among the Catholic gentry, was by carrying with them a box of trinkets, or articles of dress. Having entered the houses of the gentry and disposed of some of their goods, they cautiously intimated that they had commodities far more valuable than these—inestimable jewels, which they would show if they could be protected from the clergy. They would then give their purchasers a bible or testament; and thereby many were deluded into heresy."—*R. Saccho.*

NOTE 39, page 293.

Chalkley Hall, near Frankford, Pa., the residence of THOMAS CHALKLEY, an eminent minister of the "Friends" denomination. He was one of the early settlers of the Colony, and his Journal, which was published in 1749, presents a quaint but beautiful picture of a life of unostentatious and simple goodness. He was the master of a merchant vessel, and, in his visits to the West Indies and Great Britain, omitted no opportunity to labor for the highest interests of his fellow-men. During a temporary residence in Philadelphia, in the summer of 1838, the quiet and beautiful scenery around the ancient village of Frankford, frequently attracted me from the heat and bustle of the city.

NOTE 40, page 302.

August. Sililoq. cap. xxxi. "Interrogavi Terram," &c.

NOTE 41, page 319.

See English caricatures of America: Slaveholder and cowhide, with the motto, "Haven't I a right to wallop my nigger?"

NOTE 42, page 324.

It is recorded that the Chians, when subjugated by Mithridates of Cappadocia, were delivered up to their own slaves, to be carried away captive to Colchis. Athenæus considers this a just punishment for their wickedness in first introducing the slave-trade into Greece. From this ancient villany of the Chians the proverb arose, "The Chian hath bought himself a master."

NOTE 43, page 339.

This ballad was written on the occasion of a Horticultural Festival. Cobbler Keezar was a noted character among the first settlers in the valley of the Merrimack.

Note 44, page 374.

Lieut. Herndon's Report of the Exploration of the Amazon has a striking description of the peculiar and melancholy notes of a bird heard by night on the shores of the river. The Indian guides called it "The Cry of a lost Soul"!

END OF VOL. I.

www.ingramcontent.com/pod-product-compliance
Lightning Source LLC
LaVergne TN
LVHW020110110826
845151LV00001B/123

* 9 7 8 1 4 2 5 5 4 3 9 6 9 *